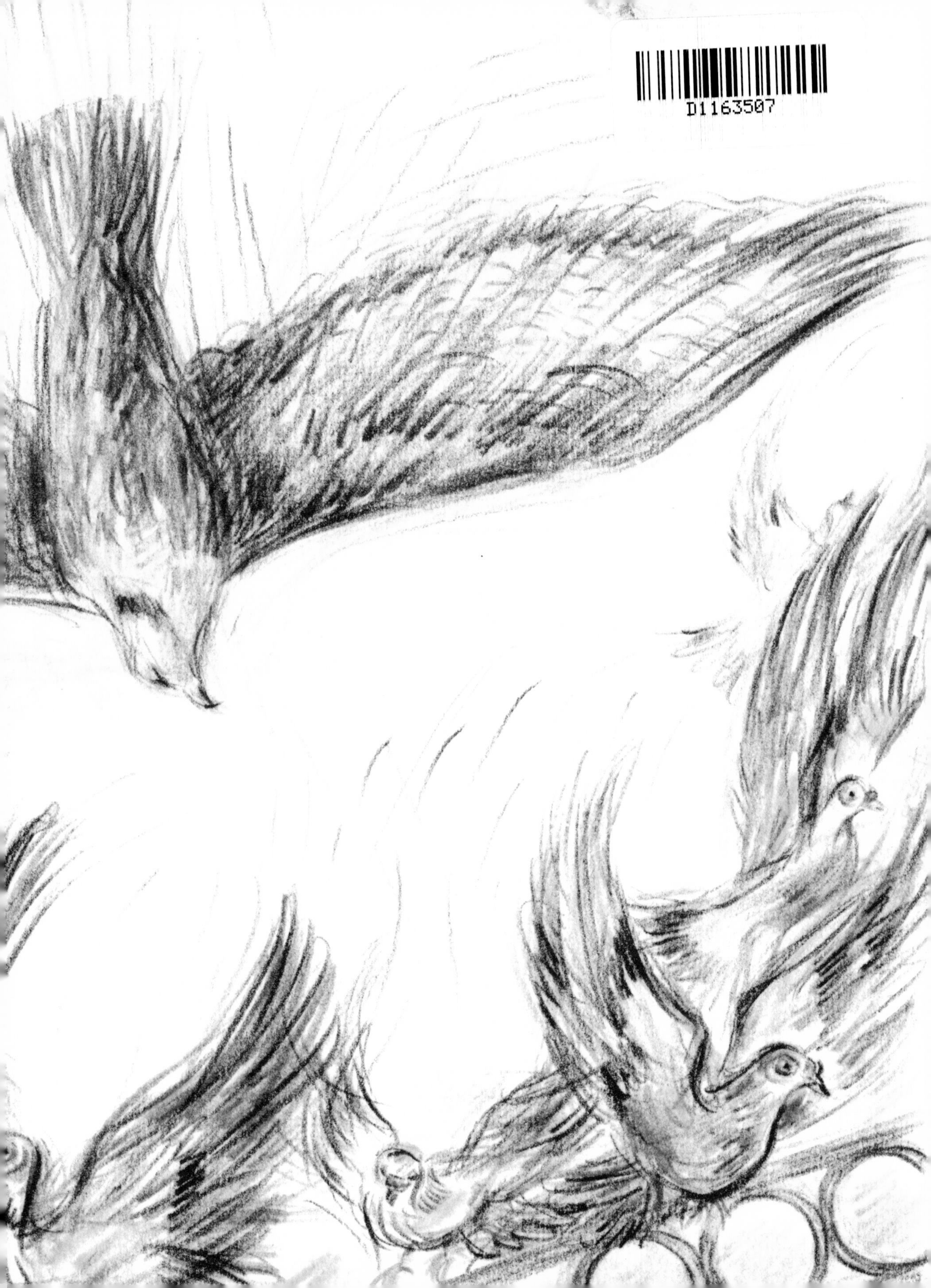

LETTING IT GO

MIRIAM KATIN

DRAWN & QUARTERLY

www.drawnandquarterly.com

First edition: March 2013
Printed in Singapore
10 9 8 7 6 5 4 3 2 1

Library and Archives Canada Cataloguing in Publication
Katin, Miriam
    Letting It Go / Miriam Katin.
ISBN 978-1-77046-103-1
    1. Graphic novels. I. Title.
PN6727.K29L48 2013   741.5'973   C2012-907118-8

Published in the USA by Drawn & Quarterly, a client publisher of
Farrar, Straus and Giroux
18 West 18th Street
New York, NY 10011
Orders: 888.330.8477

Published in Canada by Drawn & Quarterly, a client publisher of
Raincoast Books
2440 Viking Way
Richmond, BC V6V 1N2
Orders: 800.663.5714

Dedicated to the Past, Present, Future and the new Berlin

ACKNOWLEDGMENTS

Many thanks to Drawn & Quarterly for taking another chance with this manic old lady. Special thanks to Tracy Hurren for cleaning up my mess and organizing it into a book. Thanks to Tinet Elmgren and Ilan Katin for letting me get away with it, to Eileen Katin for much clear-headed advice, to Joanne Spivak for judicious editing, and to Joan Flax for additional editing. Thanks to Bryan Ackerman for his humor and for being an all around good guy, and to Serhat Ozel for the Turkish translation. To cousin Betty Schmoller, thanks for lending your name and charm to the persona in the story. Thanks to Louis Sorkin, Board Certified Entomologist at the Museum of Natural History, and to Dr. Sloane Drayson-Kniggle for her "swim, salmon, swim!" To the folks at our favorite restaurant in Berlin with the doggie bar, the Dicke Wiertel. To my friends Freya Tanz, Masako Kanayama, and Jean-Pierre Jacket for your much needed and cherished dialogue. To Joanne and Michael Spivak, thanks for the usage of your pictures from Berlin. My thanks to Chris Tashima of Cedar Grove Productions, director of "Visas and Virtue," the Academy Award winning short film inspired by the the true story of Chiune Sugihara. It was the source for my drawings about this great man. To Geoffry H. Katin, thank you for all the music in my life.

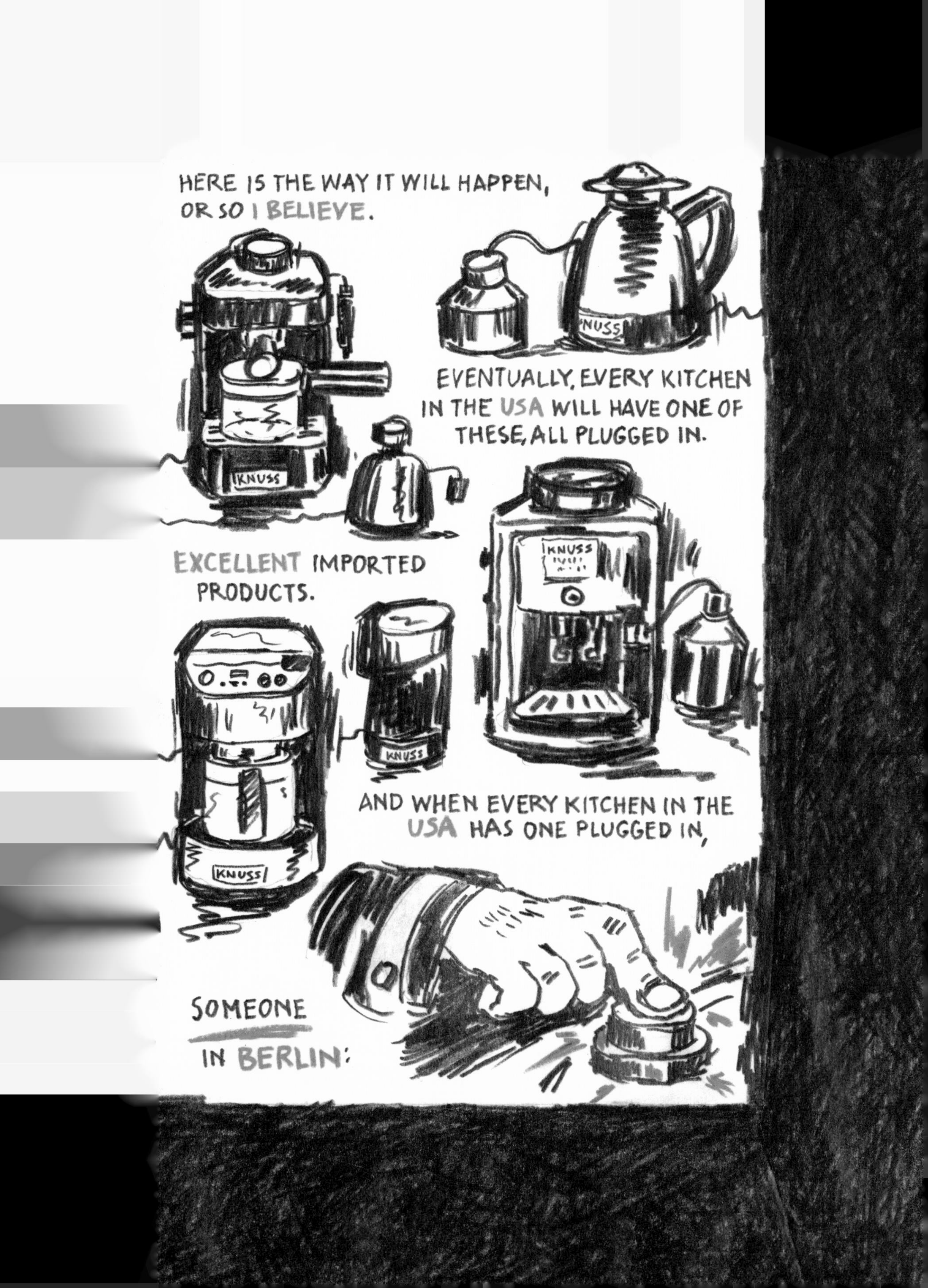
HERE IS THE WAY IT WILL HAPPEN,
OR SO I BELIEVE.
KNUSS
KNUSS
EVENTUALLY, EVERY KITCHEN
IN THE USA WILL HAVE ONE OF
THESE, ALL PLUGGED IN.
EXCELLENT IMPORTED
PRODUCTS.
KNUSS
KNUSS
KNUSS
AND WHEN EVERY KITCHEN IN THE
USA HAS ONE PLUGGED IN,
SOMEONE
IN BERLIN:

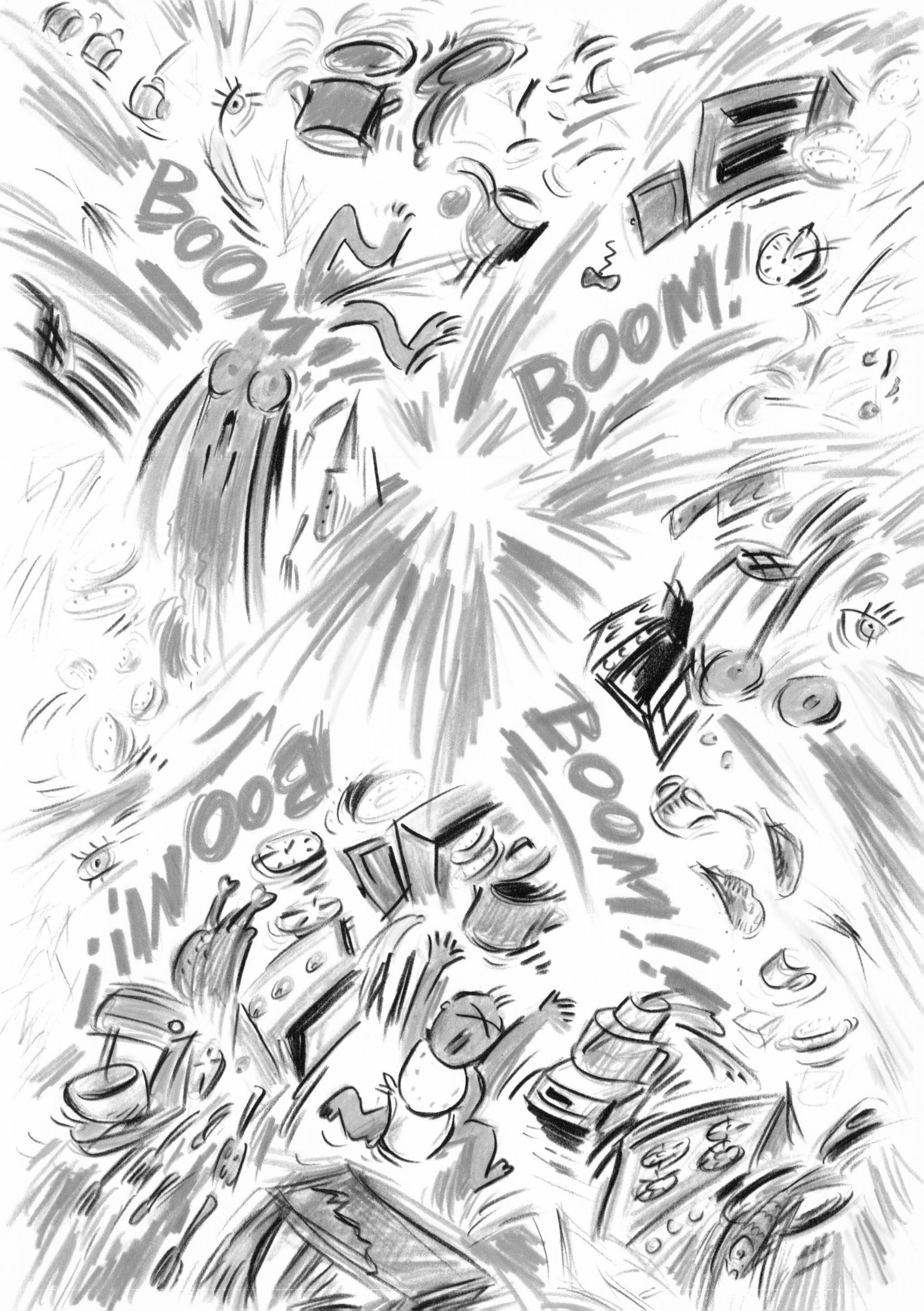
BOOM!
BOOM!
BOOM!
BOOM!

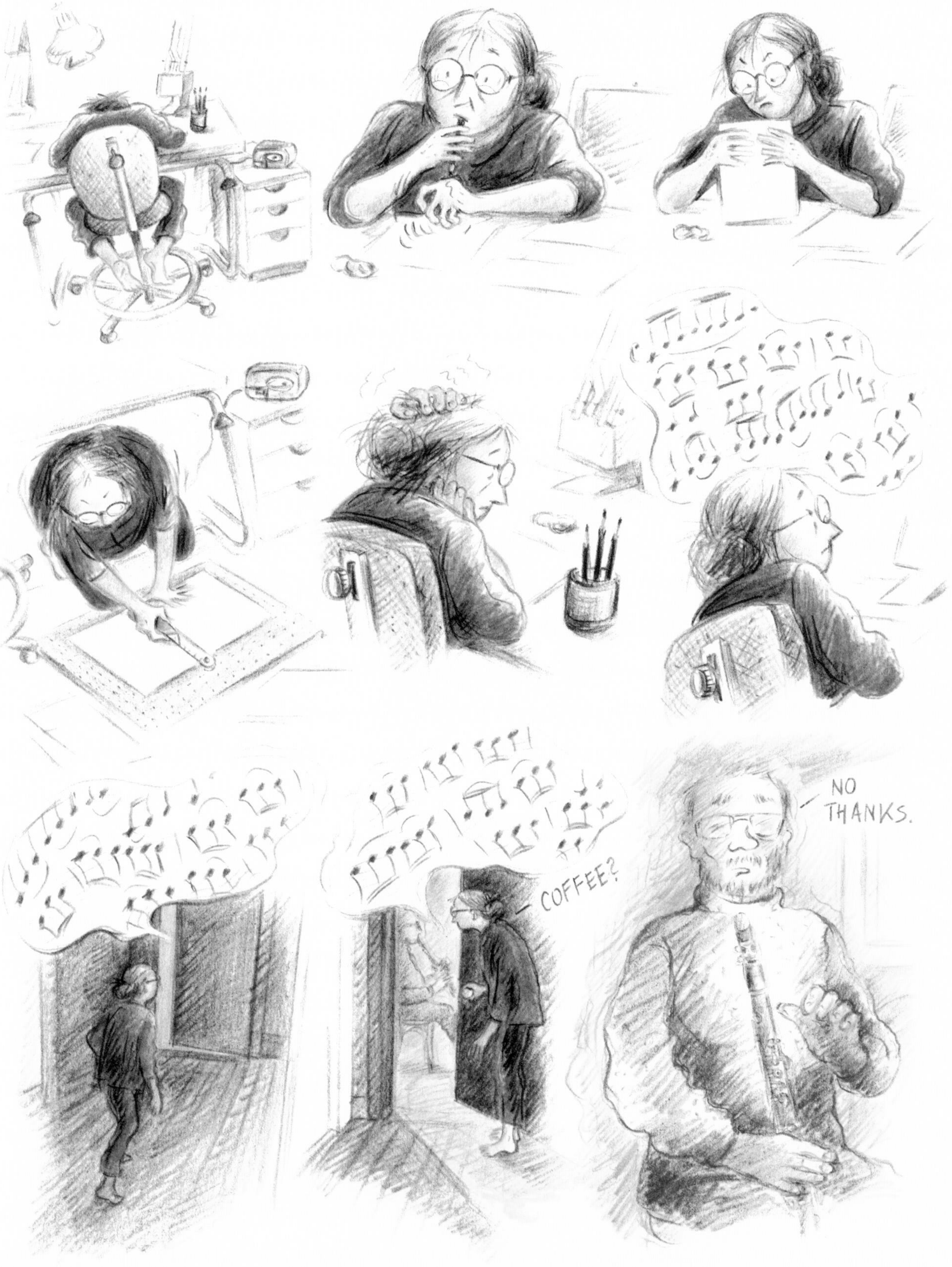
COFFEE?
NO THANKS.

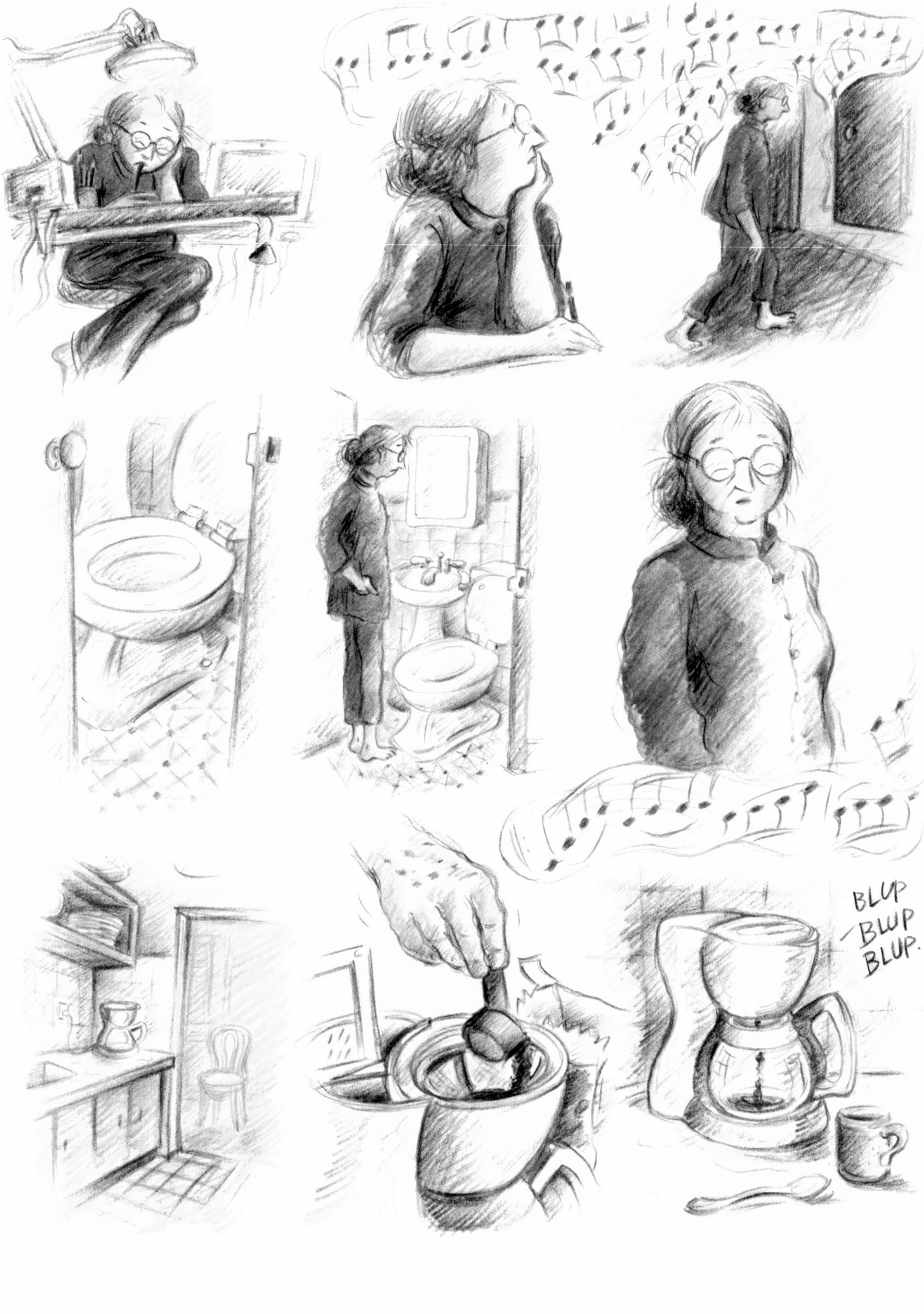
BLUP
BLUP
BLUP..

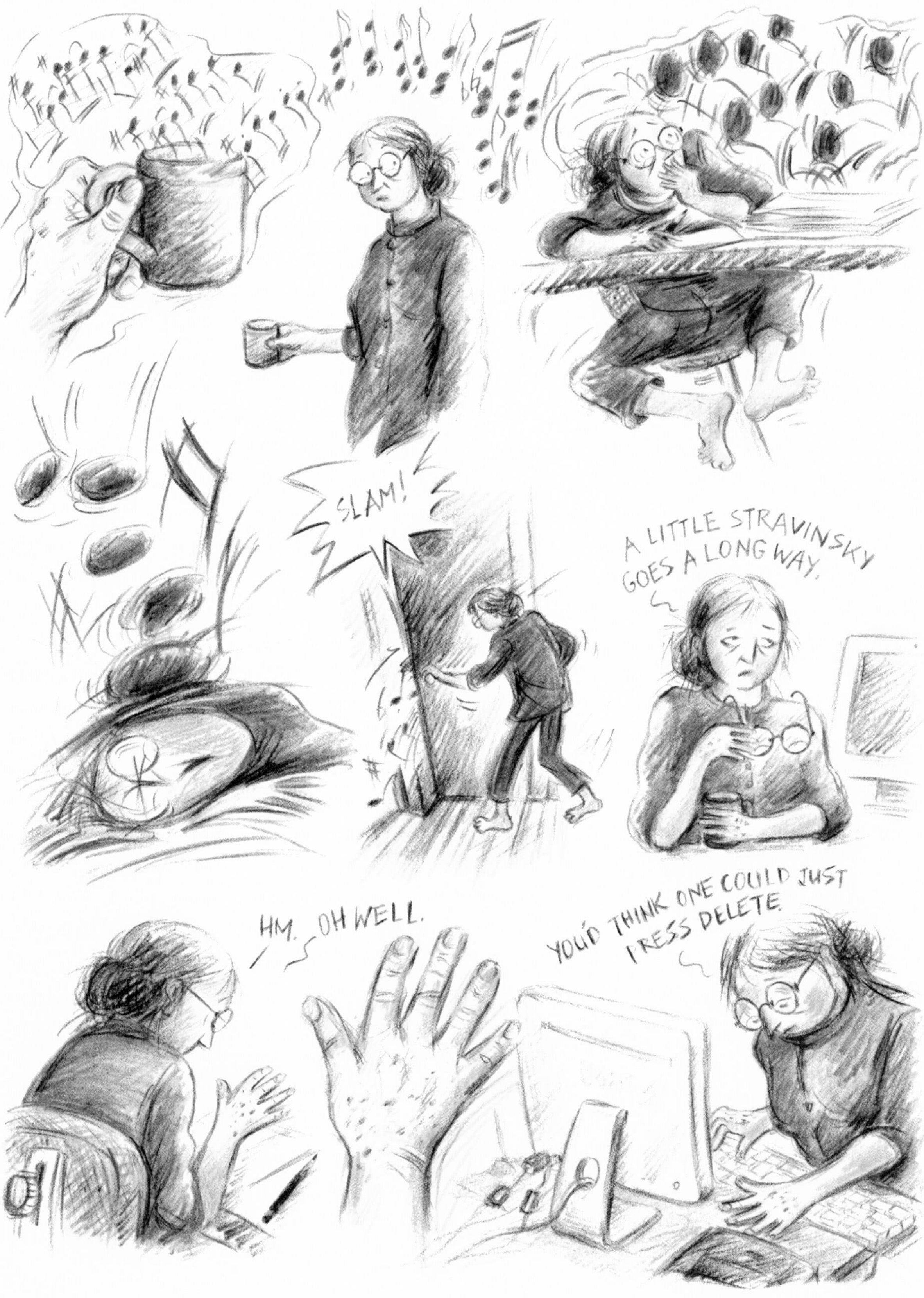
SLAM!
A LITTLE STRAVINSKY GOES A LONG WAY.
HM.
OH WELL.
YOU'D THINK ONE COULD JUST PRESS DELETE.

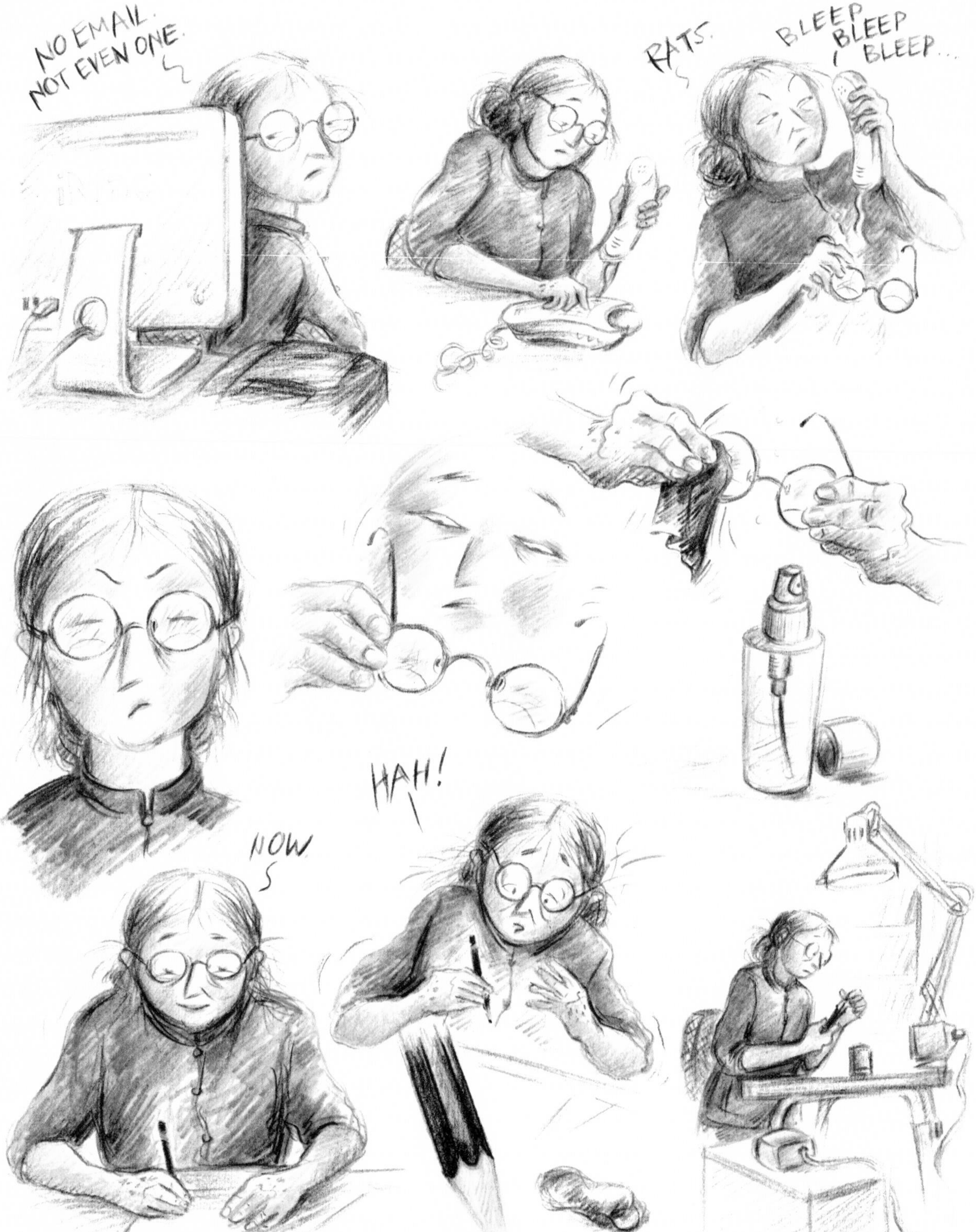
NO EMAIL. NOT EVEN ONE.
RATS.
BLEEP BLEEP BLEEP...
HAH!
NOW.

GZEE GZEE GZEE

UEUEUEUEUEUEUEUE

UEUEUEUEUEE

"TEN TIMES OVER I MUST ESSAY THE TASK, MUST LEAN DOWN OVER THE ABYSS. AND EACH TIME THE NATURAL LAZINESS WHICH DETERS US FROM EVERY DIFFICULT ENTERPRISE... HAS URGED ME TO LEAVE THE THING ALONE AND DRINK MY TEA AND TO THINK MERELY OF THE WORRIES OF TODAY... WHICH LET THEMSELVES BE PONDERED OVER WITHOUT EFFORT OR DISTRESS OF MIND."
MARCEL PROUST, SWANN'S WAY

EUEUEUEUEUEUEUEU

OR IS IT ALL JUST FEAR?

INSIDE THE TERRIFYING WORLD OF PROCRASTINATION.

SWANN'S WAY, PART ONE OF REMEMBRANCE OF THINGS PAST: À LA RECHERCHE DU TEMPS PERDU.

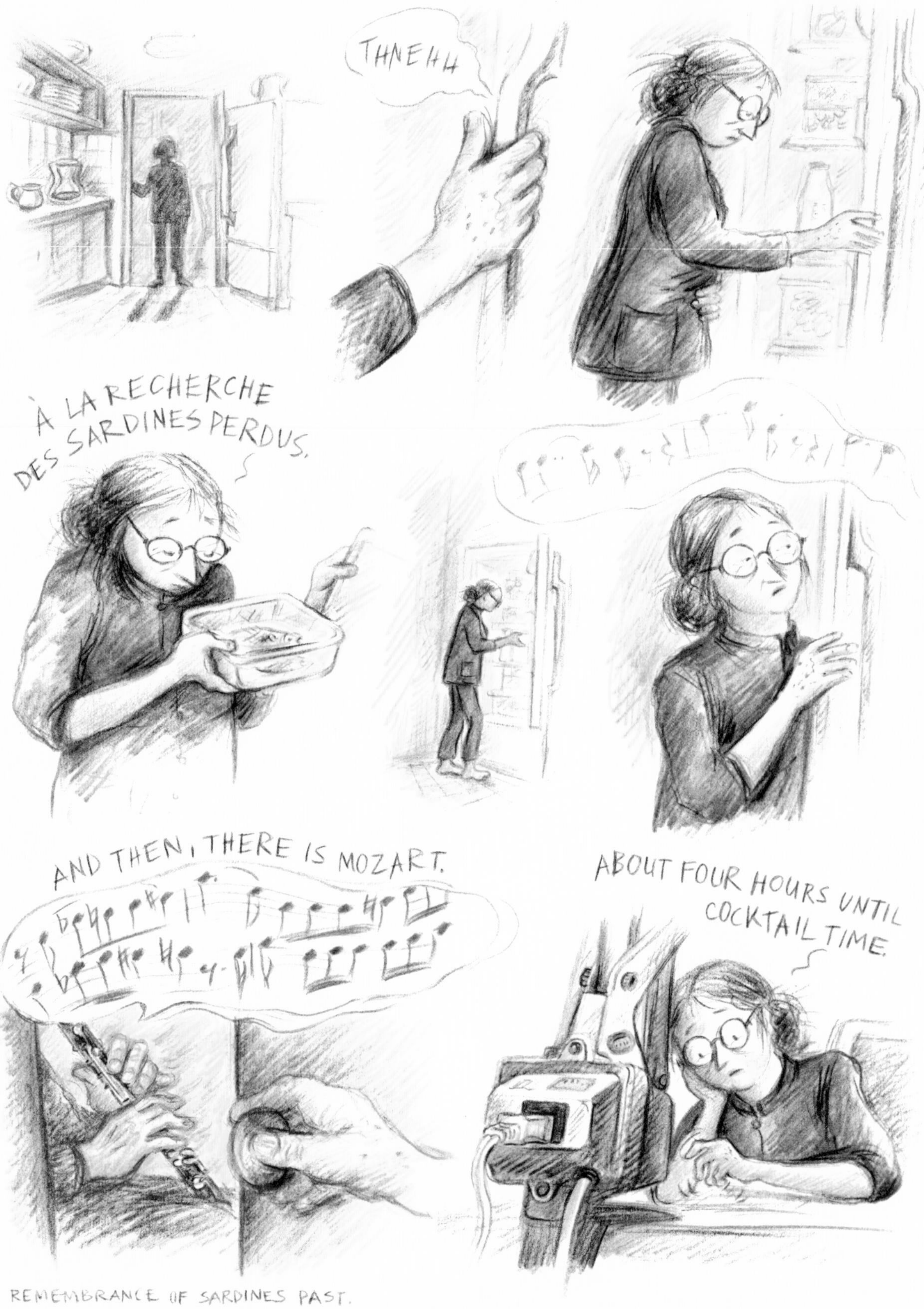
THNEHH
À LA RECHERCHE DES SARDINES PERDUS.
AND THEN, THERE IS MOZART.
ABOUT FOUR HOURS UNTIL COCKTAIL TIME.

REMEMBRANCE OF SARDINES PAST.

SO, WHERE DOES A STORY BEGIN?

AND IF YOU ARE INSIDE THAT STORY RIGHT NOW,

IN THAT SITUATION AND IT HURTS AND SAY YOU CAN DRAW,

THEN YOU MUST TRY AND DRAW YOURSELF OUT OF IT.

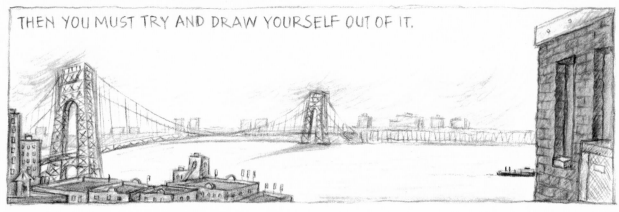

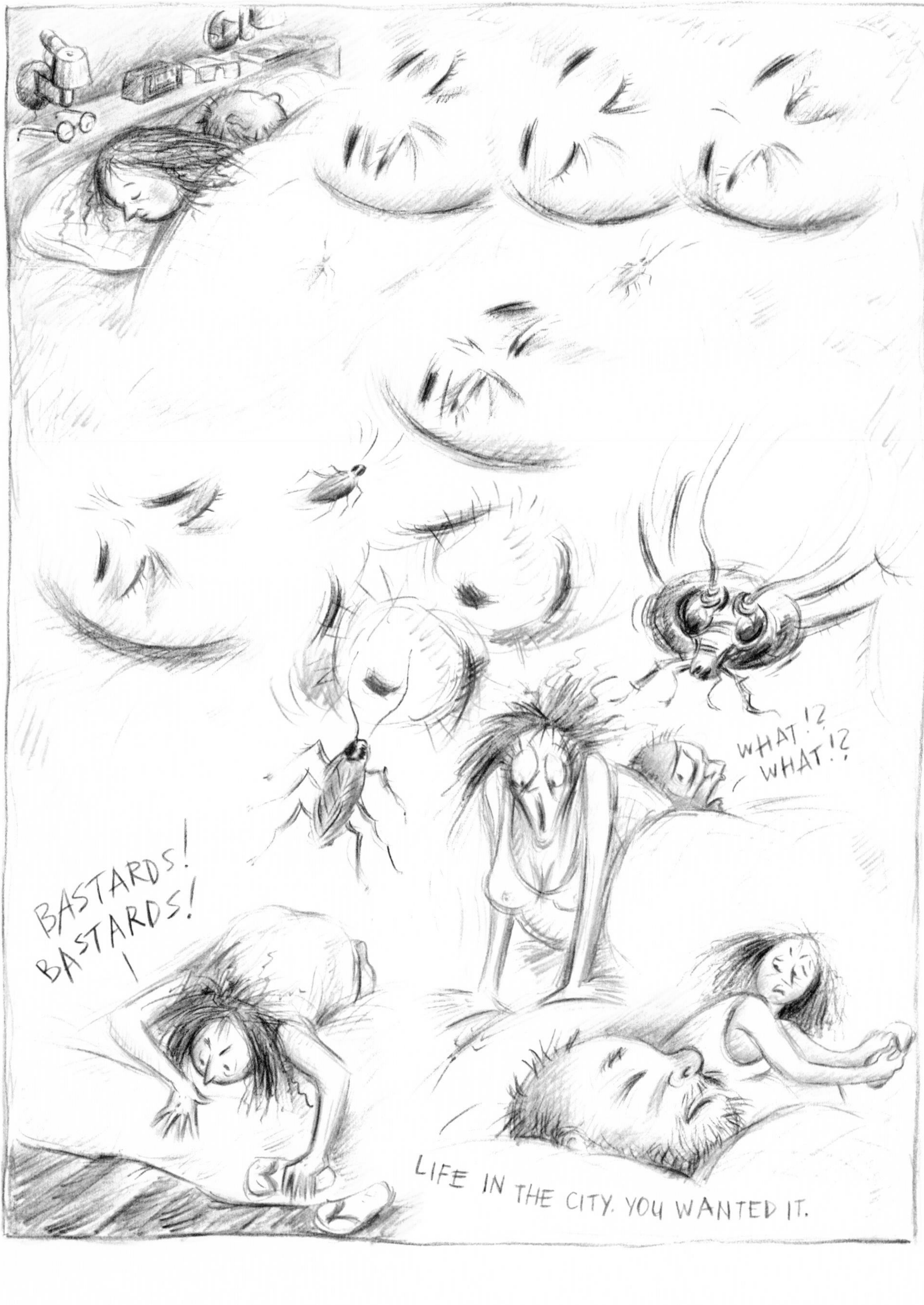
WHAT!? WHAT!?
BASTARDS! BASTARDS!
LIFE IN THE CITY. YOU WANTED IT.

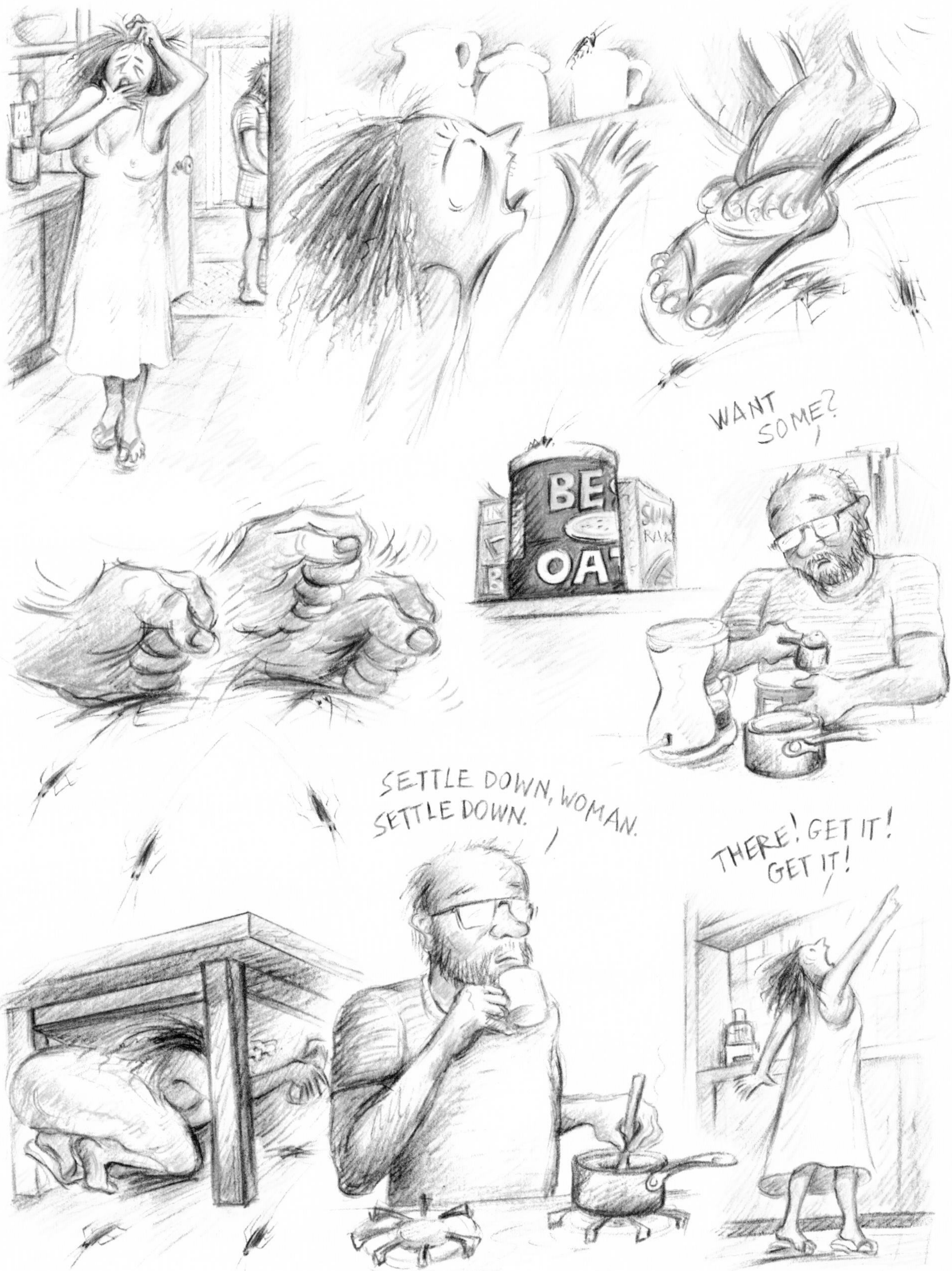
WANT SOME?
SETTLE DOWN, WOMAN. SETTLE DOWN.
THERE! GET IT! GET IT!

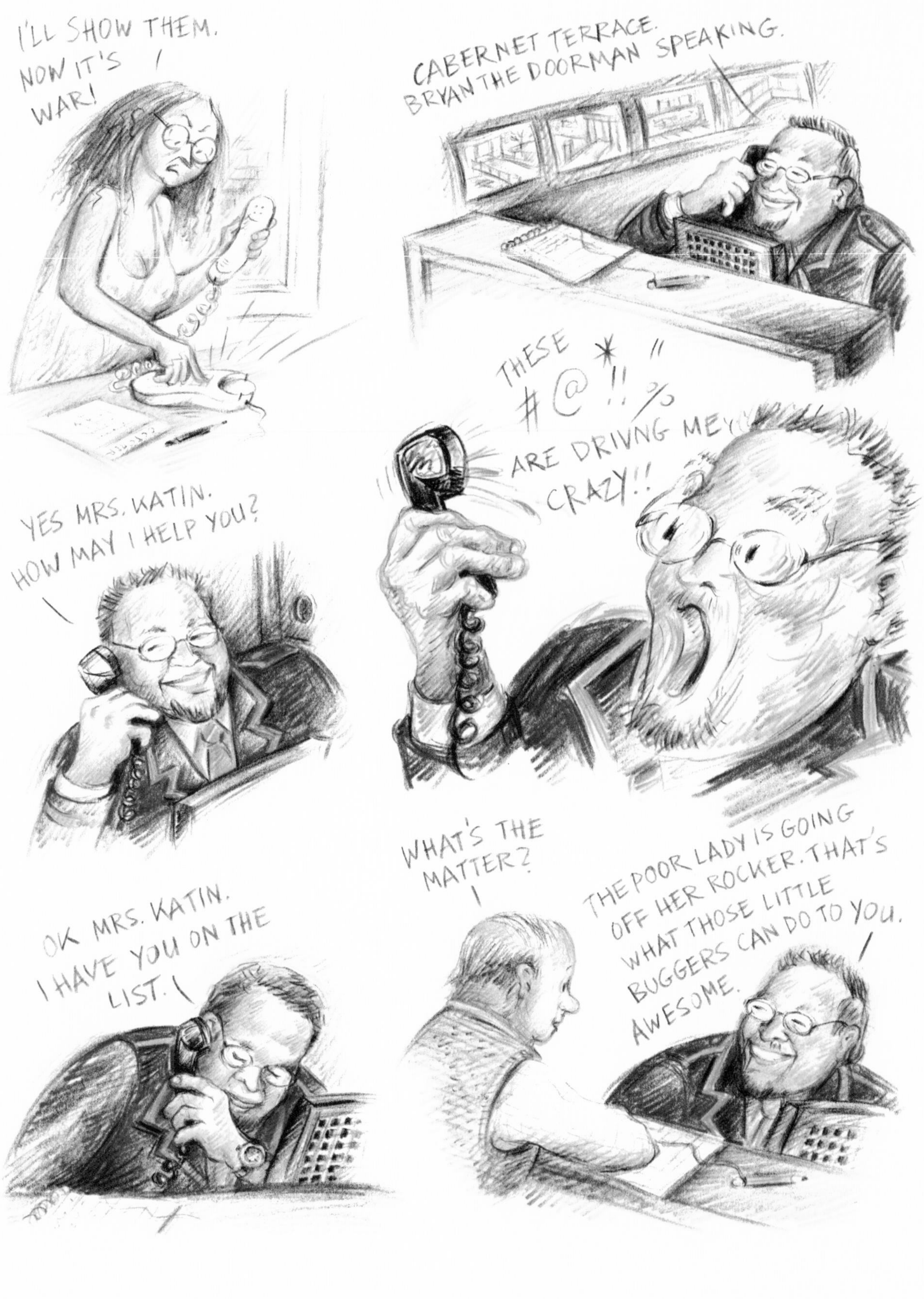
I'LL SHOW THEM. NOW IT'S WAR!
CABERNET TERRACE. BRYAN THE DOORMAN SPEAKING.
YES MRS. KATIN. HOW MAY I HELP YOU?
THESE #@*!!% ARE DRIVING ME CRAZY!!
OK MRS. KATIN. I HAVE YOU ON THE LIST.
WHAT'S THE MATTER?
THE POOR LADY IS GOING OFF HER ROCKER. THAT'S WHAT THOSE LITTLE BUGGERS CAN DO TO YOU. AWESOME.

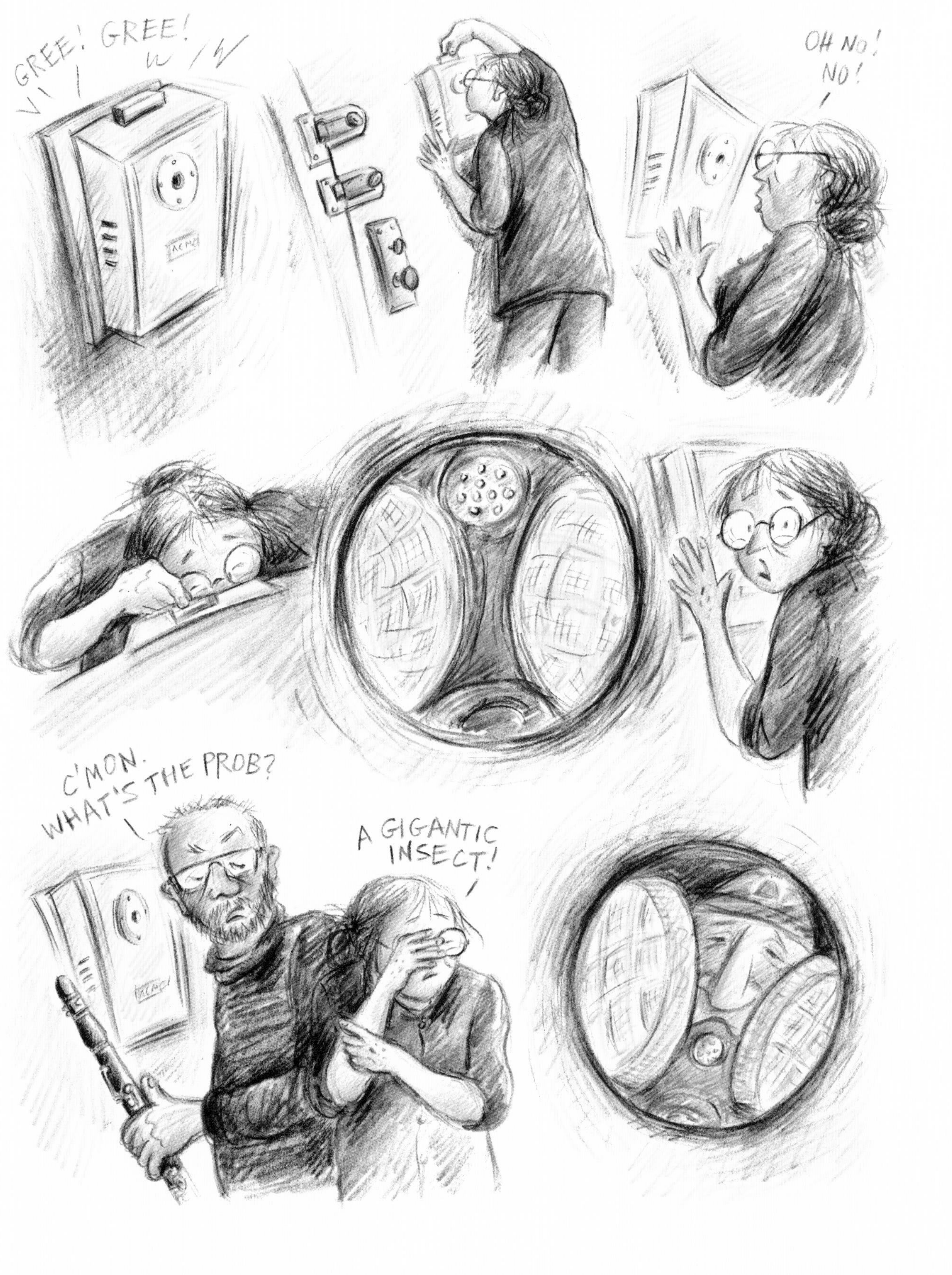
GREE! GREE!
OH NO! NO!
C'MON. WHAT'S THE PROB?
A GIGANTIC INSECT!

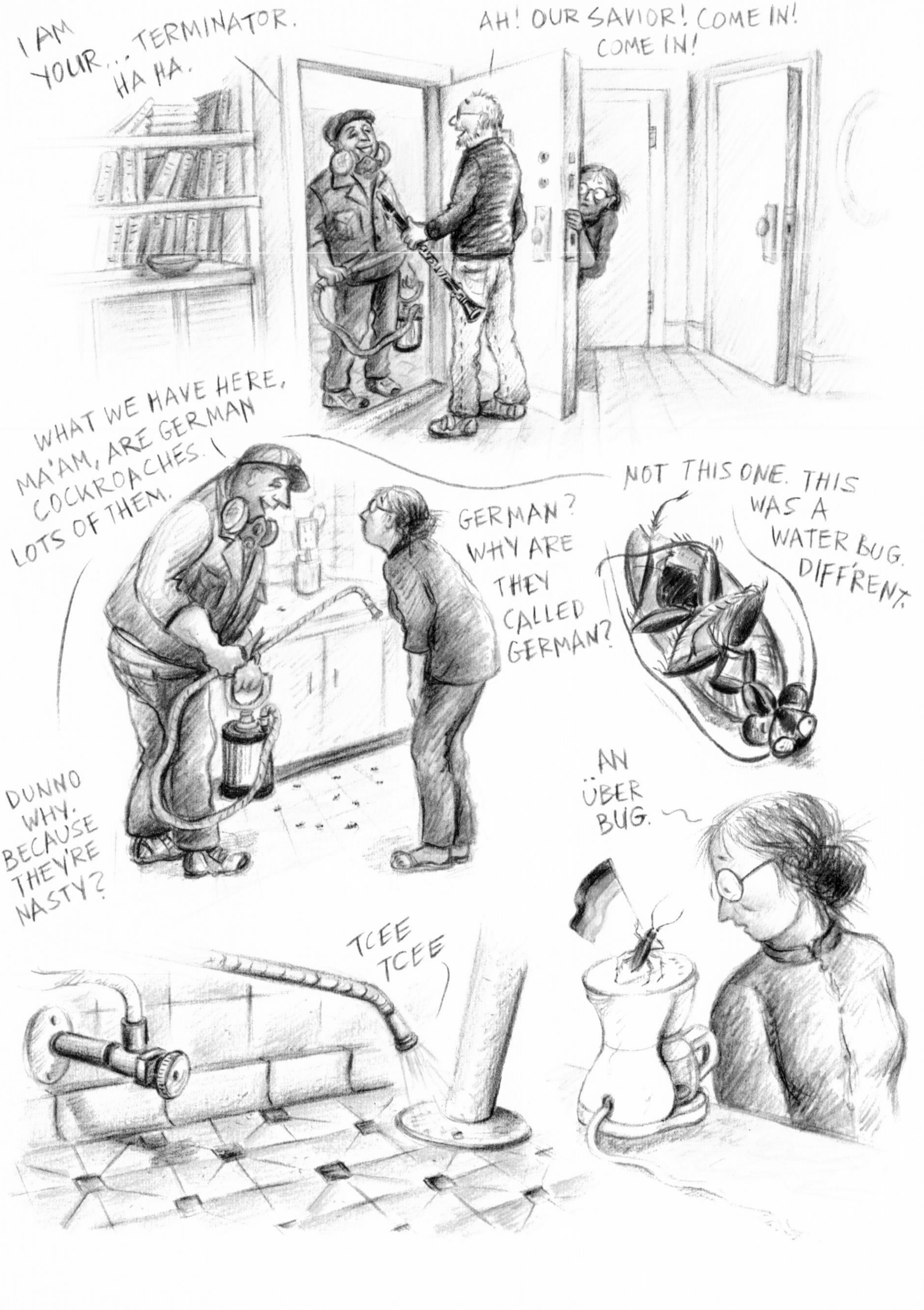
I AM YOUR... TERMINATOR. HA HA.
AH! OUR SAVIOR! COME IN! COME IN!
WHAT WE HAVE HERE, MA'AM, ARE GERMAN COCKROACHES. LOTS OF THEM.
GERMAN? WHY ARE THEY CALLED GERMAN?
NOT THIS ONE. THIS WAS A WATER BUG. DIFF'RENT.
DUNNO WHY. BECAUSE THEY'RE NASTY?
AN ÜBER BUG.
TCEE TCEE

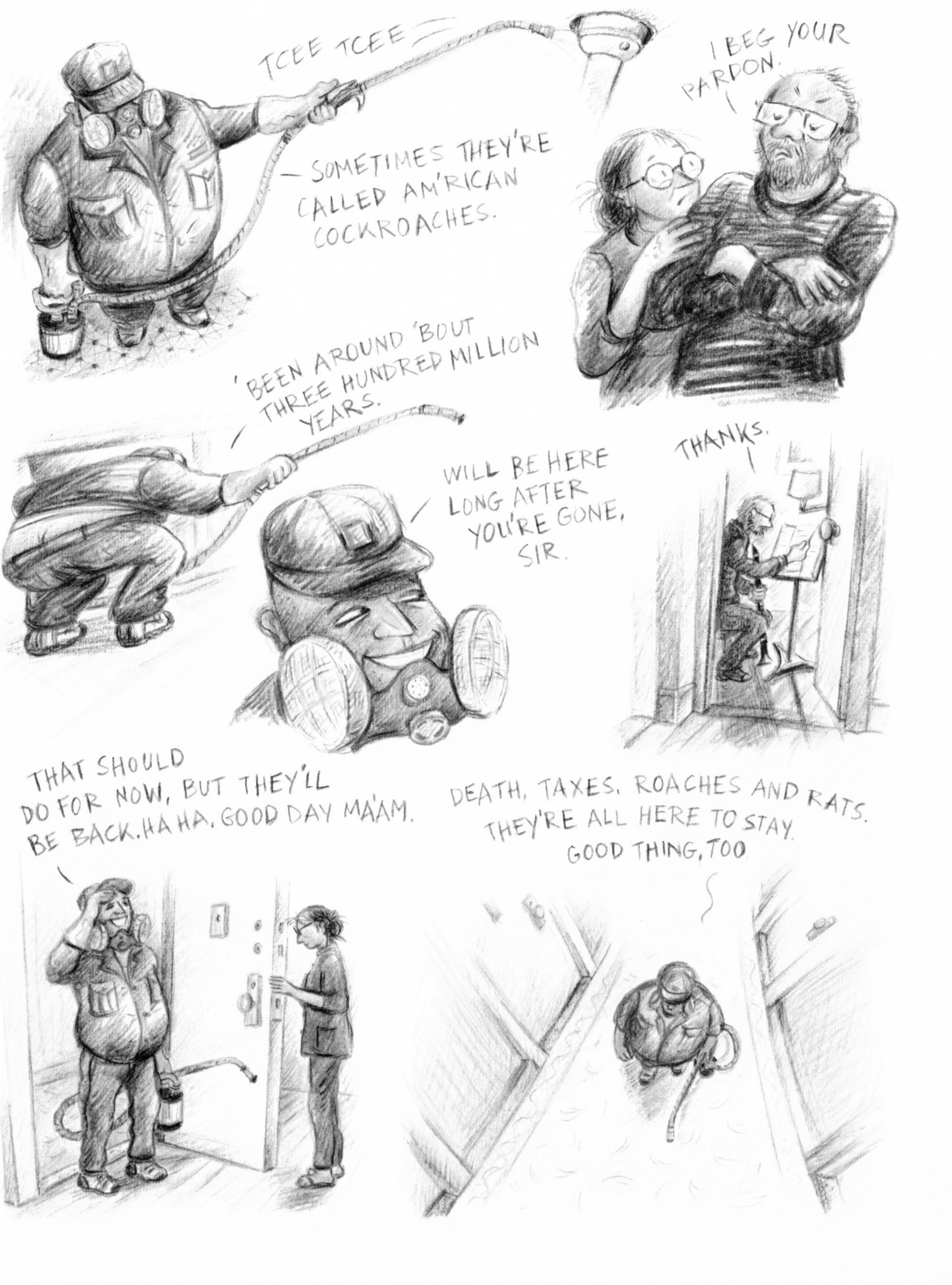
TCEE TCEE
SOMETIMES THEY'RE CALLED AM'RICAN COCKROACHES.
I BEG YOUR PARDON.
'BEEN AROUND 'BOUT THREE HUNDRED MILLION YEARS.
WILL BE HERE LONG AFTER YOU'RE GONE, SIR.
THANKS.
THAT SHOULD DO FOR NOW, BUT THEY'LL BE BACK. HA HA. GOOD DAY MA'AM.
DEATH, TAXES, ROACHES AND RATS. THEY'RE ALL HERE TO STAY. GOOD THING, TOO.

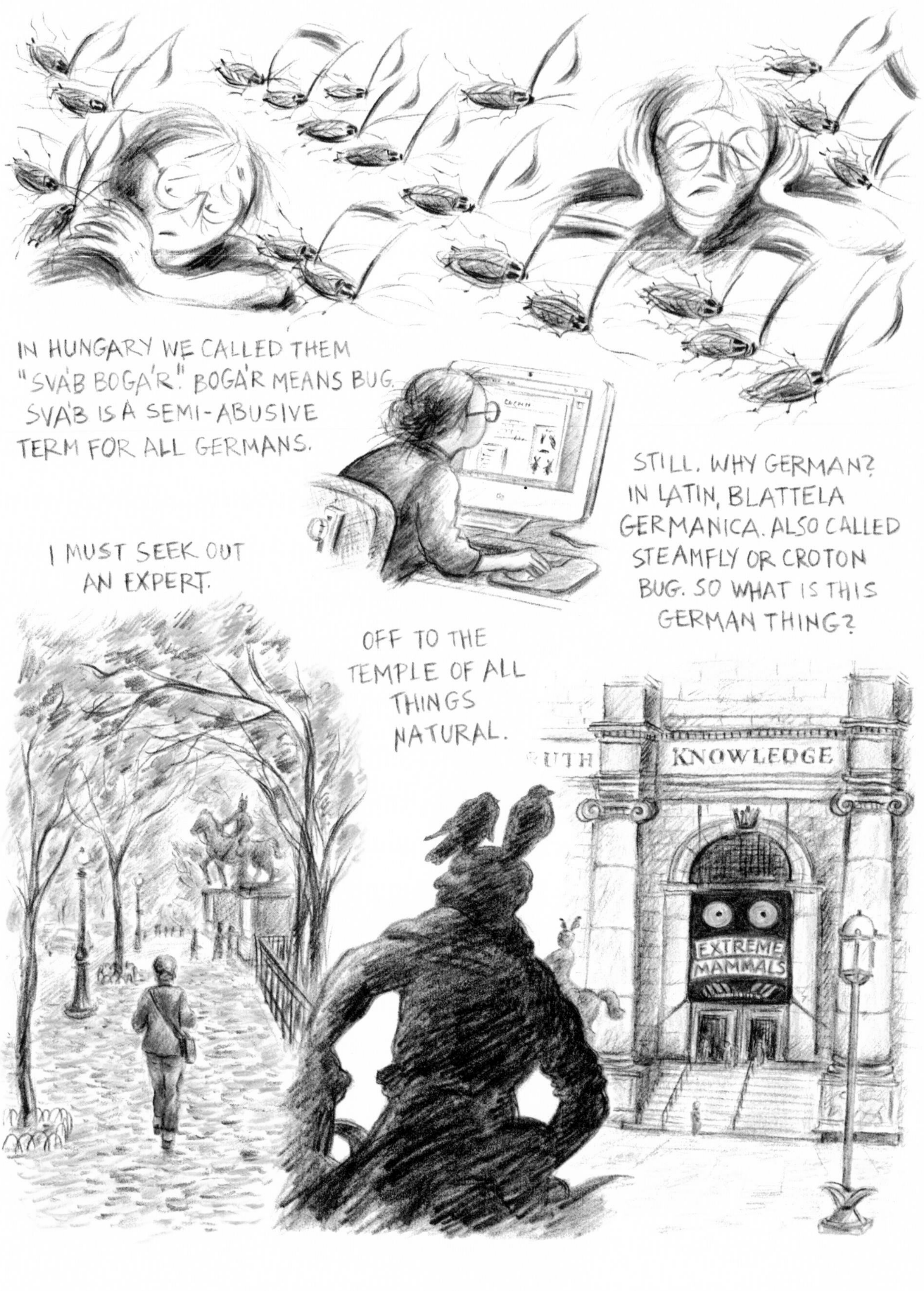
IN HUNGARY WE CALLED THEM "SVÁB BOGÁR." BOGÁR MEANS BUG. SVÁB IS A SEMI-ABUSIVE TERM FOR ALL GERMANS.
STILL. WHY GERMAN? IN LATIN, BLATTELA GERMANICA. ALSO CALLED STEAMFLY OR CROTON BUG. SO WHAT IS THIS GERMAN THING?
I MUST SEEK OUT AN EXPERT.
OFF TO THE TEMPLE OF ALL THINGS NATURAL.
KNOWLEDGE
EXTREME MAMMALS

THIS EXPERT SAID IT'S VERY POSSIBLE THAT THE GERMANS CALL THEM POLISH COCKROACHES.

IT'S THAT KIND OF A THING.

THAT POSTER UP THERE, "SUB TALK" IT'S CALLED.

A BIT OF LITERATURE TO ENTERTAIN THE WEARY TRAVELER. OR ... IS IT A MESSAGE FOR ME?

Franz Kafka (1913-1924) The Metamorphosis

As Gregor Samsa awoke one morning from uneasy dreams he found himself transformed in his bed into a giant insect.

963 WQXR

SubTalk

HERE'S ONE. OOTHECA. OR OOTHECAE, SUCH A PRETTY WORD.

OOTHECA CAN BE SEEN PROTRUDING FROM THE GENITAL CHAMBER OF THE FEMALE.

THIS JUST MIGHT BE THE RIGHT DAY TO START.

NYMPHS WILL OFTEN HATCH FROM THE OOTHECA WHILE THE FEMALE IS STILL CARRYING IT.

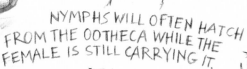

HOW VERY SWEET AND CARING.

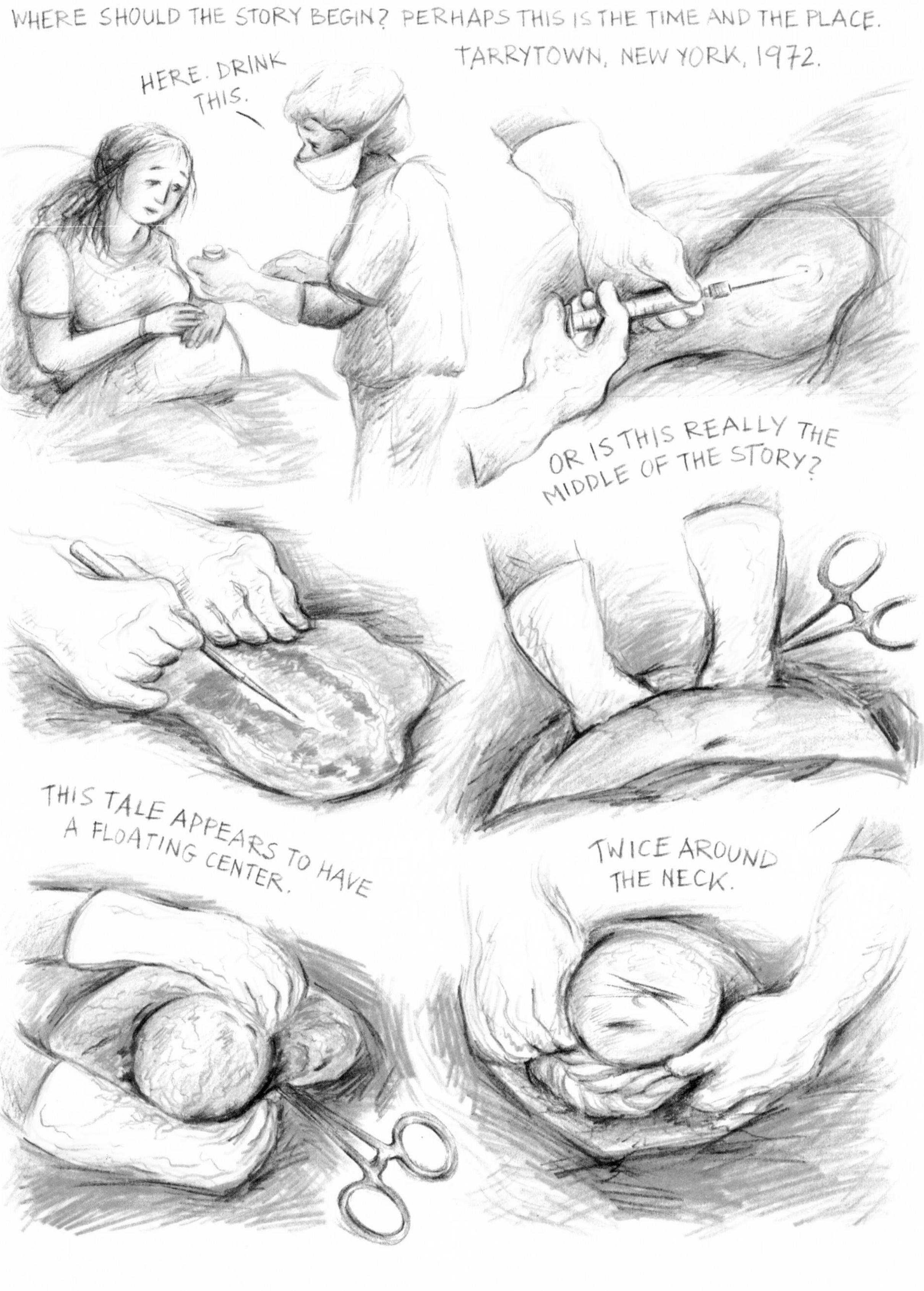
WHERE SHOULD THE STORY BEGIN? PERHAPS THIS IS THE TIME AND THE PLACE.
TARRYTOWN, NEW YORK, 1972.
HERE. DRINK THIS.
OR IS THIS REALLY THE MIDDLE OF THE STORY?
THIS TALE APPEARS TO HAVE A FLOATING CENTER.
TWICE AROUND THE NECK.

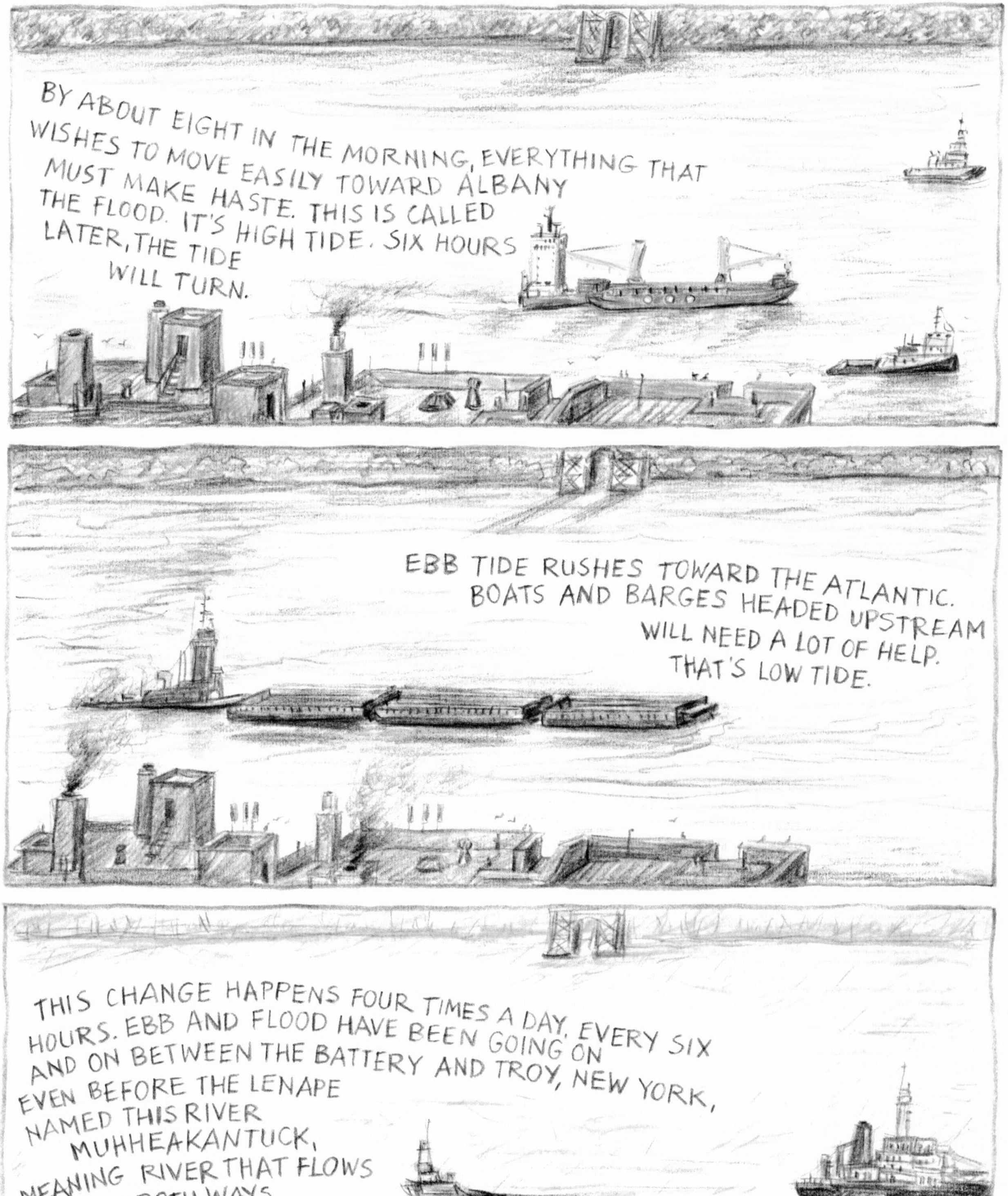
BY ABOUT EIGHT IN THE MORNING, EVERYTHING THAT WISHES TO MOVE EASILY TOWARD ALBANY MUST MAKE HASTE. THIS IS CALLED THE FLOOD. IT'S HIGH TIDE. SIX HOURS LATER, THE TIDE WILL TURN.
EBB TIDE RUSHES TOWARD THE ATLANTIC. BOATS AND BARGES HEADED UPSTREAM WILL NEED A LOT OF HELP. THAT'S LOW TIDE.
THIS CHANGE HAPPENS FOUR TIMES A DAY, EVERY SIX HOURS. EBB AND FLOOD HAVE BEEN GOING ON AND ON BETWEEN THE BATTERY AND TROY, NEW YORK, EVEN BEFORE THE LENAPE NAMED THIS RIVER MUHHEAKANTUCK, MEANING RIVER THAT FLOWS BOTH WAYS.

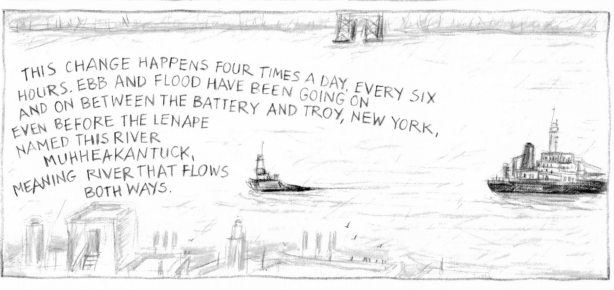

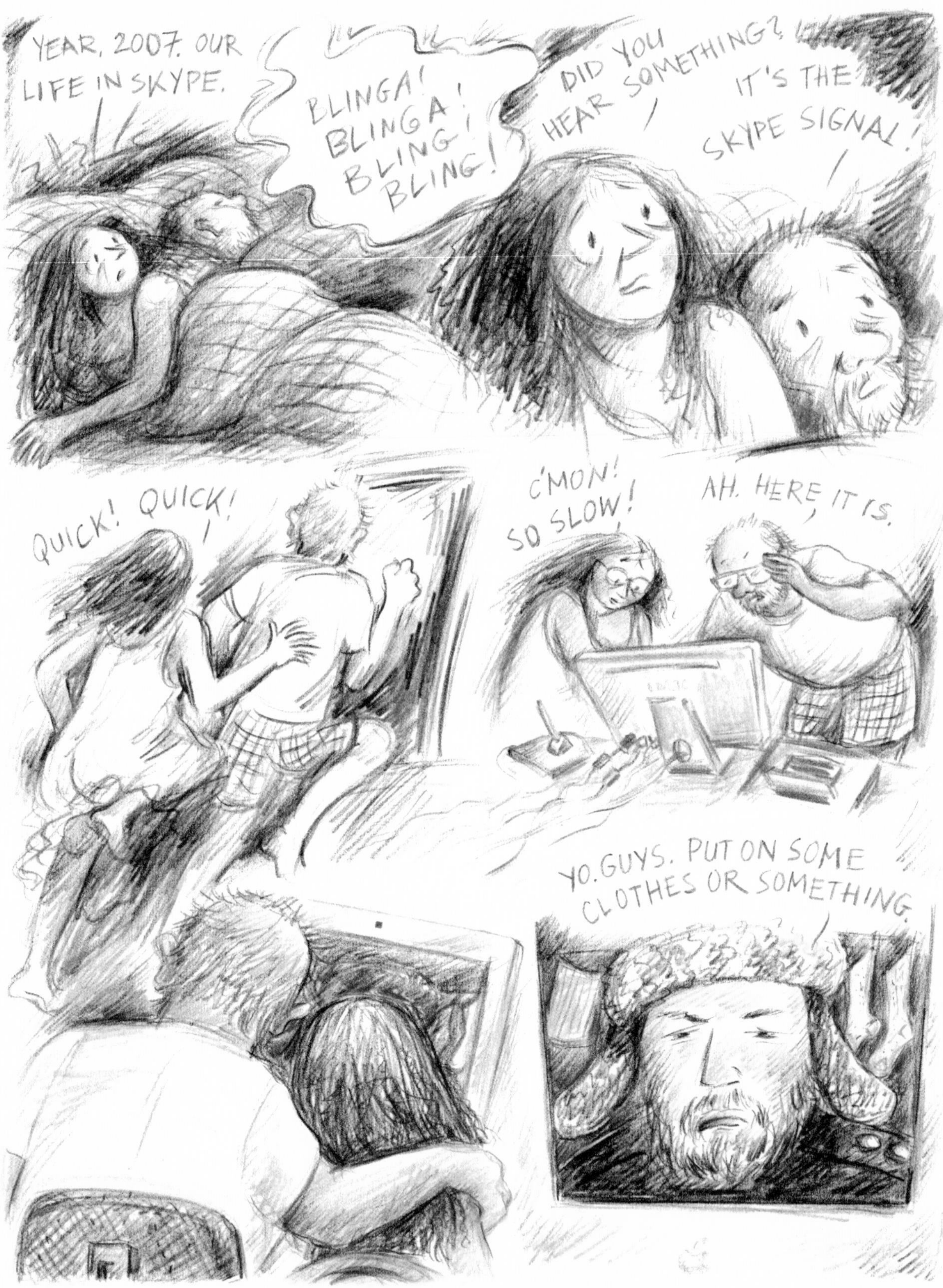
YEAR, 2007. OUR LIFE IN SKYPE.
BLINGA! BLINGA! BLING! BLING!
DID YOU HEAR SOMETHING?
IT'S THE SKYPE SIGNAL!
QUICK! QUICK!
C'MON! SO SLOW!
AH. HERE IT IS.
YO. GUYS. PUT ON SOME CLOTHES OR SOMETHING.

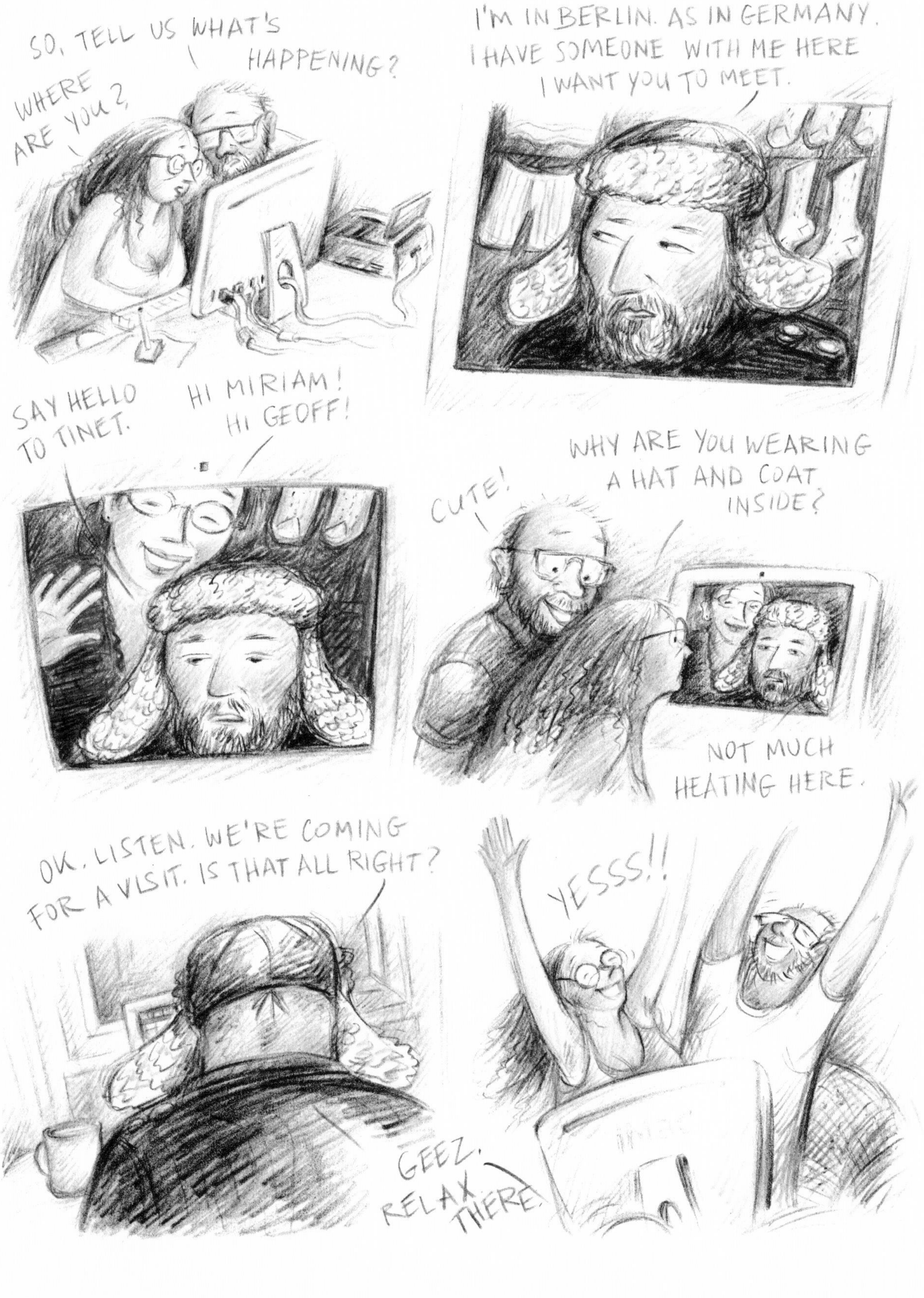
SO, TELL US WHAT'S HAPPENING?
WHERE ARE YOU?
I'M IN BERLIN. AS IN GERMANY. I HAVE SOMEONE WITH ME HERE I WANT YOU TO MEET.
SAY HELLO TO TINET.
HI MIRIAM! HI GEOFF!
CUTE!
WHY ARE YOU WEARING A HAT AND COAT INSIDE?
NOT MUCH HEATING HERE.
OK. LISTEN. WE'RE COMING FOR A VISIT. IS THAT ALL RIGHT?
YESSS!!
GEEZ. RELAX THERE.

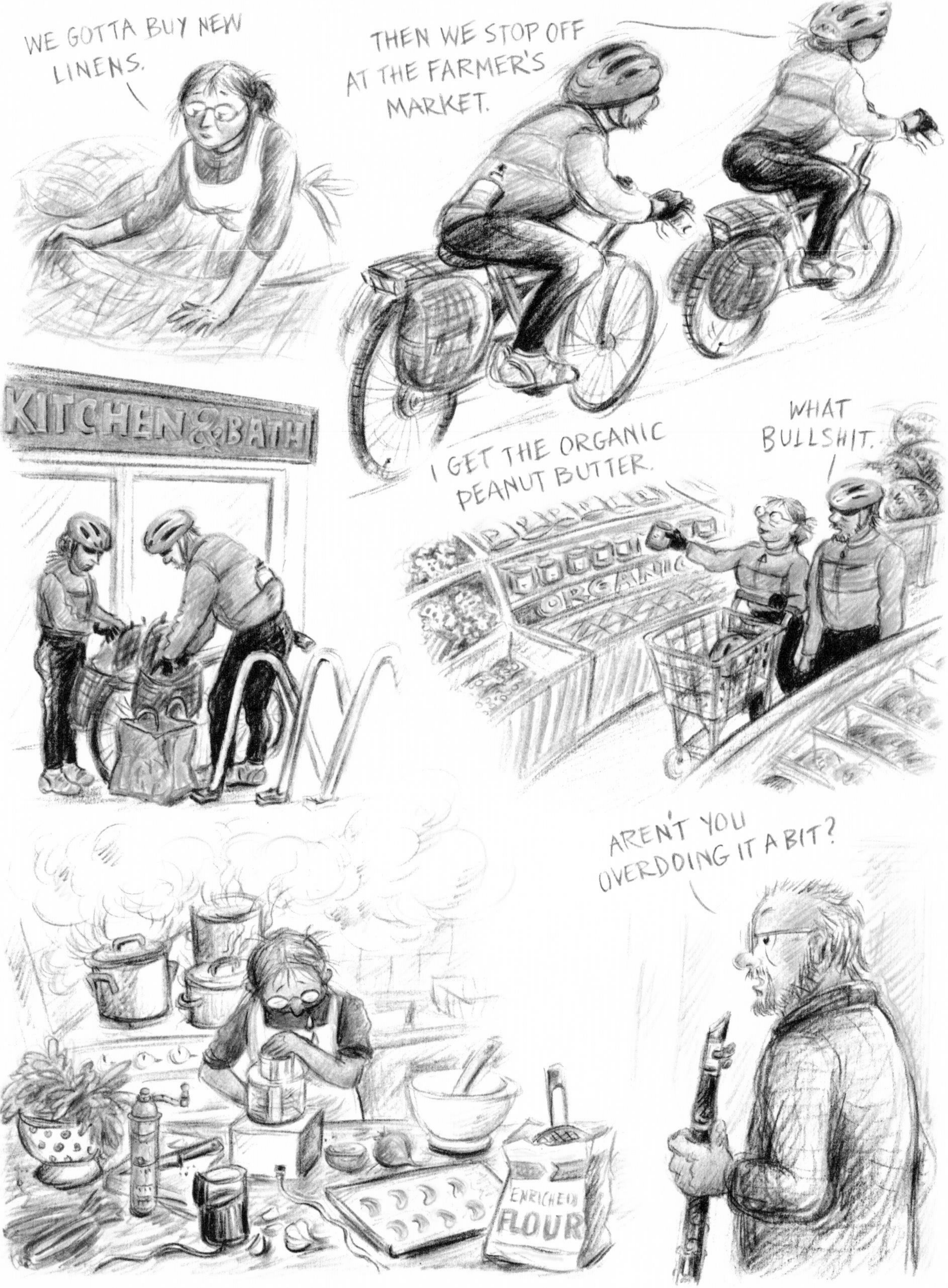
WE GOTTA BUY NEW LINENS.
THEN WE STOP OFF AT THE FARMER'S MARKET.
KITCHEN & BATH
I GET THE ORGANIC PEANUT BUTTER.
WHAT BULLSHIT.
ORGANIC
ENRICHED FLOUR
AREN'T YOU OVERDOING IT A BIT?

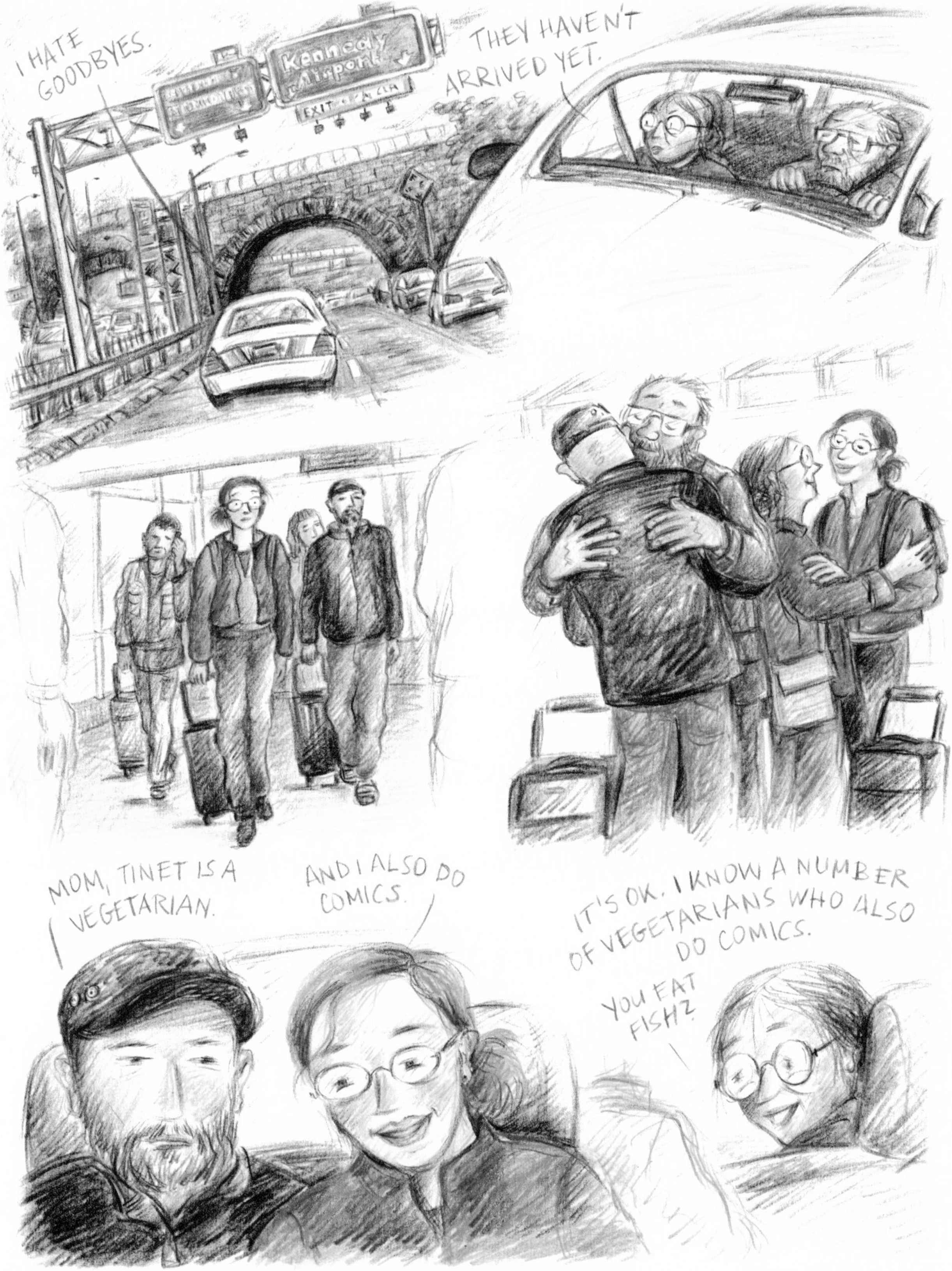
I HATE GOODBYES.
Kennedy Airport
THEY HAVEN'T ARRIVED YET.
MOM, TINET IS A VEGETARIAN.
AND I ALSO DO COMICS.
IT'S OK. I KNOW A NUMBER OF VEGETARIANS WHO ALSO DO COMICS.
YOU EAT FISH?

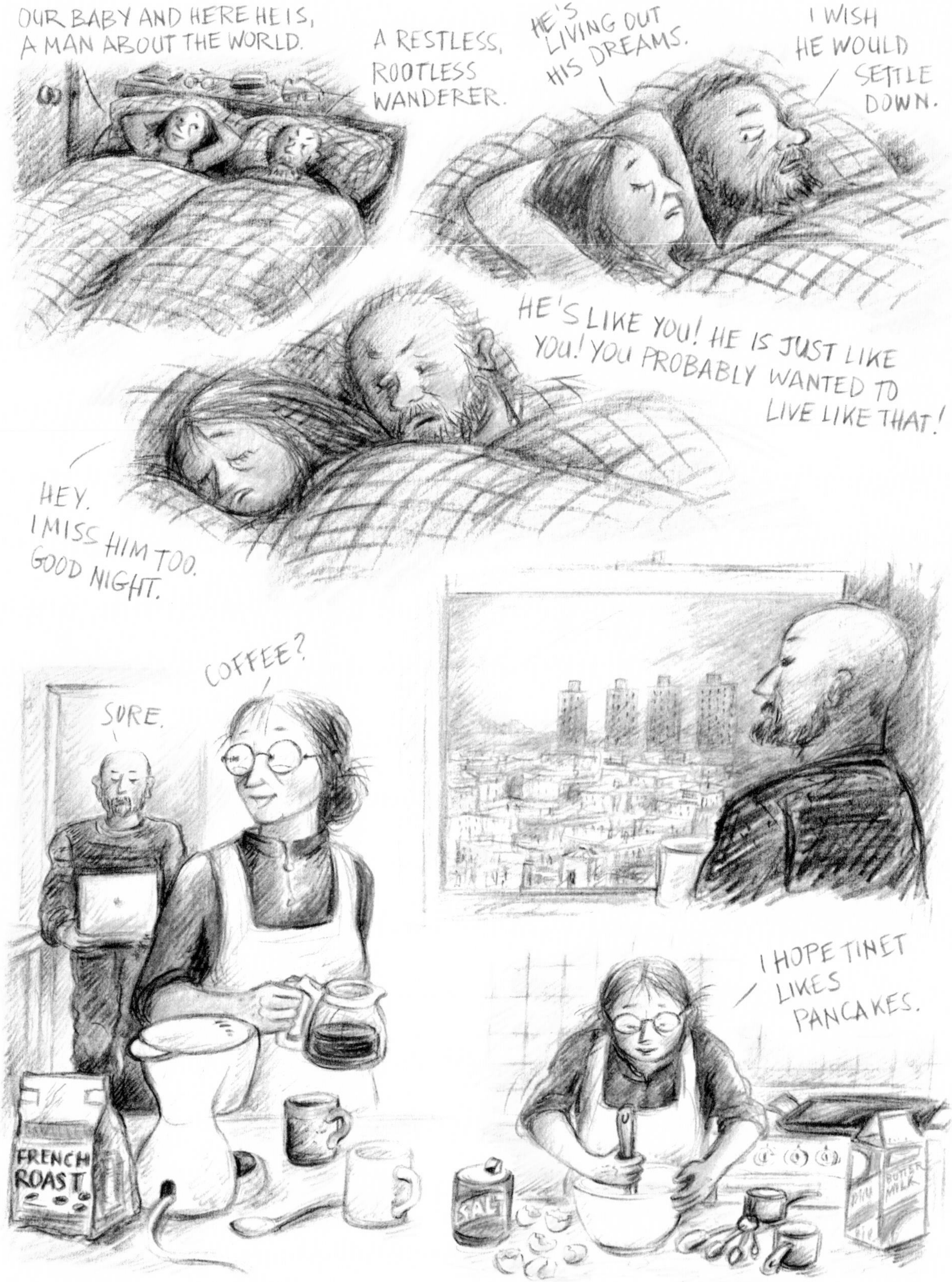
OUR BABY AND HERE HE IS, A MAN ABOUT THE WORLD.
A RESTLESS, ROOTLESS WANDERER.
HE'S LIVING OUT HIS DREAMS.
I WISH HE WOULD SETTLE DOWN.
HE'S LIKE YOU! HE IS JUST LIKE YOU! YOU PROBABLY WANTED TO LIVE LIKE THAT!
HEY. I MISS HIM TOO. GOOD NIGHT.
COFFEE?
SURE.
FRENCH ROAST
I HOPE TINET LIKES PANCAKES.
SALT
BUTTER MILK

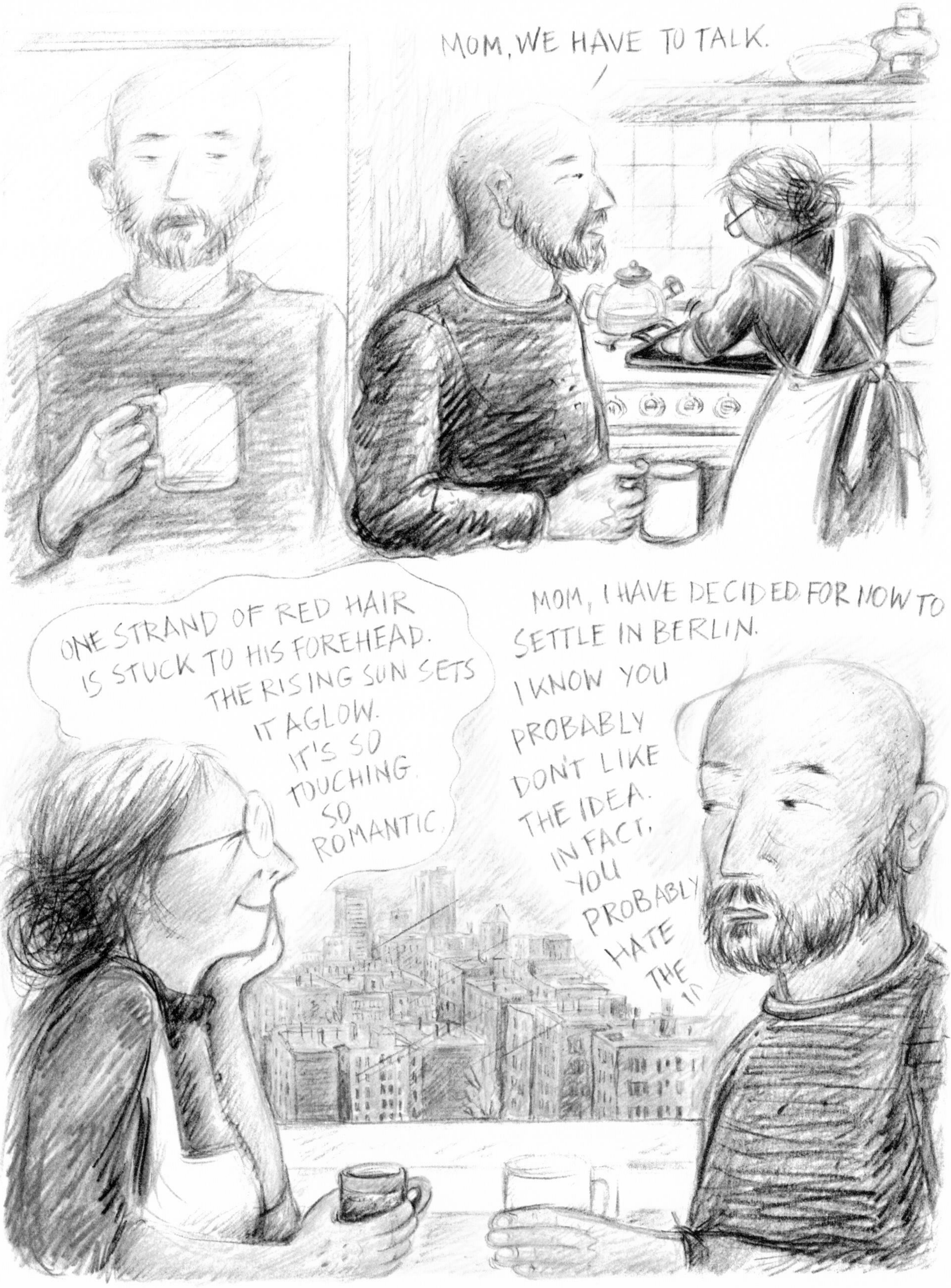
MOM, WE HAVE TO TALK.
ONE STRAND OF RED HAIR IS STUCK TO HIS FOREHEAD. THE RISING SUN SETS IT AGLOW. IT'S SO TOUCHING. SO ROMANTIC.
MOM, I HAVE DECIDED FOR NOW TO SETTLE IN BERLIN.
I KNOW YOU PROBABLY DON'T LIKE THE IDEA. IN FACT, YOU PROBABLY HATE THE

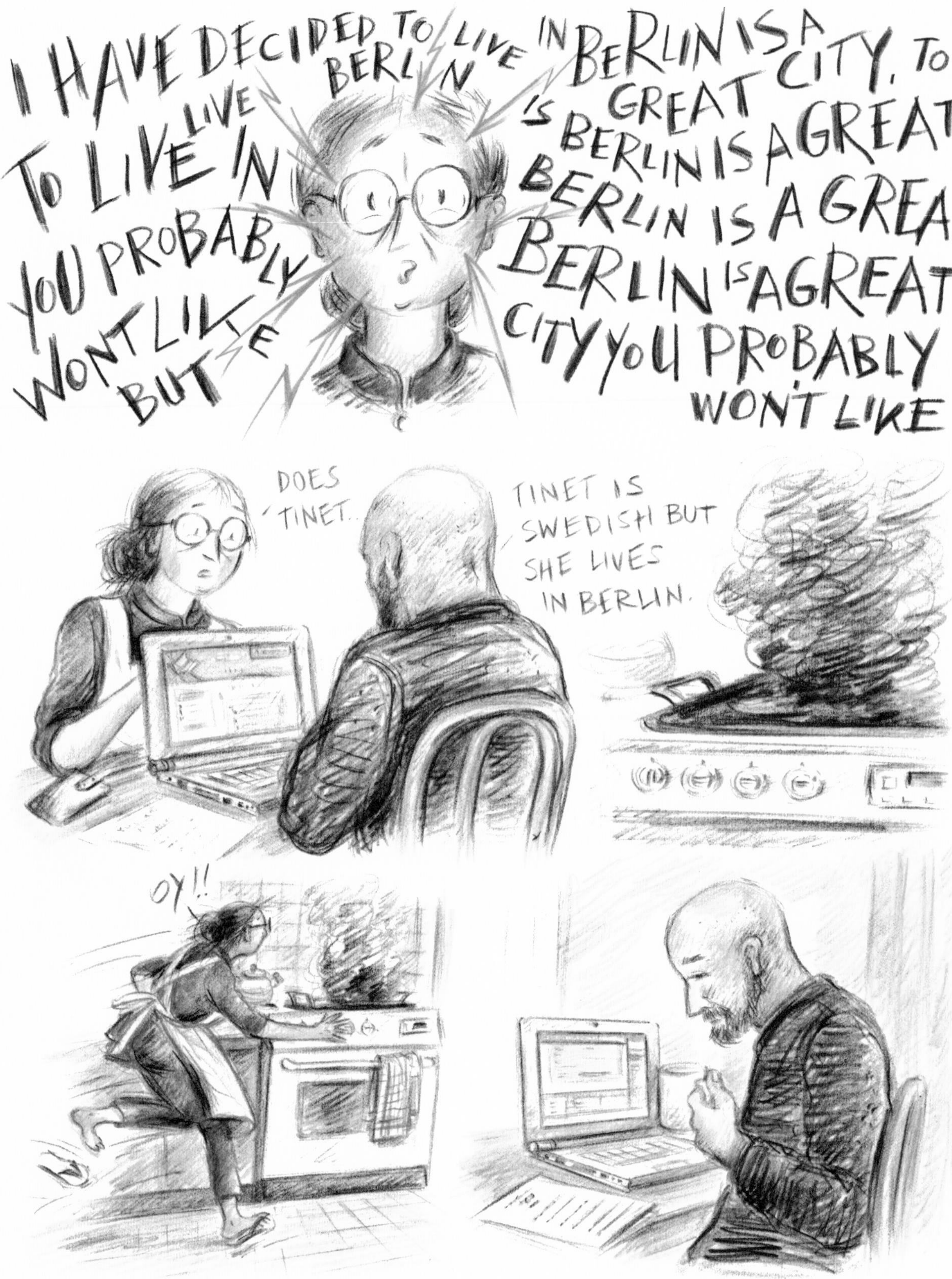
I HAVE DECIDED TO LIVE IN
BERLIN
BERLIN IS A GREAT CITY. TO
TO LIVE LIVE IN
YOU PROBABLY WONT LIVE BUT
IS BERLIN IS A GREAT
BERLIN IS A GREA
BERLIN IS A GREAT CITY YOU PROBABLY WON'T LIKE
DOES TINET..
TINET IS SWEDISH BUT SHE LIVES IN BERLIN.
OY!!

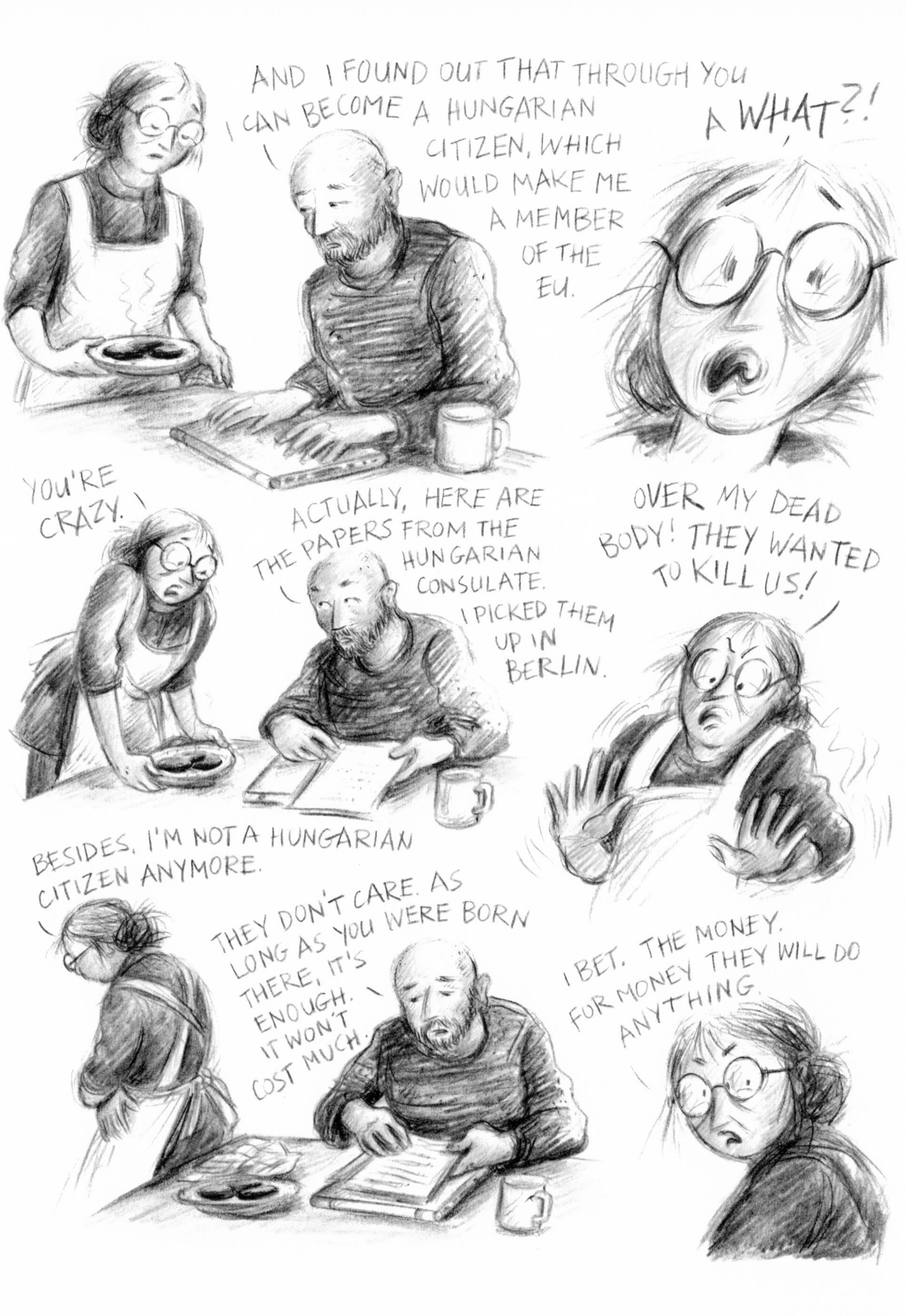
AND I FOUND OUT THAT THROUGH YOU I CAN BECOME A HUNGARIAN CITIZEN, WHICH WOULD MAKE ME A MEMBER OF THE EU.
A WHAT?!
YOU'RE CRAZY.
ACTUALLY, HERE ARE THE PAPERS FROM THE HUNGARIAN CONSULATE. I PICKED THEM UP IN BERLIN.
OVER MY DEAD BODY! THEY WANTED TO KILL US!
BESIDES, I'M NOT A HUNGARIAN CITIZEN ANYMORE.
THEY DON'T CARE. AS LONG AS YOU WERE BORN THERE, IT'S ENOUGH. IT WON'T COST MUCH.
I BET. THE MONEY. FOR MONEY THEY WILL DO ANYTHING.

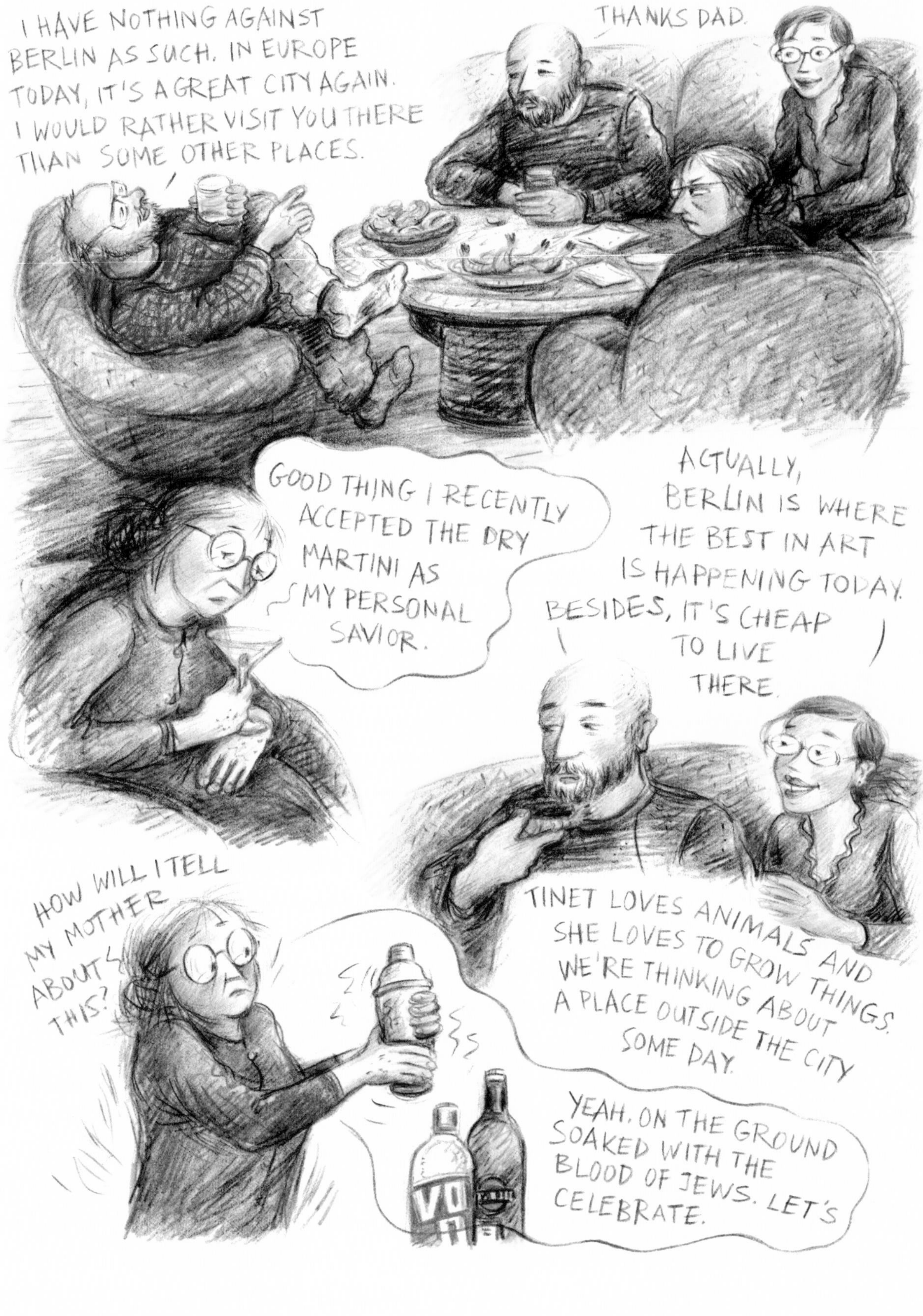
I HAVE NOTHING AGAINST BERLIN AS SUCH. IN EUROPE TODAY, IT'S A GREAT CITY AGAIN. I WOULD RATHER VISIT YOU THERE THAN SOME OTHER PLACES.
THANKS DAD.
GOOD THING I RECENTLY ACCEPTED THE DRY MARTINI AS MY PERSONAL SAVIOR.
ACTUALLY, BERLIN IS WHERE THE BEST IN ART IS HAPPENING TODAY. BESIDES, IT'S CHEAP TO LIVE THERE.
TINET LOVES ANIMALS AND SHE LOVES TO GROW THINGS. WE'RE THINKING ABOUT A PLACE OUTSIDE THE CITY SOME DAY.
HOW WILL I TELL MY MOTHER ABOUT THIS?
YEAH. ON THE GROUND SOAKED WITH THE BLOOD OF JEWS. LET'S CELEBRATE.

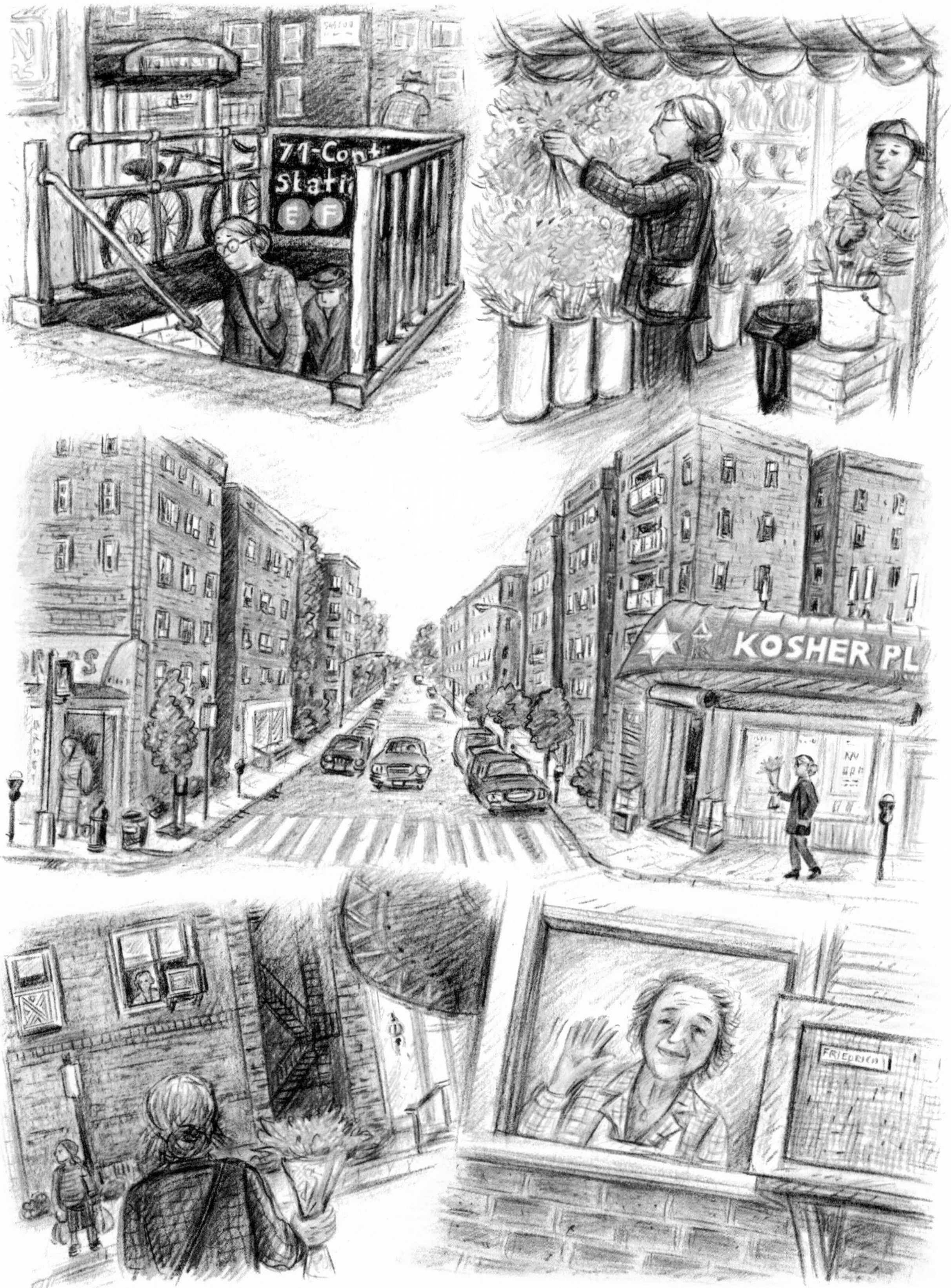

71-Cont
Stati
E F
KOSHER PL
FRIEDRICH

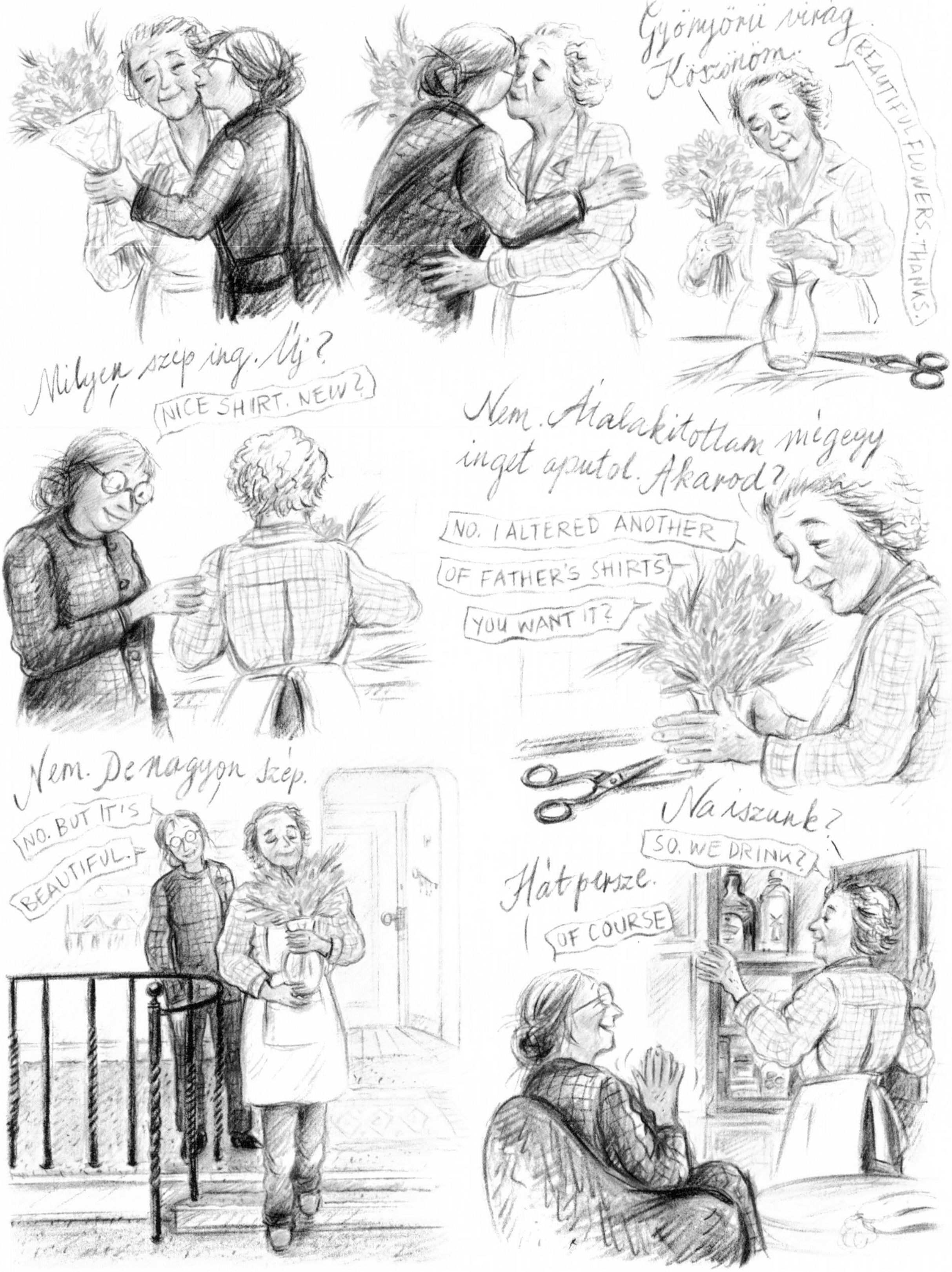
Gyönyörü virág. Köszönöm.
BEAUTIFUL FLOWERS. THANKS.
Milyen szép ing. Új?
NICE SHIRT. NEW?
Nem. Átalakitottam mégegy inget aputol. Akarod?
NO. I ALTERED ANOTHER
OF FATHER'S SHIRTS.
YOU WANT IT?
Nem. De nagyon szép.
NO. BUT IT'S
BEAUTIFUL.
Na iszunk?
SO. WE DRINK?
Hát persze.
OF COURSE

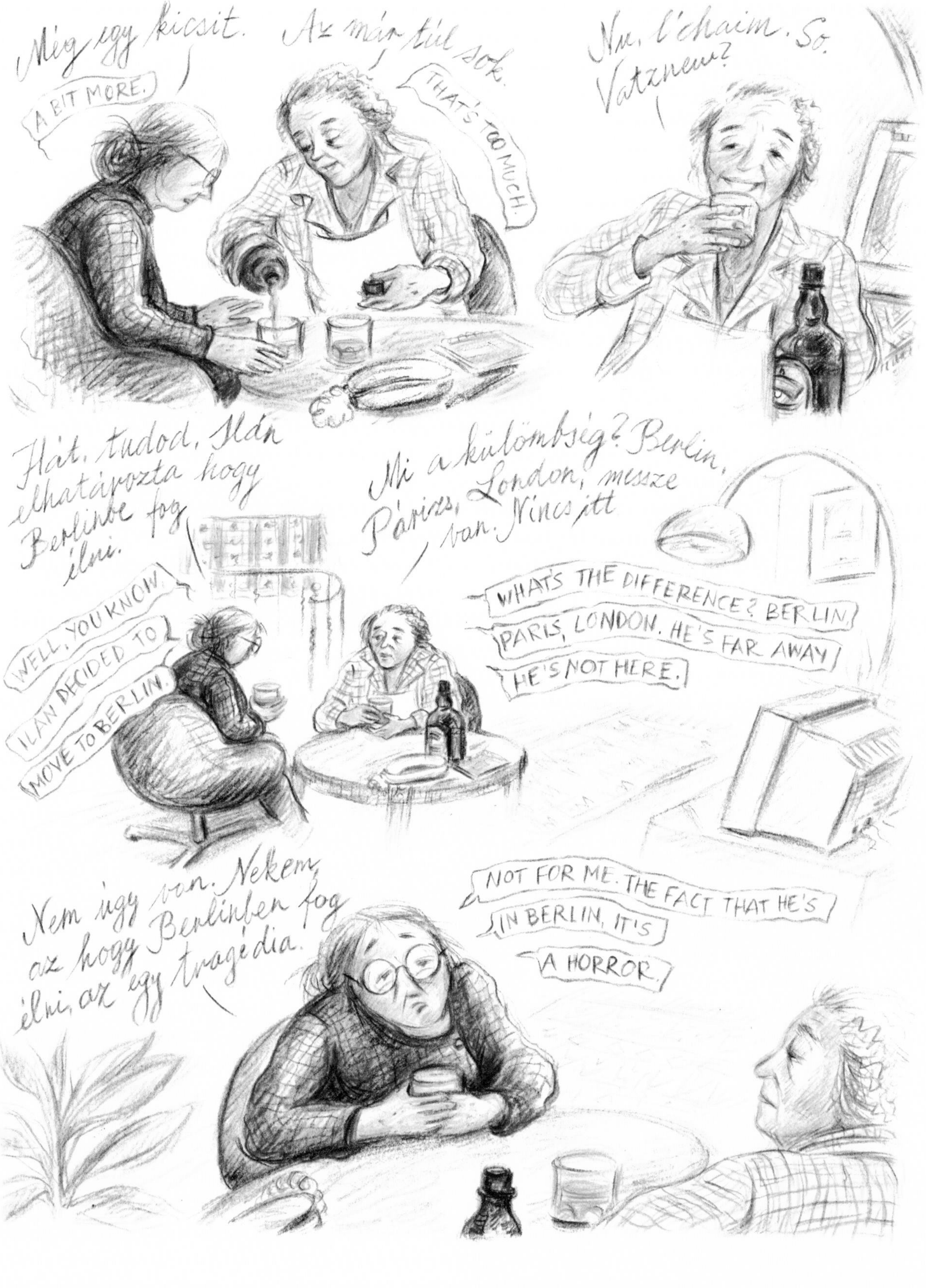
Még egy kicsit.
A BIT MORE.
Az már túl sok.
THAT'S TOO MUCH.
Nu, l'chaim. So. Vatznew?
Hát, tudod, Ilán elhatározta hogy Berlinbe fog élni.
WELL, YOU KNOW, ILAN DECIDED TO MOVE TO BERLIN.
Mi a külömbség? Berlin, Páriss, London, messze van. Nincs itt
WHAT'S THE DIFFERENCE? BERLIN, PARIS, LONDON. HE'S FAR AWAY HE'S NOT HERE.
Nem úgy van. Nekem, az hogy Berlinben fog élni, az egy tragédia.
NOT FOR ME. THE FACT THAT HE'S IN BERLIN, IT'S A HORROR.

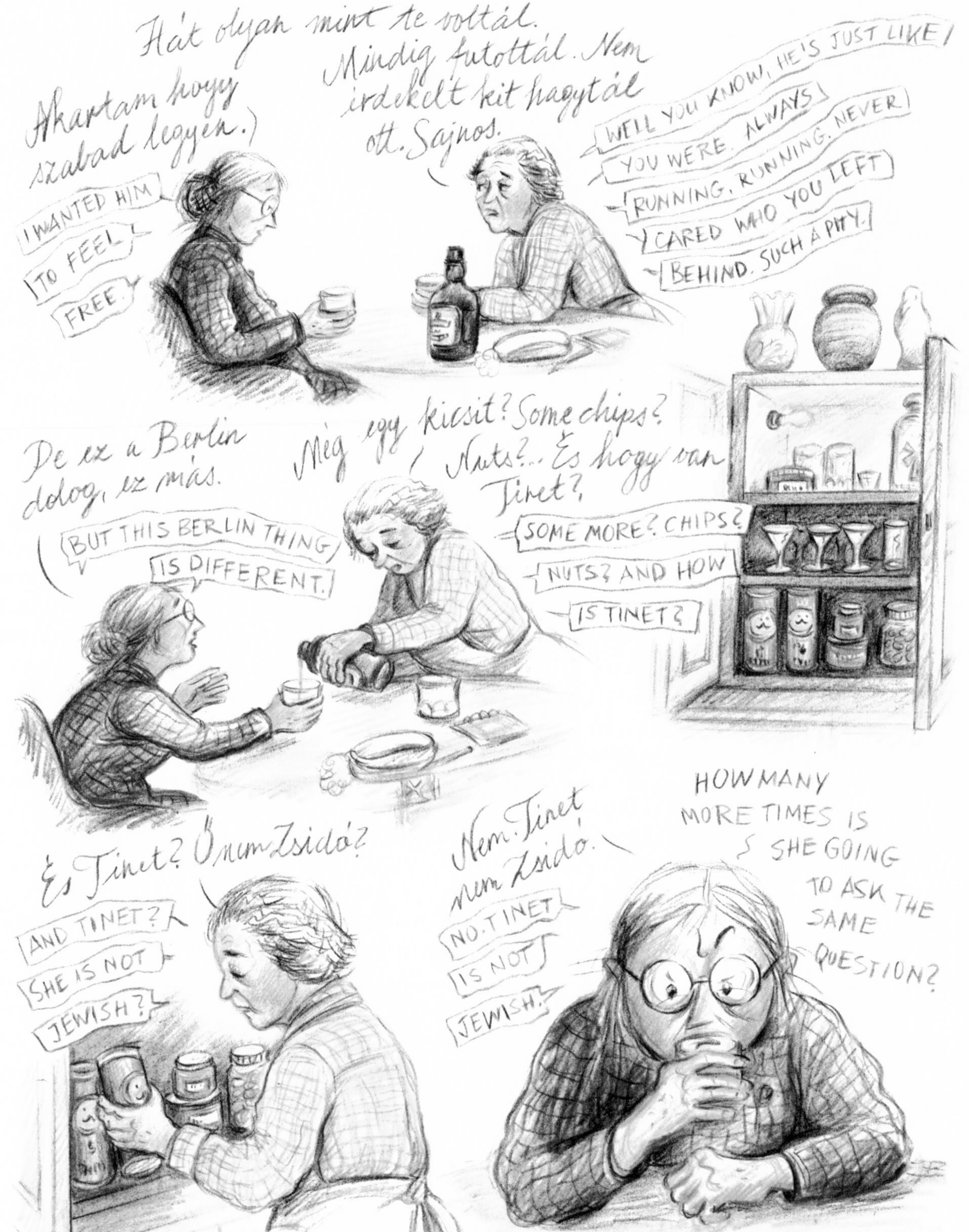

Hát olyan mint te voltál. Mindig futottál. Nem érdekelt kit hagytál ott. Sajnos.
WELL YOU KNOW, HE'S JUST LIKE YOU WERE. ALWAYS RUNNING, RUNNING. NEVER CARED WHO YOU LEFT BEHIND. SUCH A PITY.
Akartam hogy szabad legyen.
I WANTED HIM TO FEEL FREE.
Még egy kicsit? Some chips? Nuts?... És hogy van Tinet?
SOME MORE? CHIPS? NUTS? AND HOW IS TINET?
De ez a Berlin dolog, ez más.
BUT THIS BERLIN THING IS DIFFERENT.
És Tinet? Ő nem Zsidó?
AND TINET? SHE IS NOT JEWISH?
Nem. Tinet nem Zsidó.
NO. TINET IS NOT JEWISH.
HOW MANY MORE TIMES IS SHE GOING TO ASK THE SAME QUESTION?

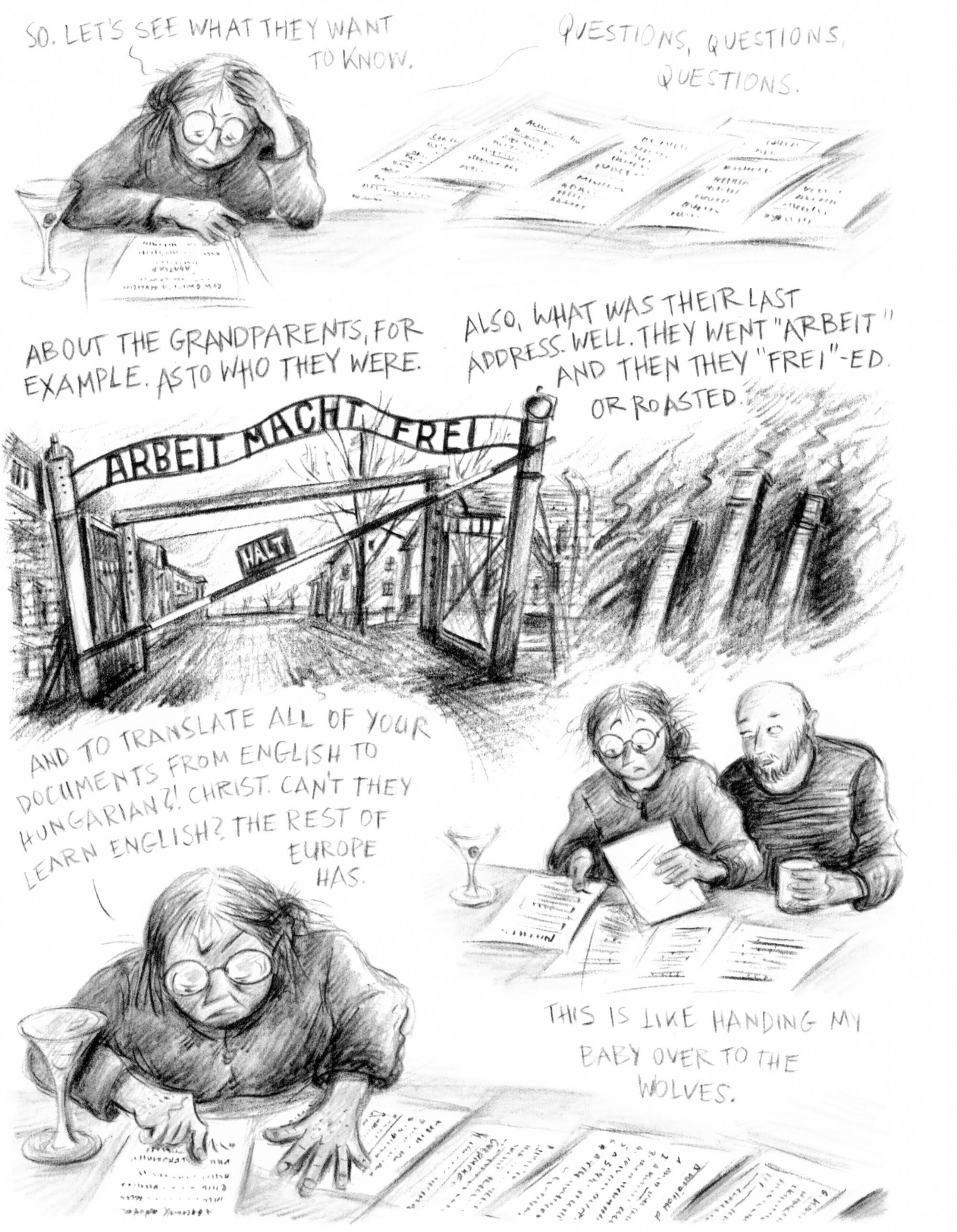
SO. LET'S SEE WHAT THEY WANT TO KNOW.
QUESTIONS, QUESTIONS, QUESTIONS.
ABOUT THE GRANDPARENTS, FOR EXAMPLE. AS TO WHO THEY WERE.
ALSO, WHAT WAS THEIR LAST ADDRESS. WELL. THEY WENT "ARBEIT" AND THEN THEY "FREI"-ED. OR ROASTED.
ARBEIT MACHT FREI
HALT
AND TO TRANSLATE ALL OF YOUR DOCUMENTS FROM ENGLISH TO HUNGARIAN?! CHRIST. CAN'T THEY LEARN ENGLISH? THE REST OF EUROPE HAS.
THIS IS LIKE HANDING MY BABY OVER TO THE WOLVES.

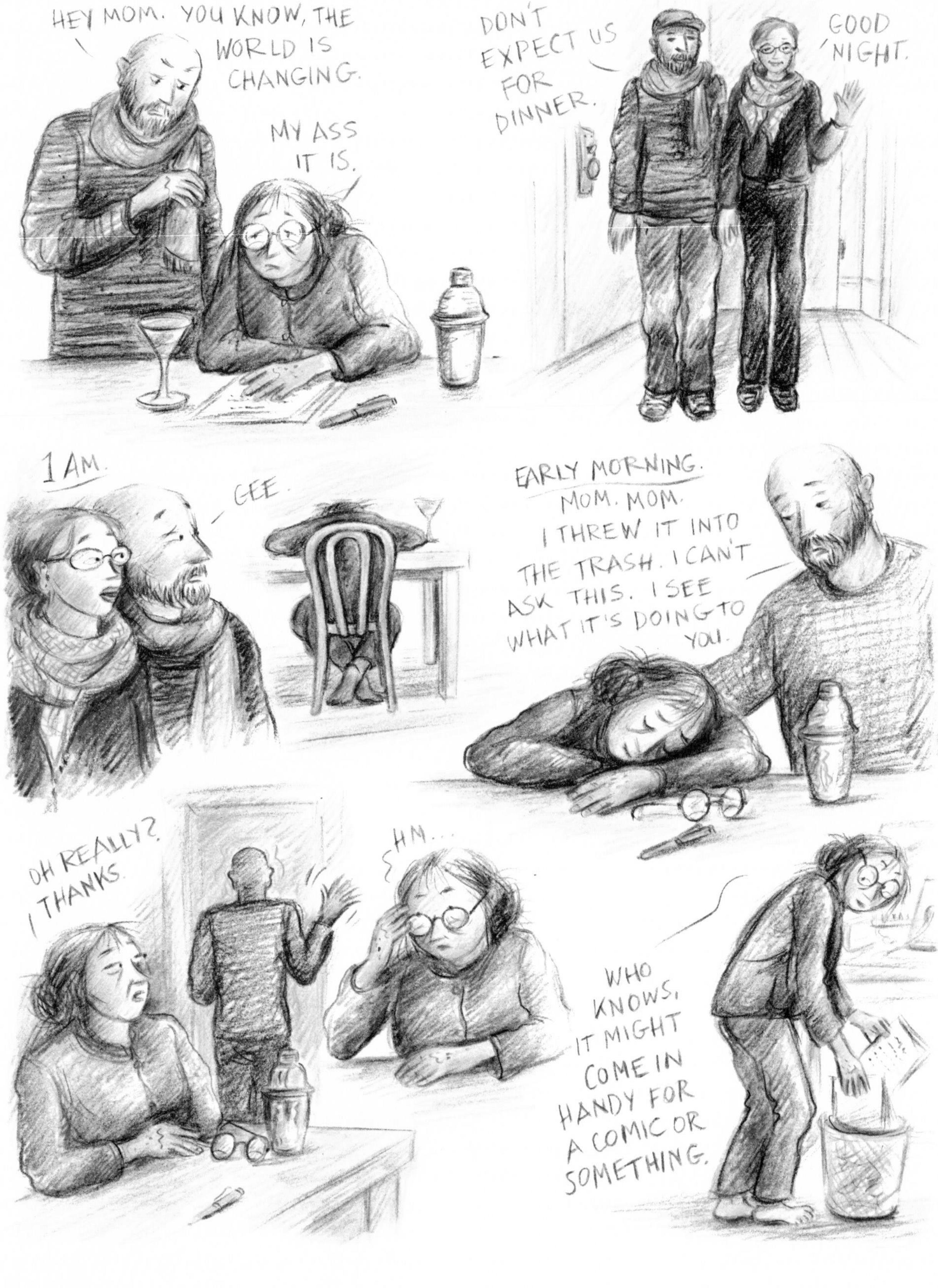
HEY MOM. YOU KNOW, THE WORLD IS CHANGING.
MY ASS IT IS.
DON'T EXPECT US FOR DINNER.
GOOD NIGHT.
1 AM.
GEE.
EARLY MORNING.
MOM. MOM. I THREW IT INTO THE TRASH. I CAN'T ASK THIS. I SEE WHAT IT'S DOING TO YOU.
OH REALLY? THANKS.
HM...
WHO KNOWS, IT MIGHT COME IN HANDY FOR A COMIC OR SOMETHING.

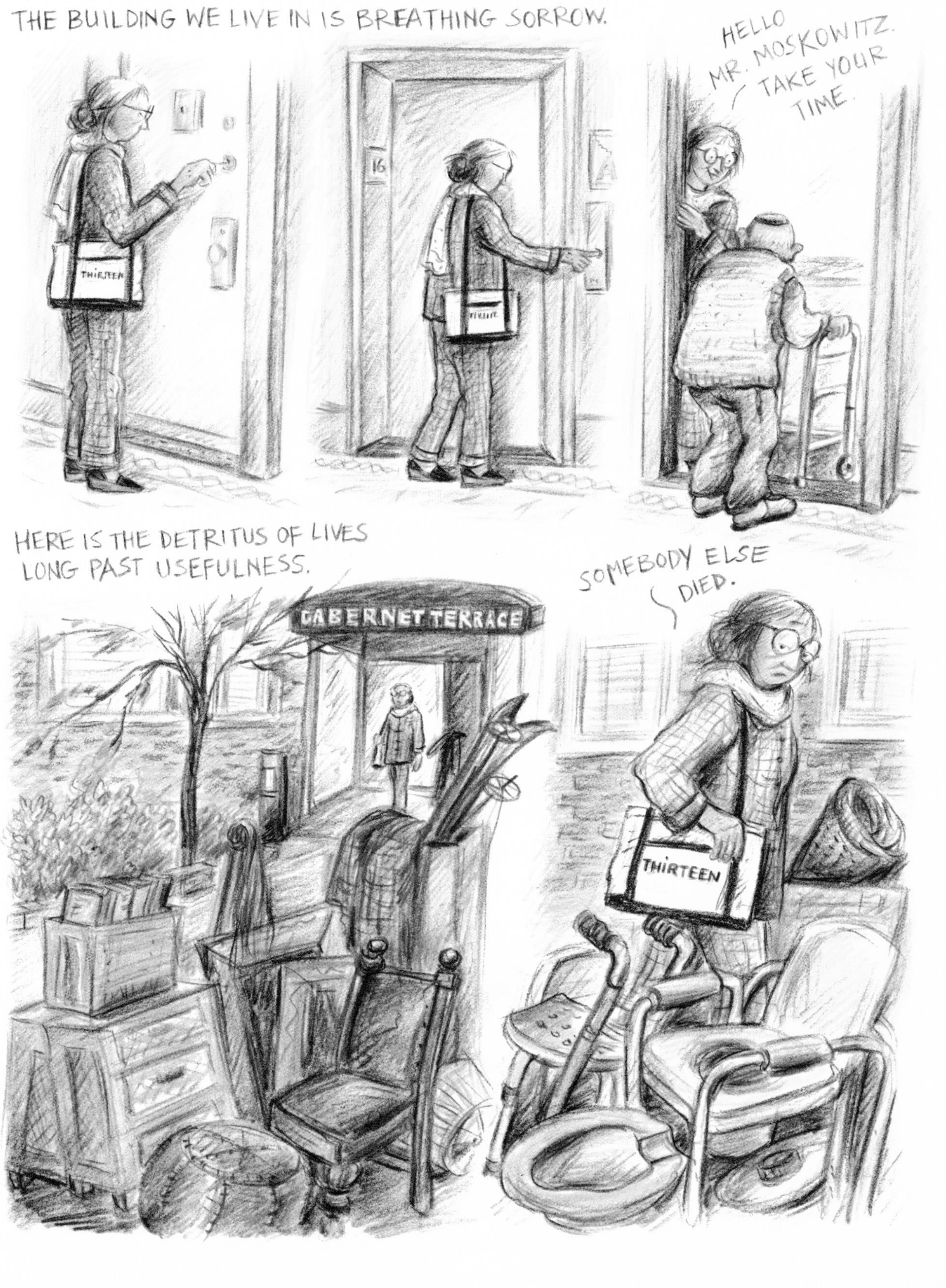
THE BUILDING WE LIVE IN IS BREATHING SORROW.
THIRTEEN
16
HELLO MR. MOSKOWITZ. TAKE YOUR TIME.
HERE IS THE DETRITUS OF LIVES LONG PAST USEFULNESS.
CABERNET TERRACE
SOMEBODY ELSE DIED.
THIRTEEN

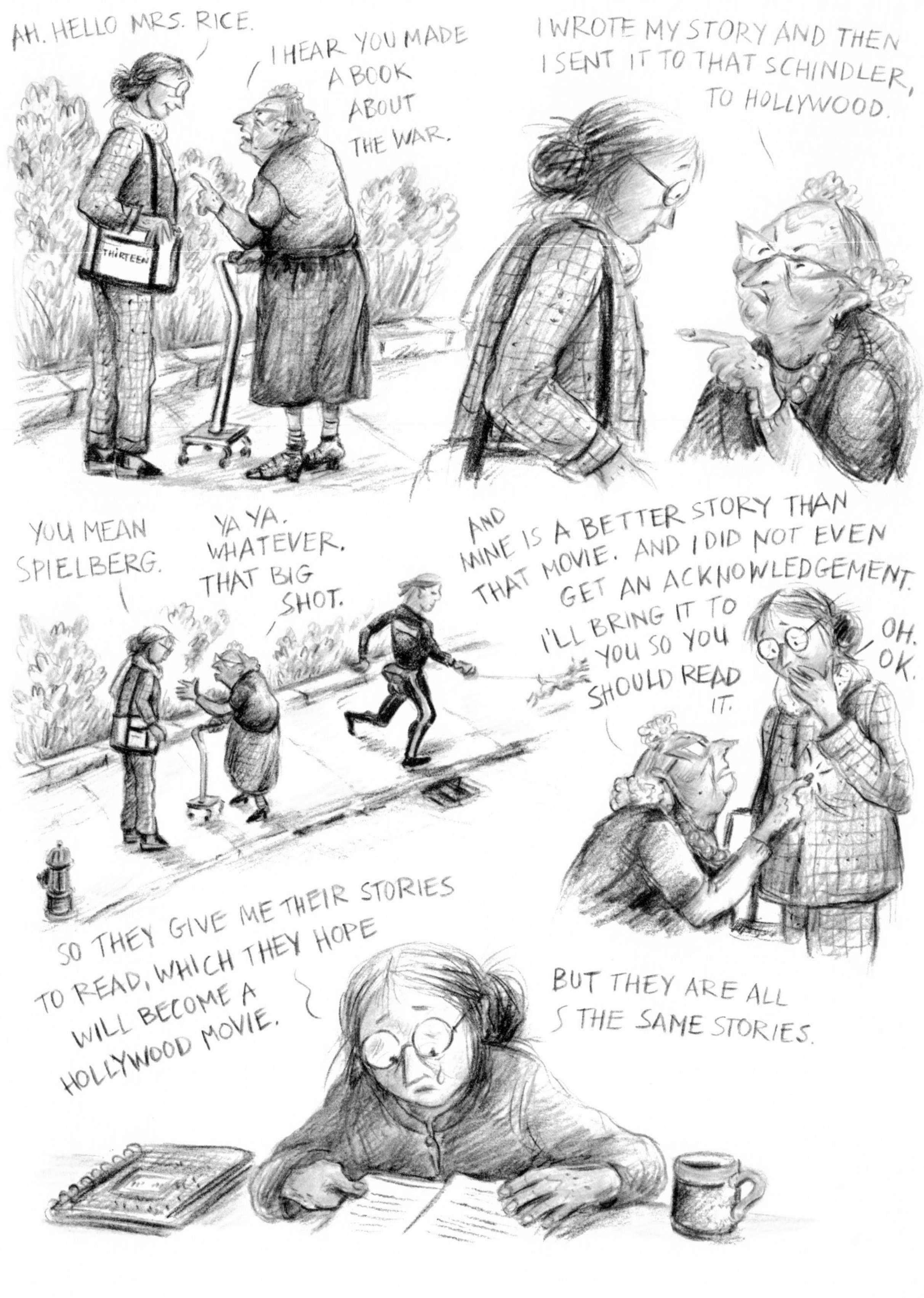
AH. HELLO MRS. RICE.
I HEAR YOU MADE A BOOK ABOUT THE WAR.
THIRTEEN
I WROTE MY STORY AND THEN I SENT IT TO THAT SCHINDLER, TO HOLLYWOOD.
YOU MEAN SPIELBERG.
YA YA. WHATEVER. THAT BIG SHOT.
AND MINE IS A BETTER STORY THAN THAT MOVIE. AND I DID NOT EVEN GET AN ACKNOWLEDGEMENT.
I'LL BRING IT TO YOU SO YOU SHOULD READ IT.
OH. OK.
SO THEY GIVE ME THEIR STORIES TO READ, WHICH THEY HOPE WILL BECOME A HOLLYWOOD MOVIE.
BUT THEY ARE ALL THE SAME STORIES.

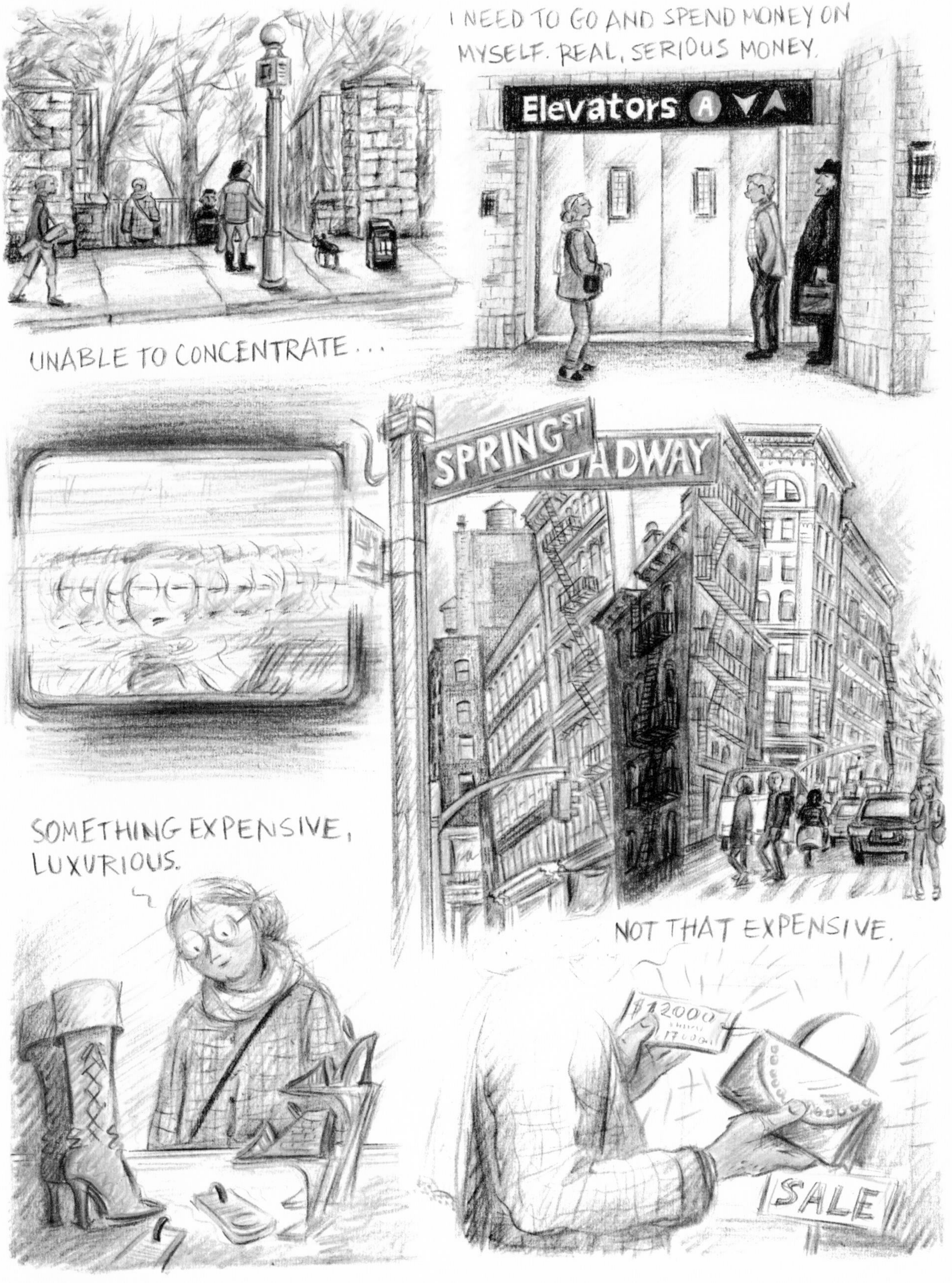
UNABLE TO CONCENTRATE . . .
I NEED TO GO AND SPEND MONEY ON MYSELF. REAL, SERIOUS MONEY.
Elevators A
SPRING ST
ADWAY
SOMETHING EXPENSIVE, LUXURIOUS.
NOT THAT EXPENSIVE.
SALE

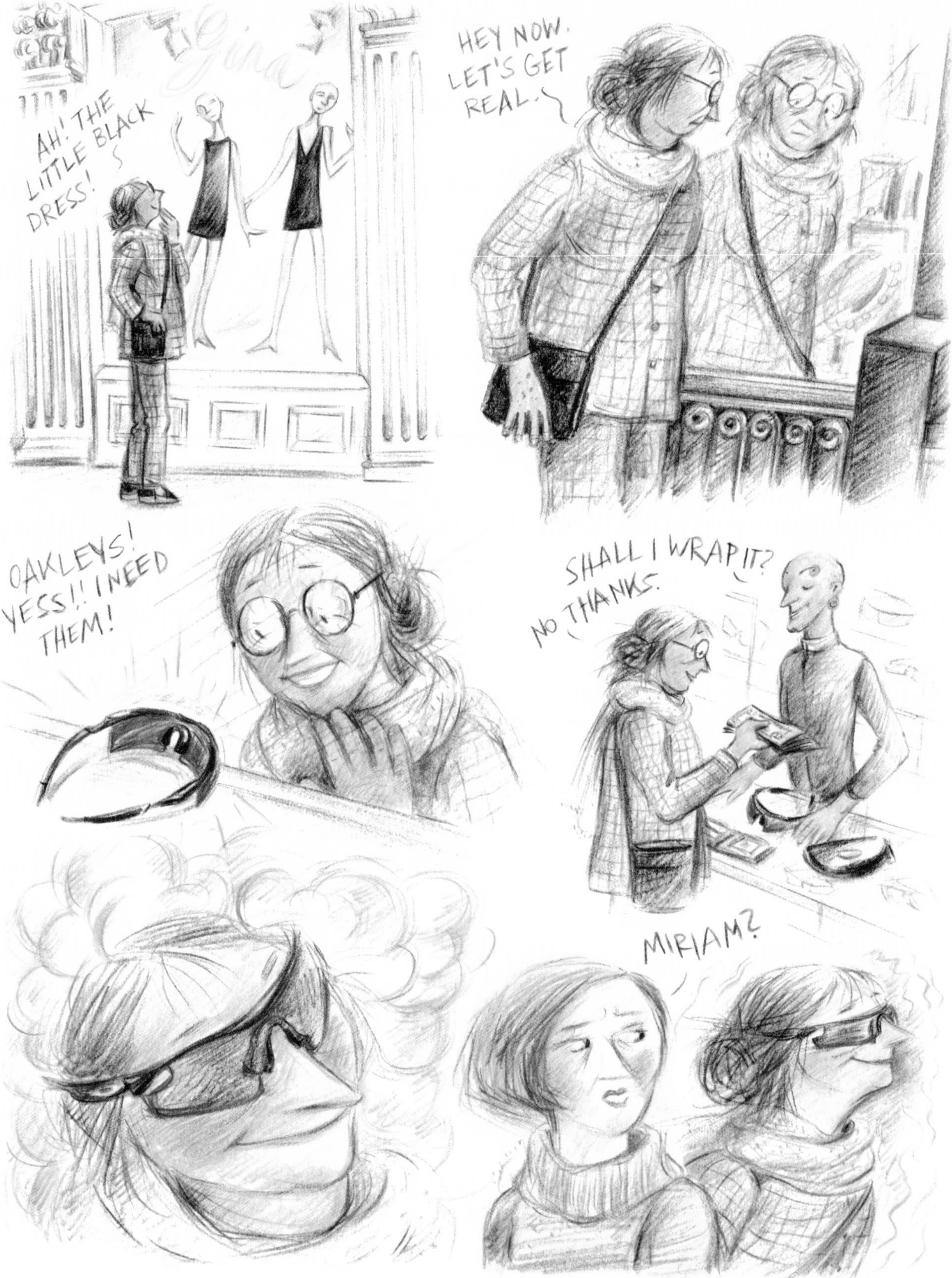
AH! THE LITTLE BLACK DRESS!
HEY NOW. LET'S GET REAL.
OAKLEYS! YESS!! I NEED THEM!
SHALL I WRAP IT?
NO THANKS.
MIRIAM?

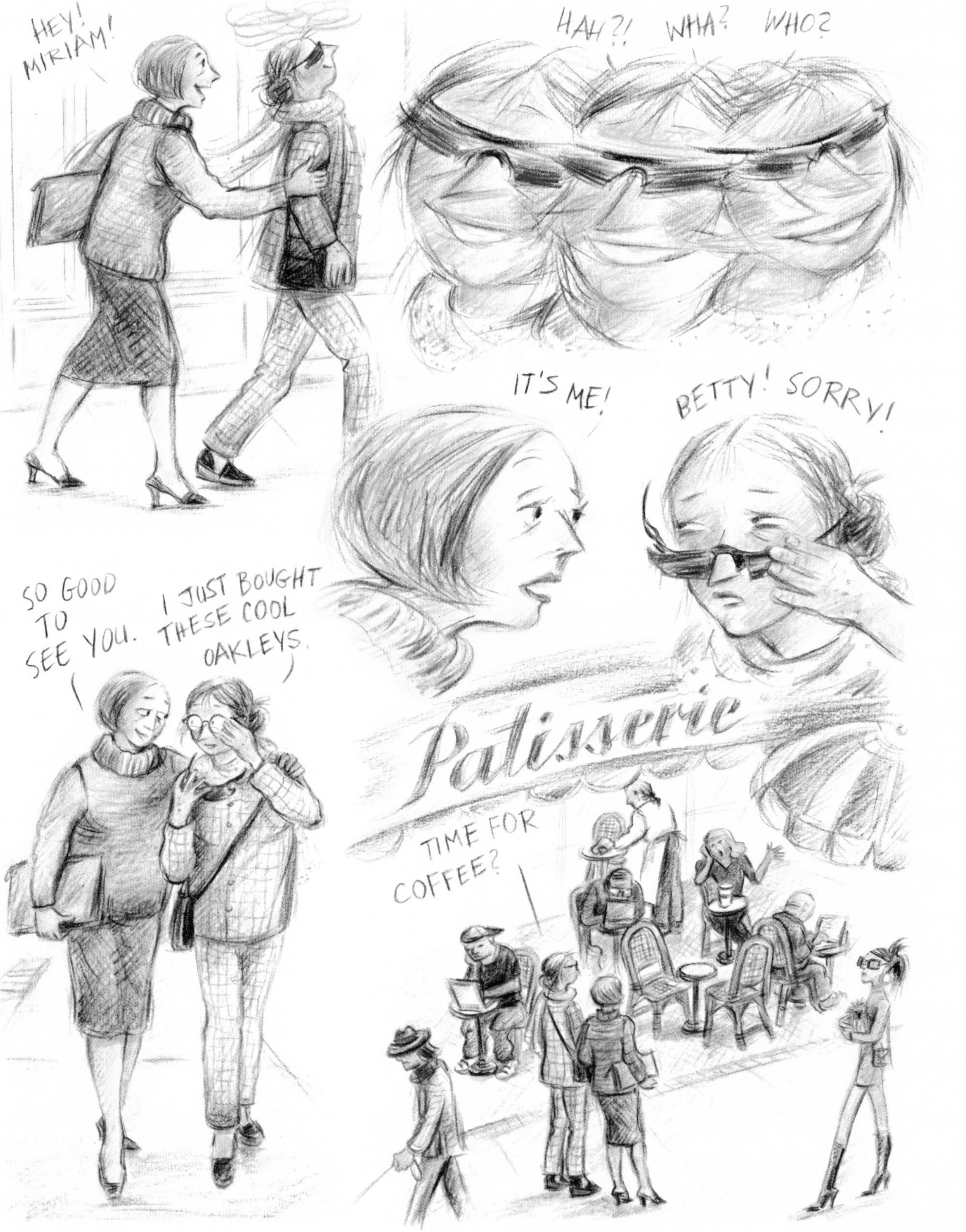
HEY! MIRIAM!
HAH?! WHA? WHO?
IT'S ME!
BETTY! SORRY!
SO GOOD TO SEE YOU.
I JUST BOUGHT THESE COOL OAKLEYS.
Patisserie
TIME FOR COFFEE?

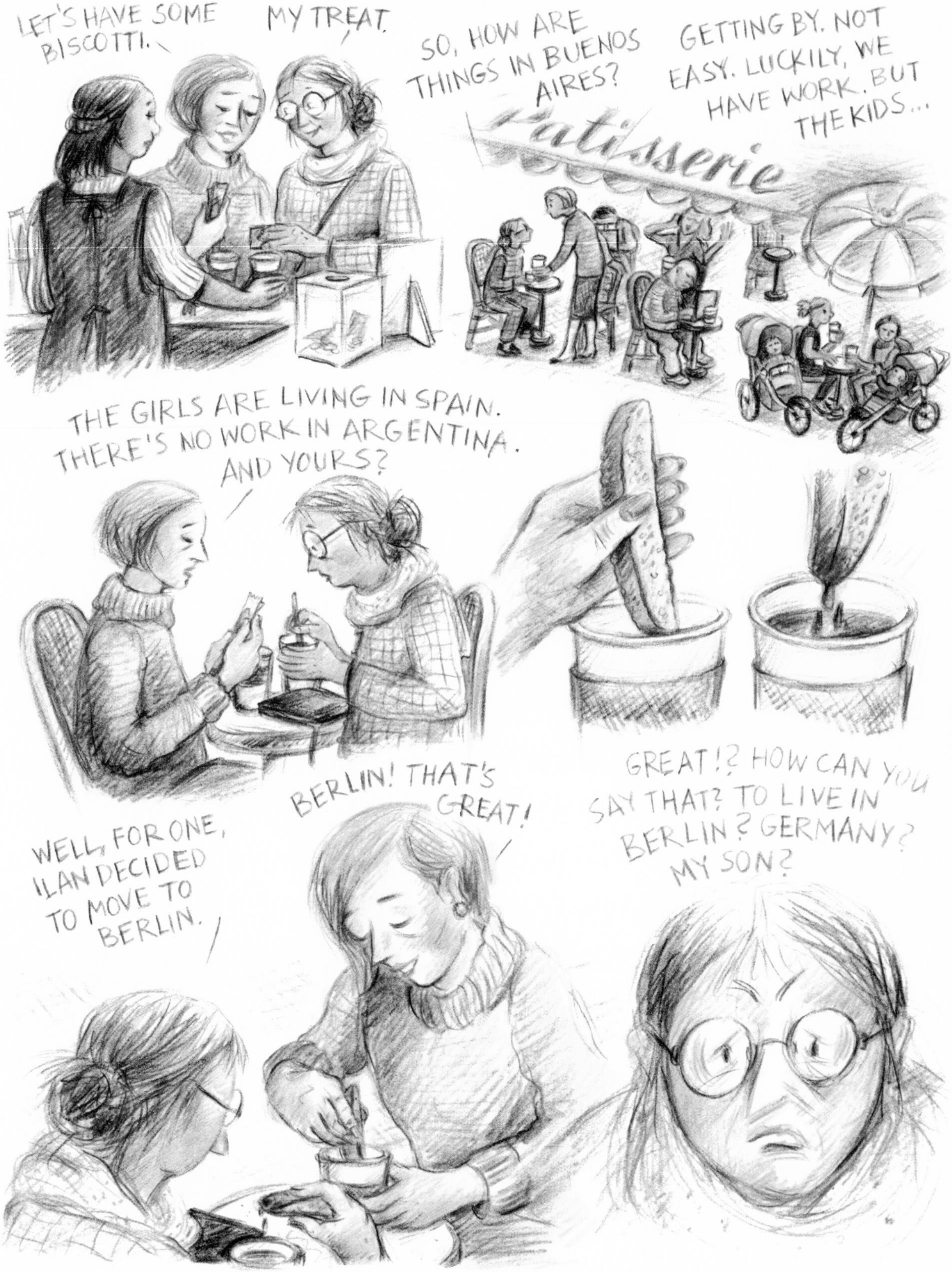
LET'S HAVE SOME BISCOTTI.
MY TREAT.
SO, HOW ARE THINGS IN BUENOS AIRES?
GETTING BY. NOT EASY. LUCKILY, WE HAVE WORK. BUT THE KIDS...
Patisserie
THE GIRLS ARE LIVING IN SPAIN. THERE'S NO WORK IN ARGENTINA. AND YOURS?
WELL, FOR ONE, ILAN DECIDED TO MOVE TO BERLIN.
BERLIN! THAT'S GREAT!
GREAT!? HOW CAN YOU SAY THAT? TO LIVE IN BERLIN? GERMANY? MY SON?

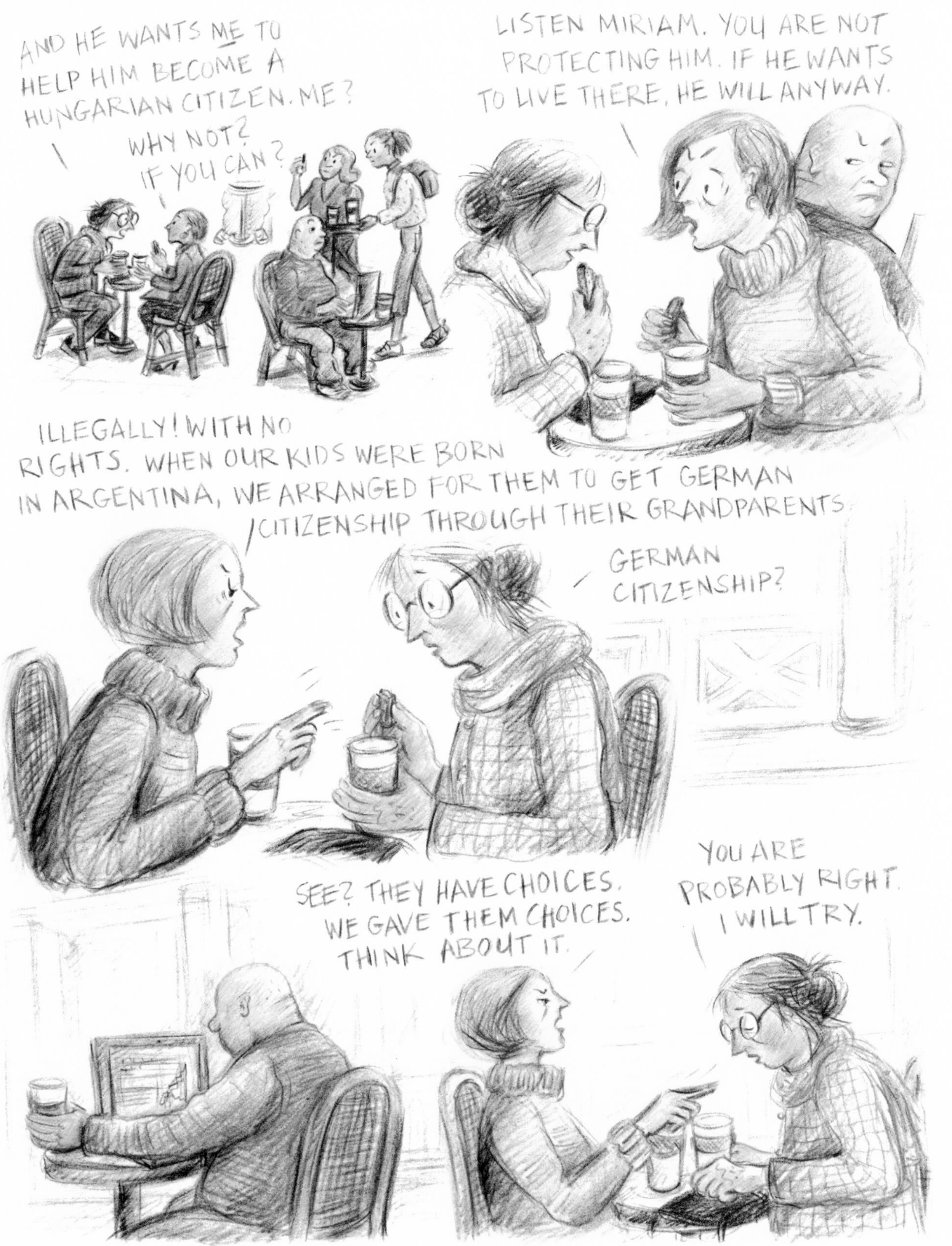
AND HE WANTS ME TO HELP HIM BECOME A HUNGARIAN CITIZEN. ME?
WHY NOT? IF YOU CAN?
LISTEN MIRIAM. YOU ARE NOT PROTECTING HIM. IF HE WANTS TO LIVE THERE, HE WILL ANYWAY.
ILLEGALLY! WITH NO RIGHTS. WHEN OUR KIDS WERE BORN IN ARGENTINA, WE ARRANGED FOR THEM TO GET GERMAN CITIZENSHIP THROUGH THEIR GRANDPARENTS.
GERMAN CITIZENSHIP?
SEE? THEY HAVE CHOICES. WE GAVE THEM CHOICES. THINK ABOUT IT.
YOU ARE PROBABLY RIGHT. I WILL TRY.

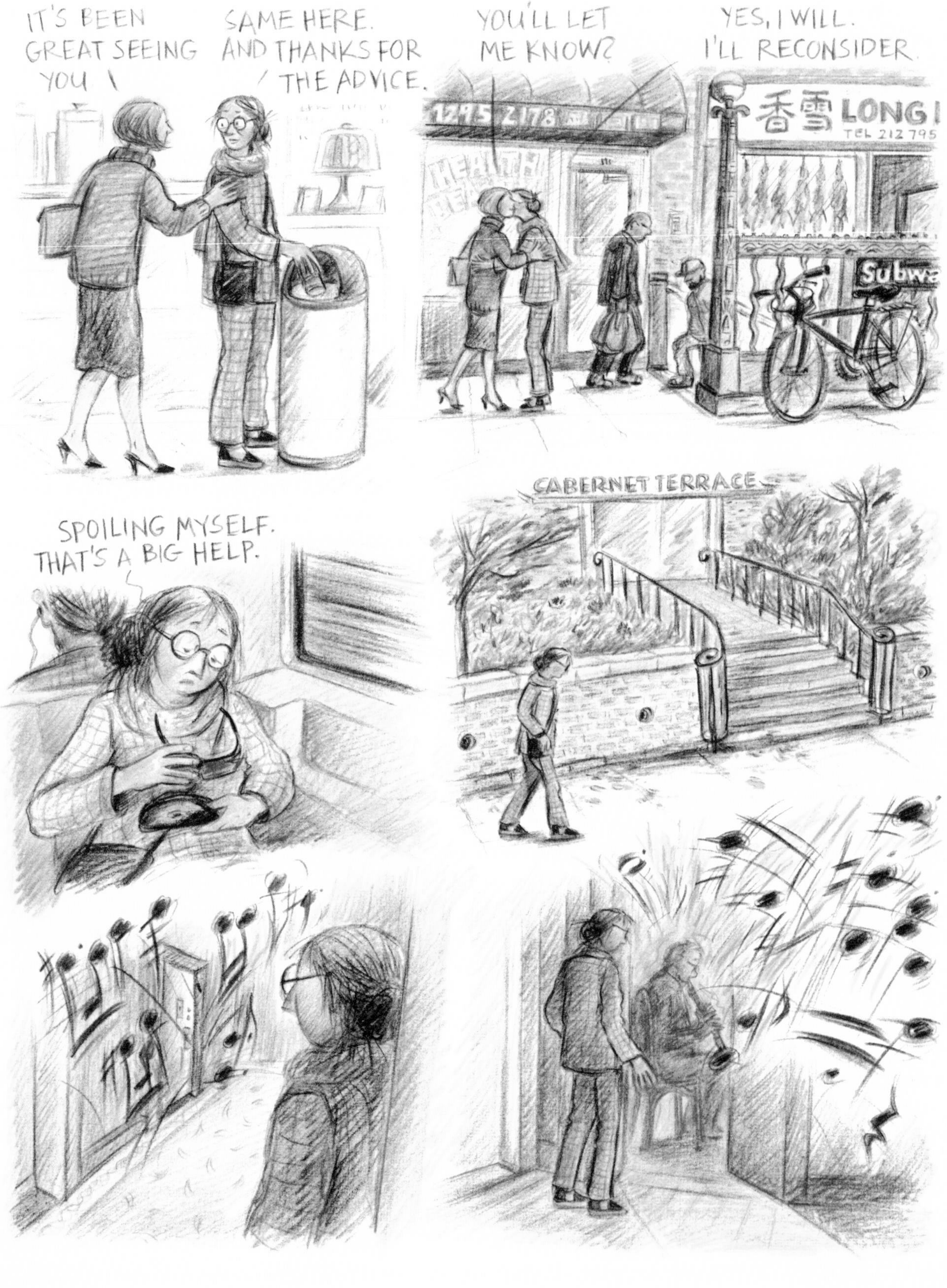
IT'S BEEN GREAT SEEING YOU.
SAME HERE. AND THANKS FOR THE ADVICE.
YOU'LL LET ME KNOW?
YES, I WILL. I'LL RECONSIDER.
香雪 LONG
TEL 212 795
Subwa
CABERNET TERRACE
SPOILING MYSELF. THAT'S A BIG HELP.

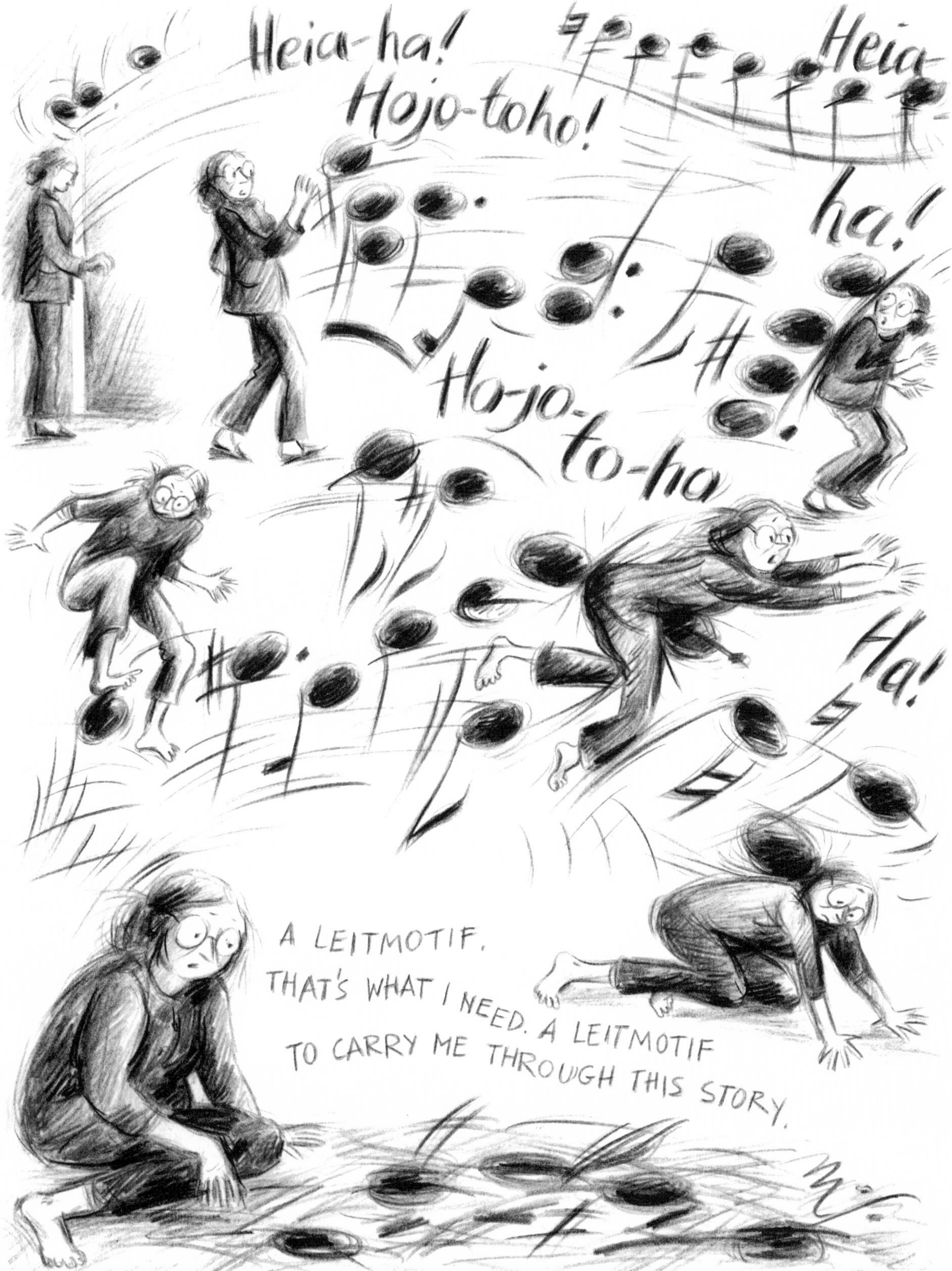
Heia-ha!
Hojo-toho!
Heia-
ha!
Ho-jo-to-ha
Ha!
A LEITMOTIF. THAT'S WHAT I NEED. A LEITMOTIF TO CARRY ME THROUGH THIS STORY.

ASSOCIATED WITH THE OPERAS OF RICHARD WAGNER, LEITMOTIF IS A MUSICAL TERM REFERRING TO A RECURRING THEME INDICATING A PARTICULAR PERSON, PLACE OR IDEA. THE ABOVE THEME IS FROM THE "RIDE OF THE VALKYRIES."

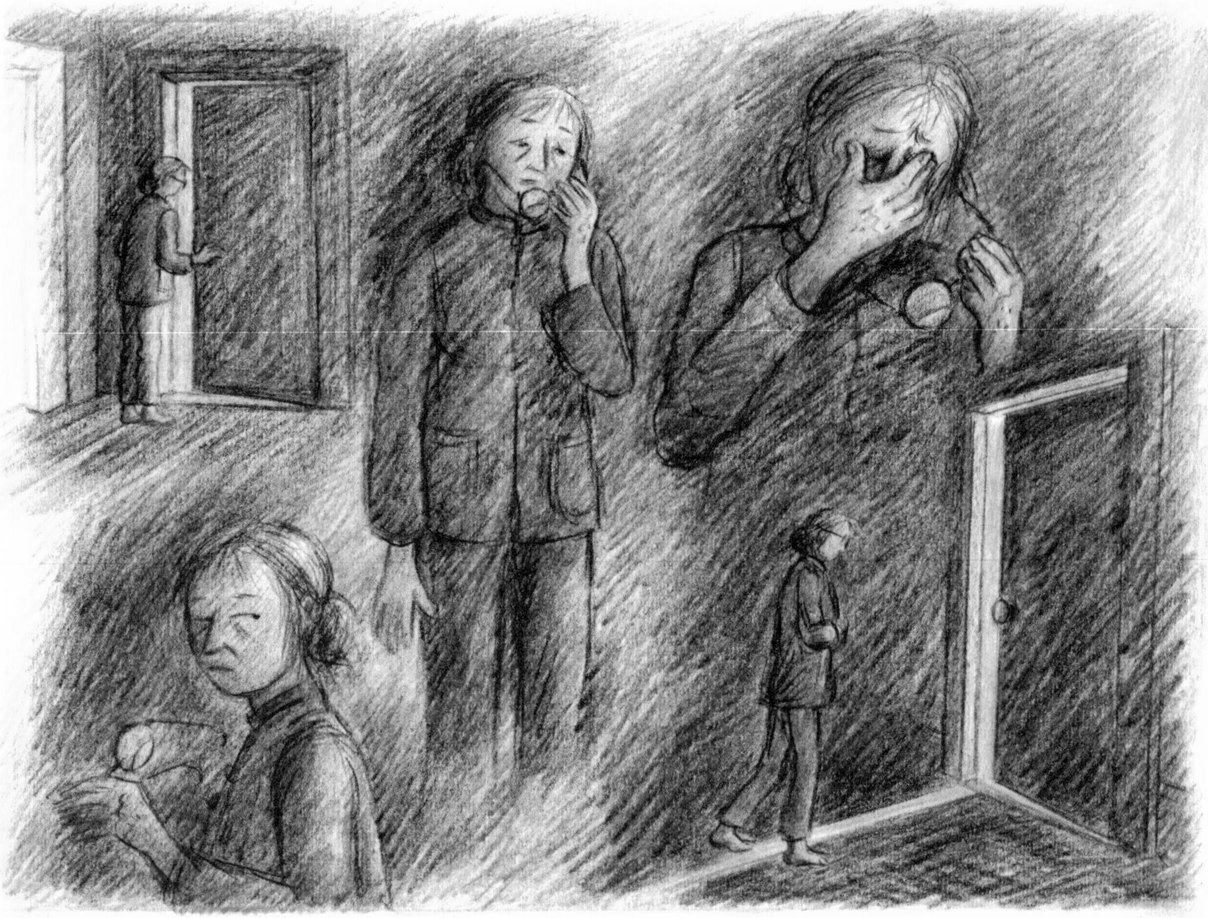
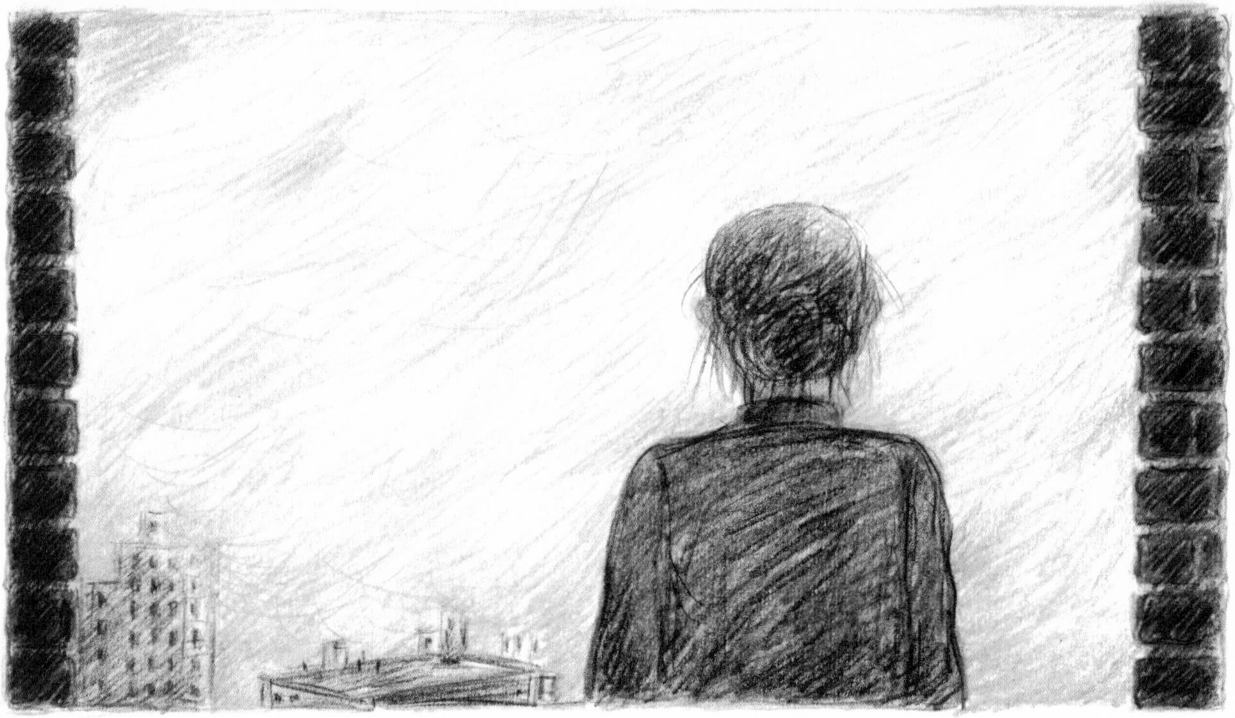

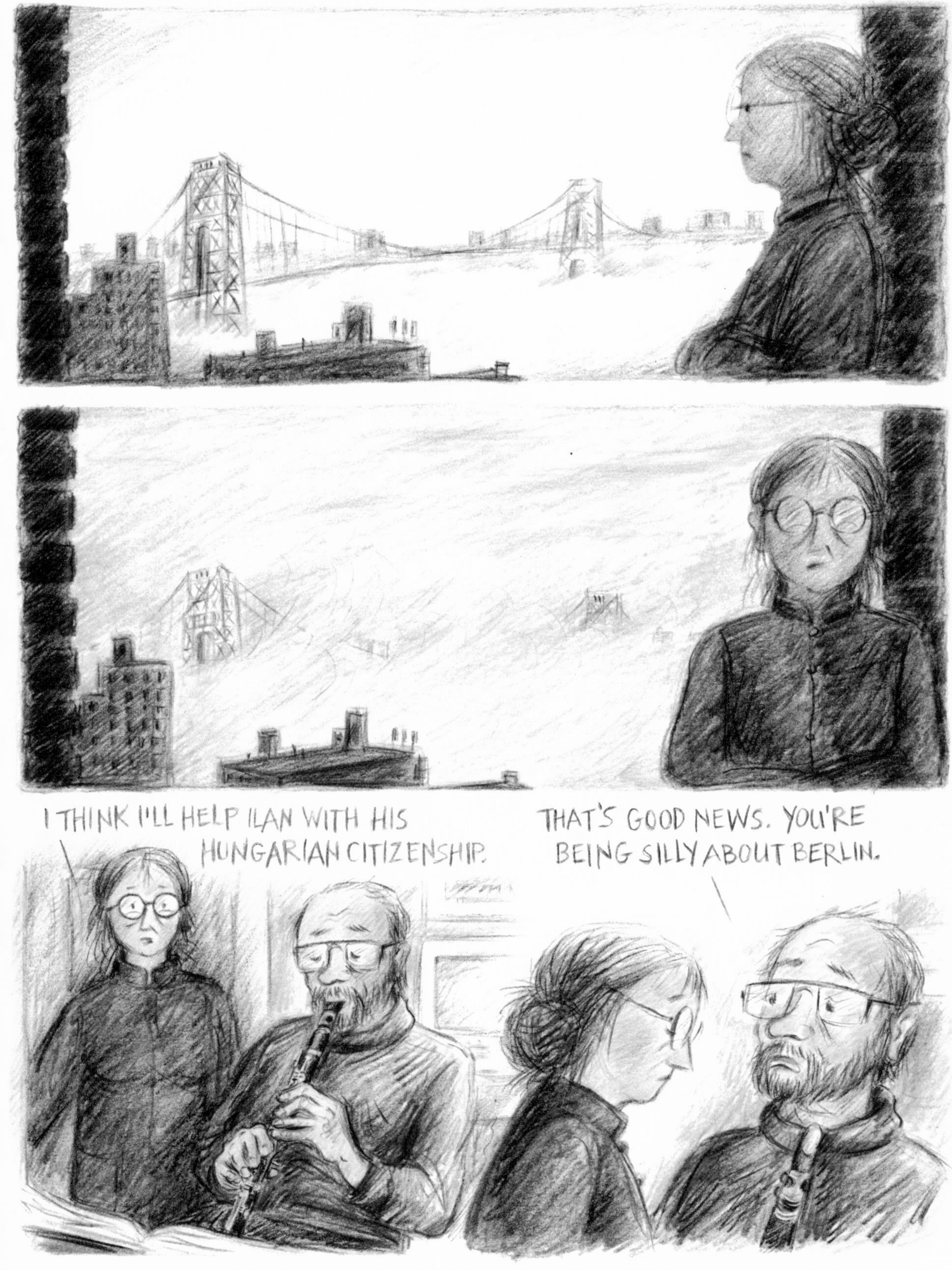
I THINK I'LL HELP ILAN WITH HIS HUNGARIAN CITIZENSHIP.
THAT'S GOOD NEWS. YOU'RE BEING SILLY ABOUT BERLIN.

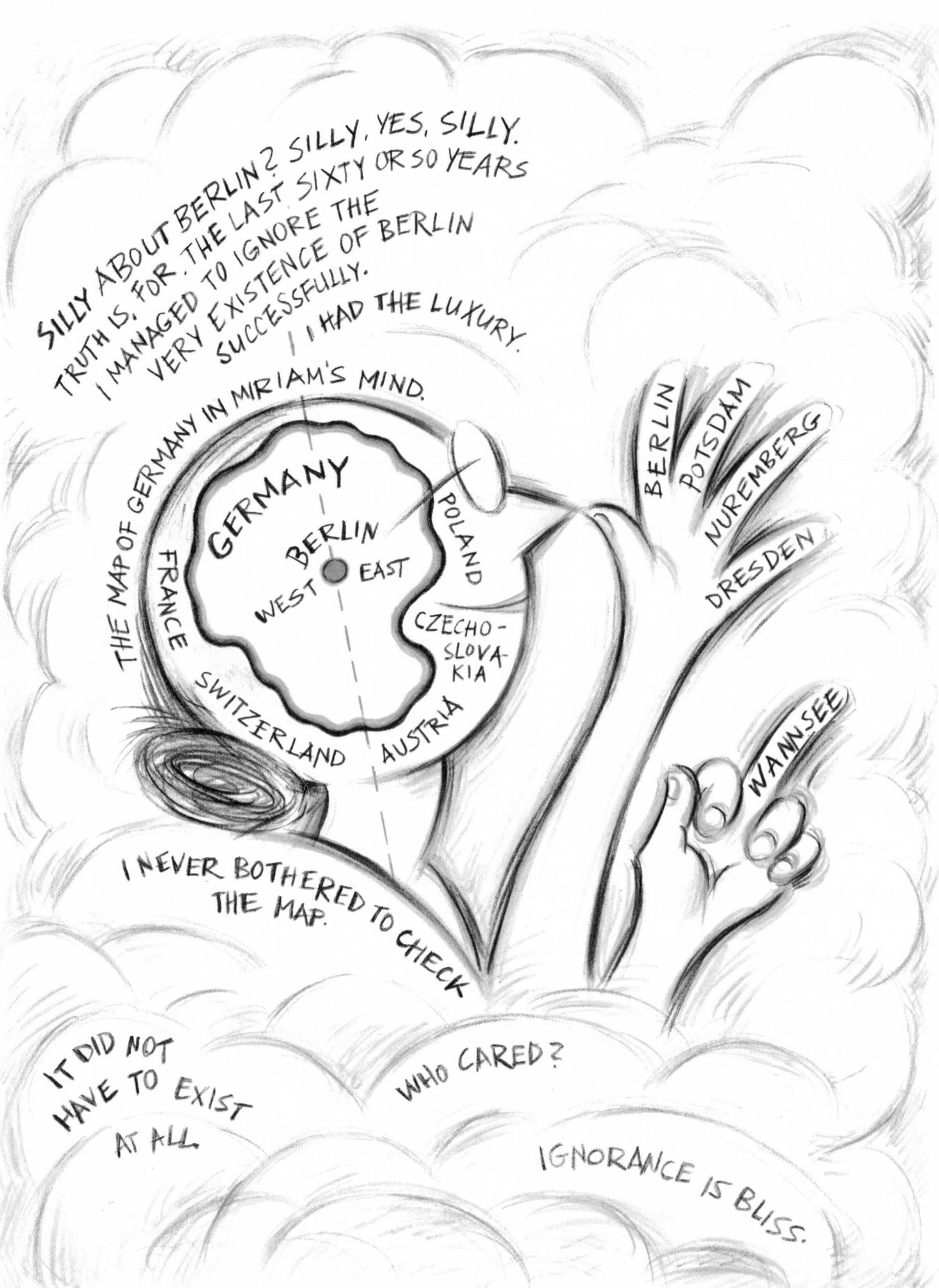
SILLY ABOUT BERLIN? SILLY. YES. SILLY.
TRUTH IS, FOR THE LAST SIXTY OR SO YEARS
I MANAGED TO IGNORE THE
VERY EXISTENCE OF BERLIN
SUCCESSFULLY.
I HAD THE LUXURY.
THE MAP OF GERMANY IN MIRIAM'S MIND.
GERMANY
BERLIN
WEST
EAST
FRANCE
POLAND
CZECHO-
SLOVA-
KIA
SWITZERLAND
AUSTRIA
BERLIN
POTSDAM
NUREMBERG
DRESDEN
WANNSEE
I NEVER BOTHERED TO CHECK THE MAP.
IT DID NOT HAVE TO EXIST AT ALL.
WHO CARED?
IGNORANCE IS BLISS.

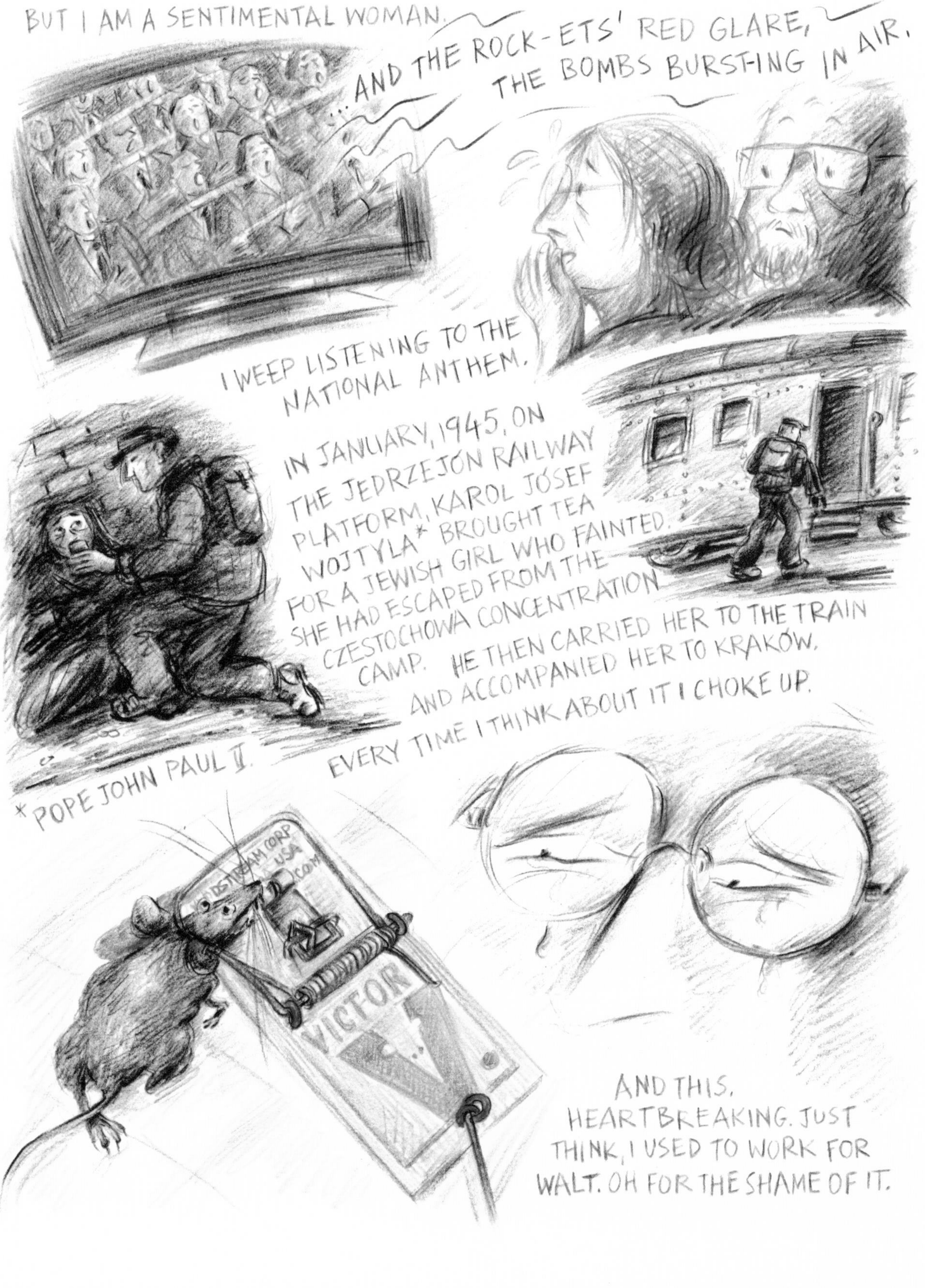
BUT I AM A SENTIMENTAL WOMAN.
...AND THE ROCK-ETS' RED GLARE, THE BOMBS BURST-ING IN AIR.
I WEEP LISTENING TO THE NATIONAL ANTHEM.
IN JANUARY, 1945, ON THE JEDRZEJÓW RAILWAY PLATFORM, KAROL JÓSEF WOJTYLA* BROUGHT TEA FOR A JEWISH GIRL WHO FAINTED. SHE HAD ESCAPED FROM THE CZESTOCHOWA CONCENTRATION CAMP. HE THEN CARRIED HER TO THE TRAIN AND ACCOMPANIED HER TO KRAKÓW.
EVERY TIME I THINK ABOUT IT I CHOKE UP.
*POPE JOHN PAUL II.
VICTOR
AND THIS. HEARTBREAKING. JUST THINK, I USED TO WORK FOR WALT. OH FOR THE SHAME OF IT.

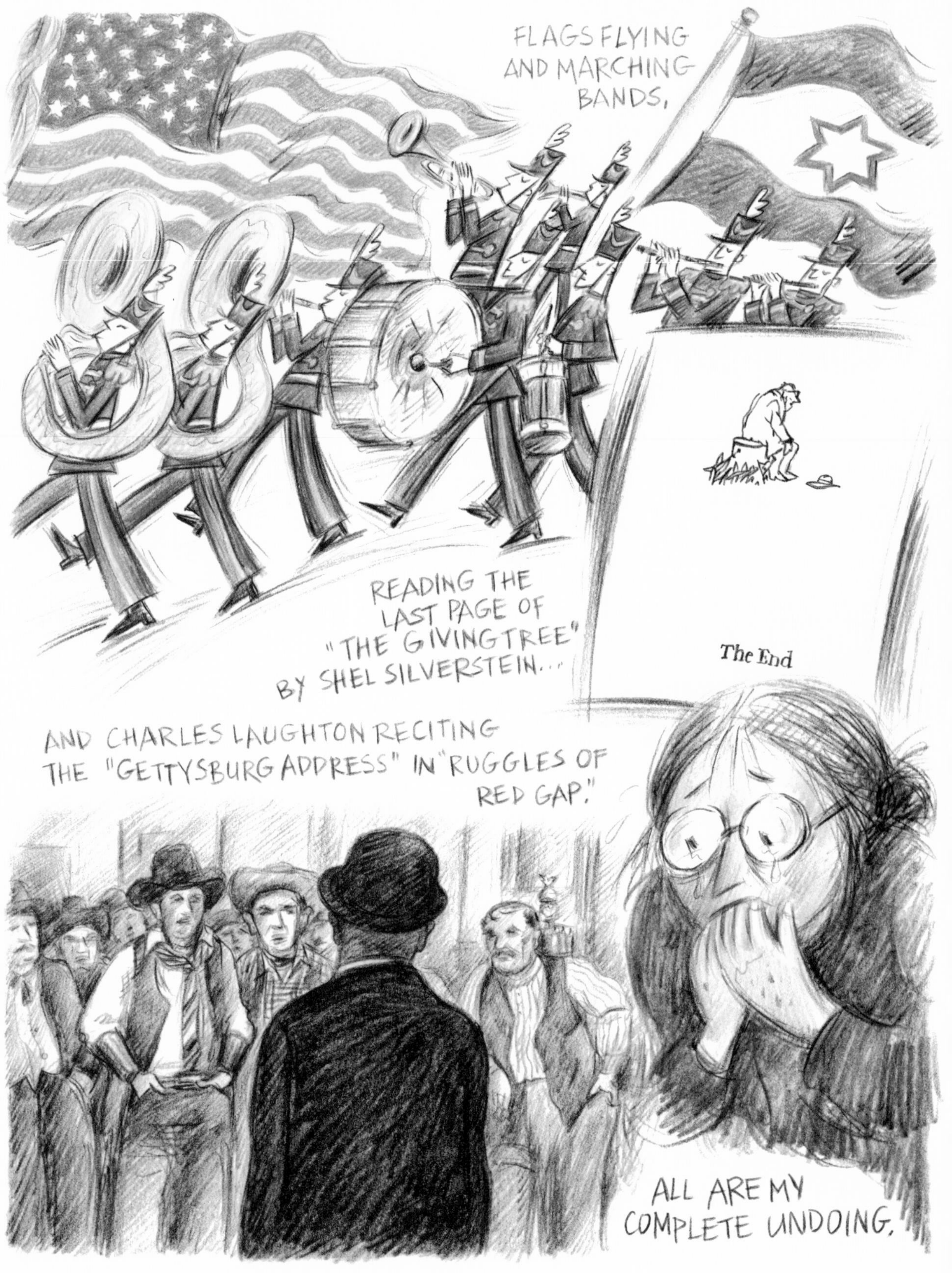
FLAGS FLYING AND MARCHING BANDS,
READING THE LAST PAGE OF "THE GIVINGTREE" BY SHEL SILVERSTEIN...
The End
AND CHARLES LAUGHTON RECITING THE "GETTYSBURG ADDRESS" IN "RUGGLES OF RED GAP."
ALL ARE MY COMPLETE UNDOING.

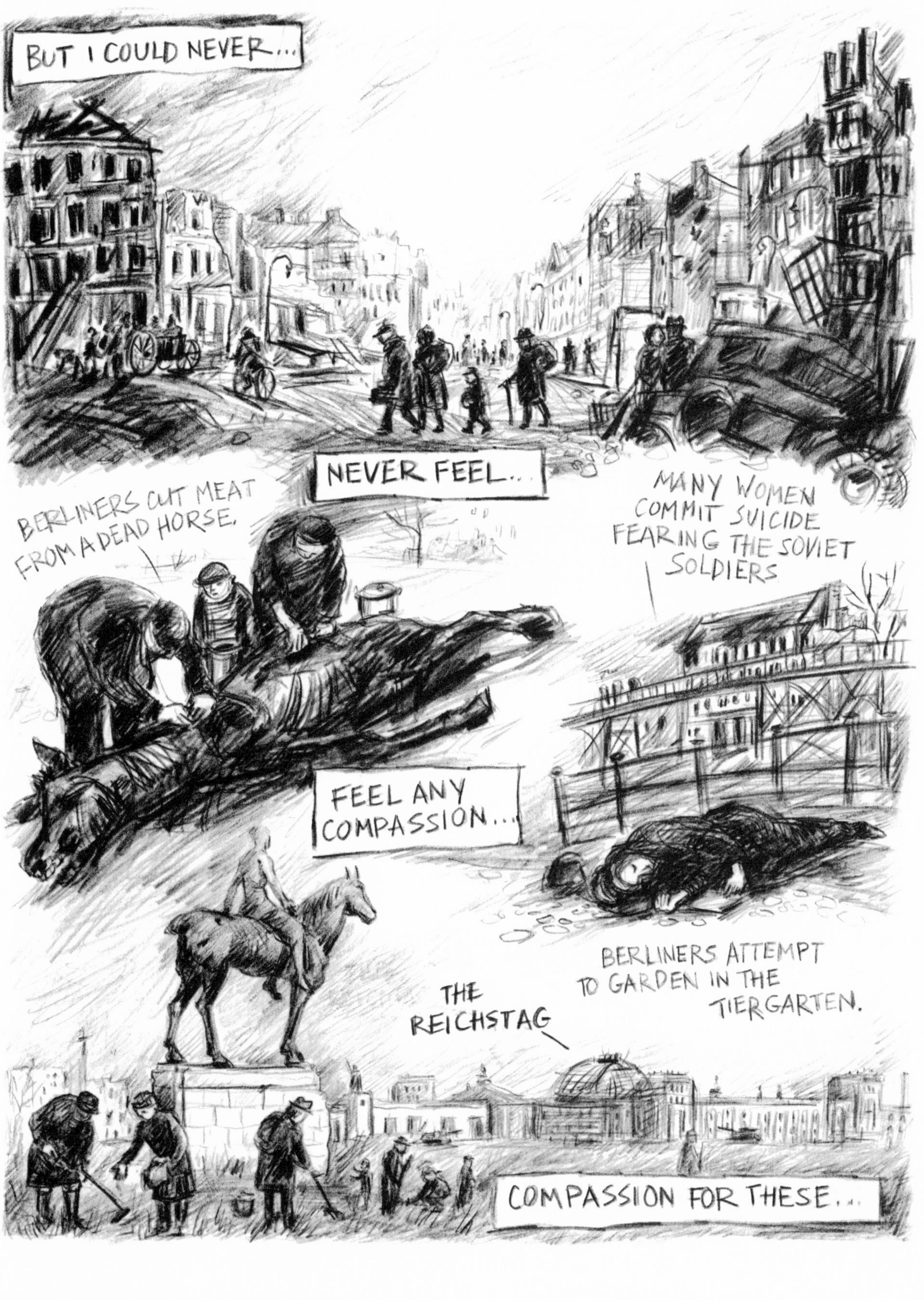
BUT I COULD NEVER...
NEVER FEEL...
BERLINERS CUT MEAT FROM A DEAD HORSE.
MANY WOMEN COMMIT SUICIDE FEARING THE SOVIET SOLDIERS
FEEL ANY COMPASSION...
BERLINERS ATTEMPT TO GARDEN IN THE TIERGARTEN.
THE REICHSTAG
COMPASSION FOR THESE...

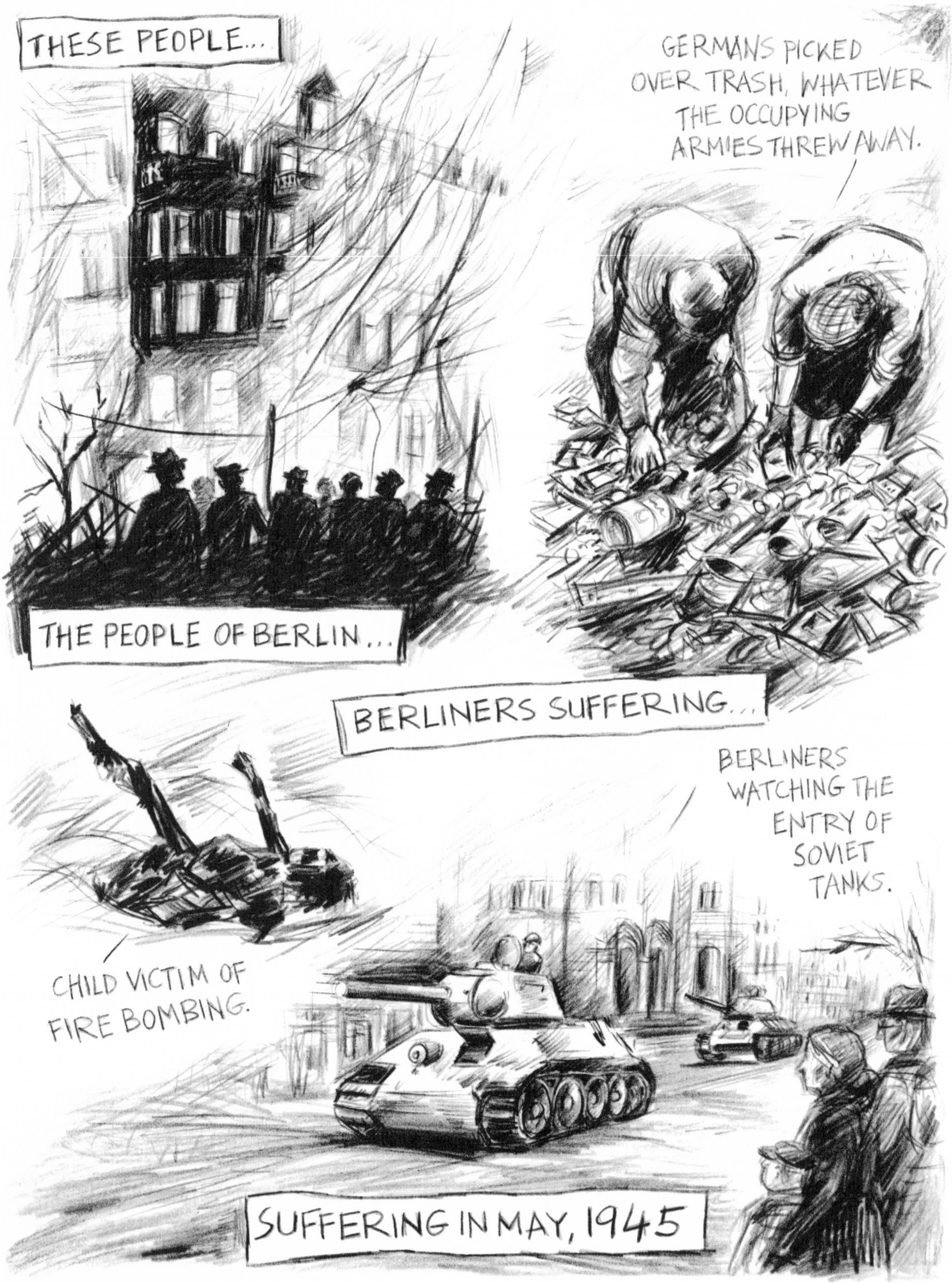
THESE PEOPLE...
THE PEOPLE OF BERLIN...
GERMANS PICKED OVER TRASH, WHATEVER THE OCCUPYING ARMIES THREW AWAY.
BERLINERS SUFFERING...
CHILD VICTIM OF FIRE BOMBING.
BERLINERS WATCHING THE ENTRY OF SOVIET TANKS.
SUFFERING IN MAY, 1945

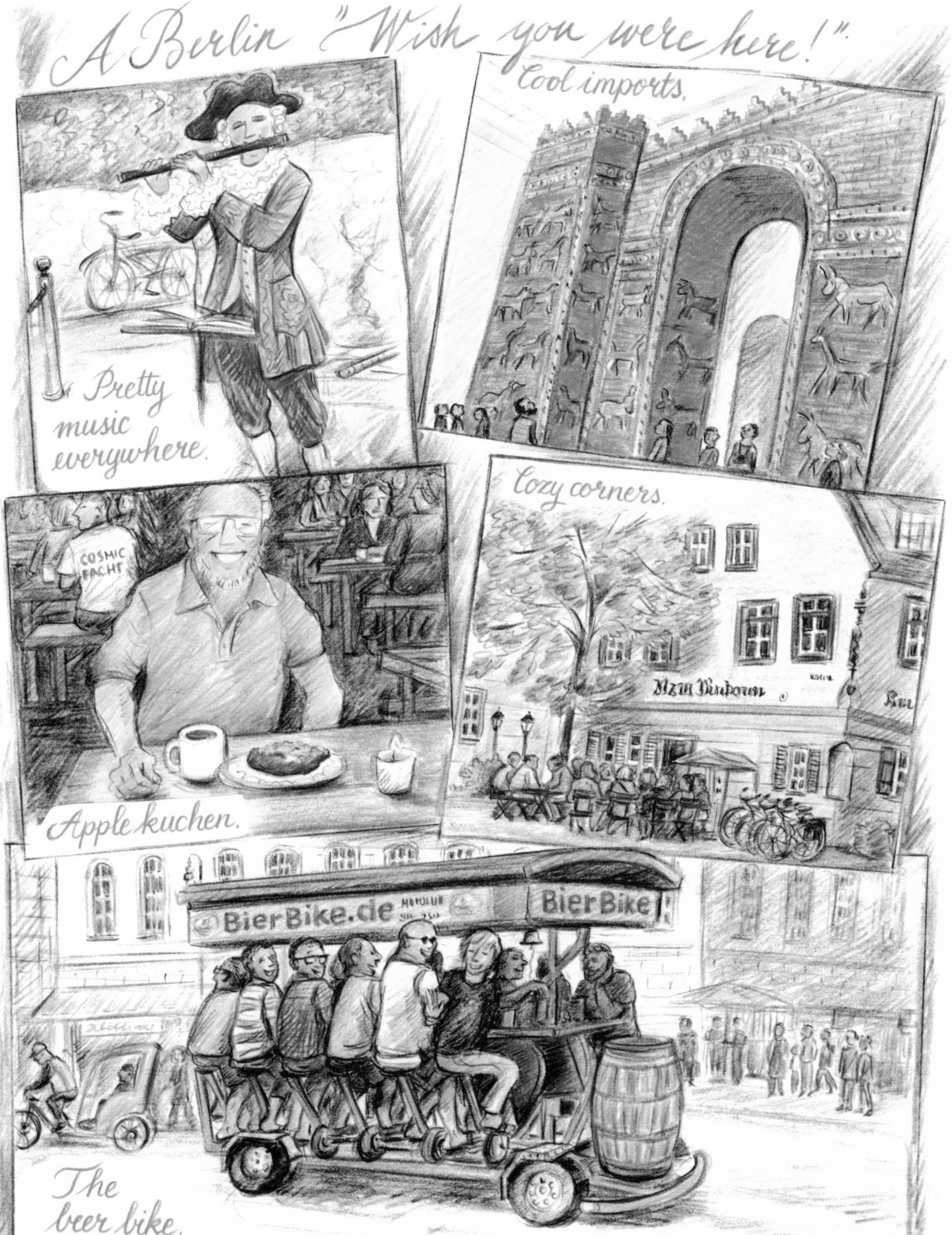
A Berlin "Wish you were here!"
Pretty music everywhere.
Cool imports.
COSMIC FACHT
Apple kuchen.
Cozy corners.
BierBike.de
Bier Bike
The beer bike.

KUCHEN: CAKE (GERMAN)

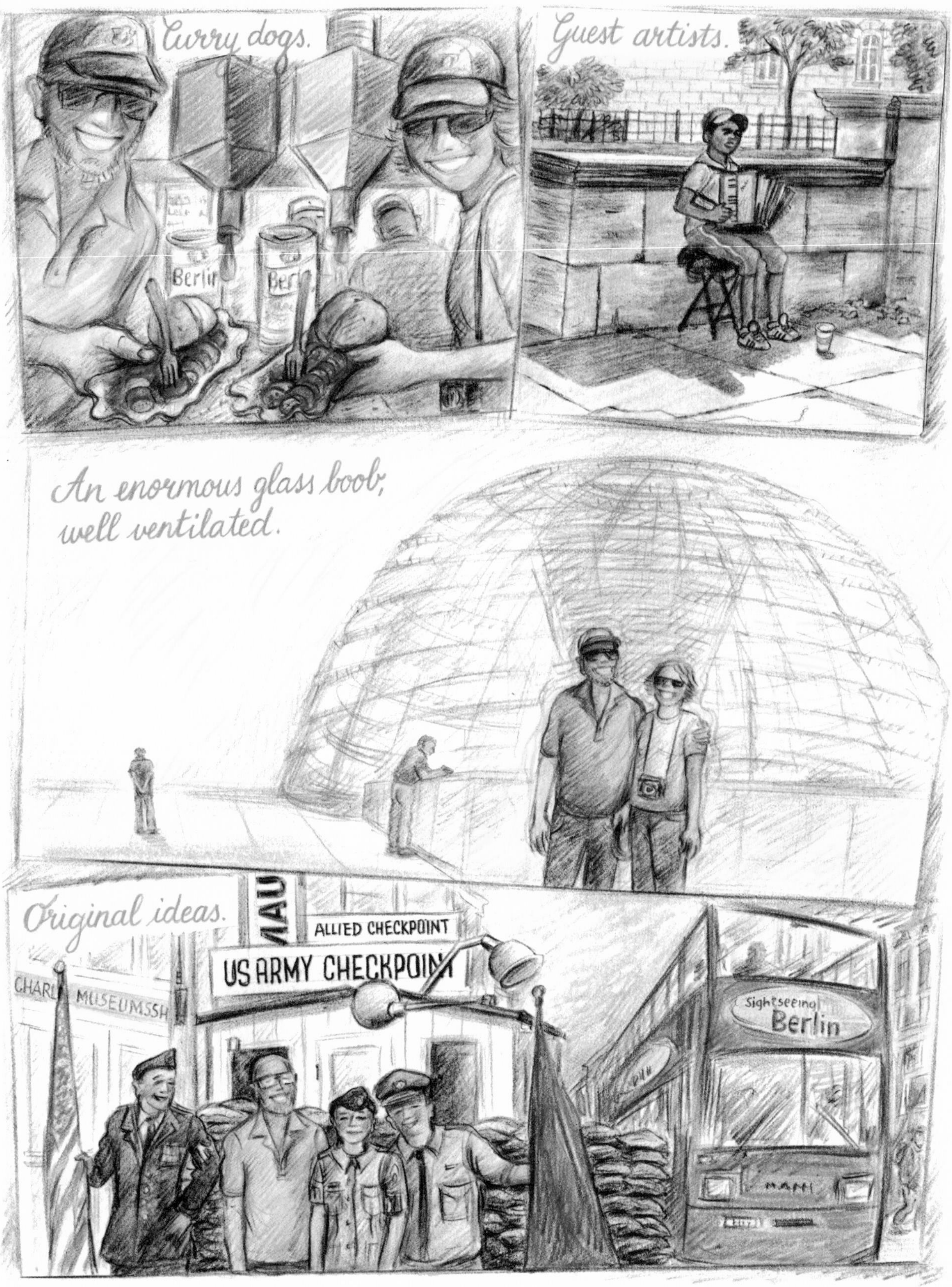
Curry dogs.
Berlin
Berlin
Guest artists.
An enormous glass boob,
well ventilated.
Original ideas.
MAU
ALLIED CHECKPOINT
US ARMY CHECKPOIN
CHARL
MUSEUMSSH
Sightseeing
Berlin

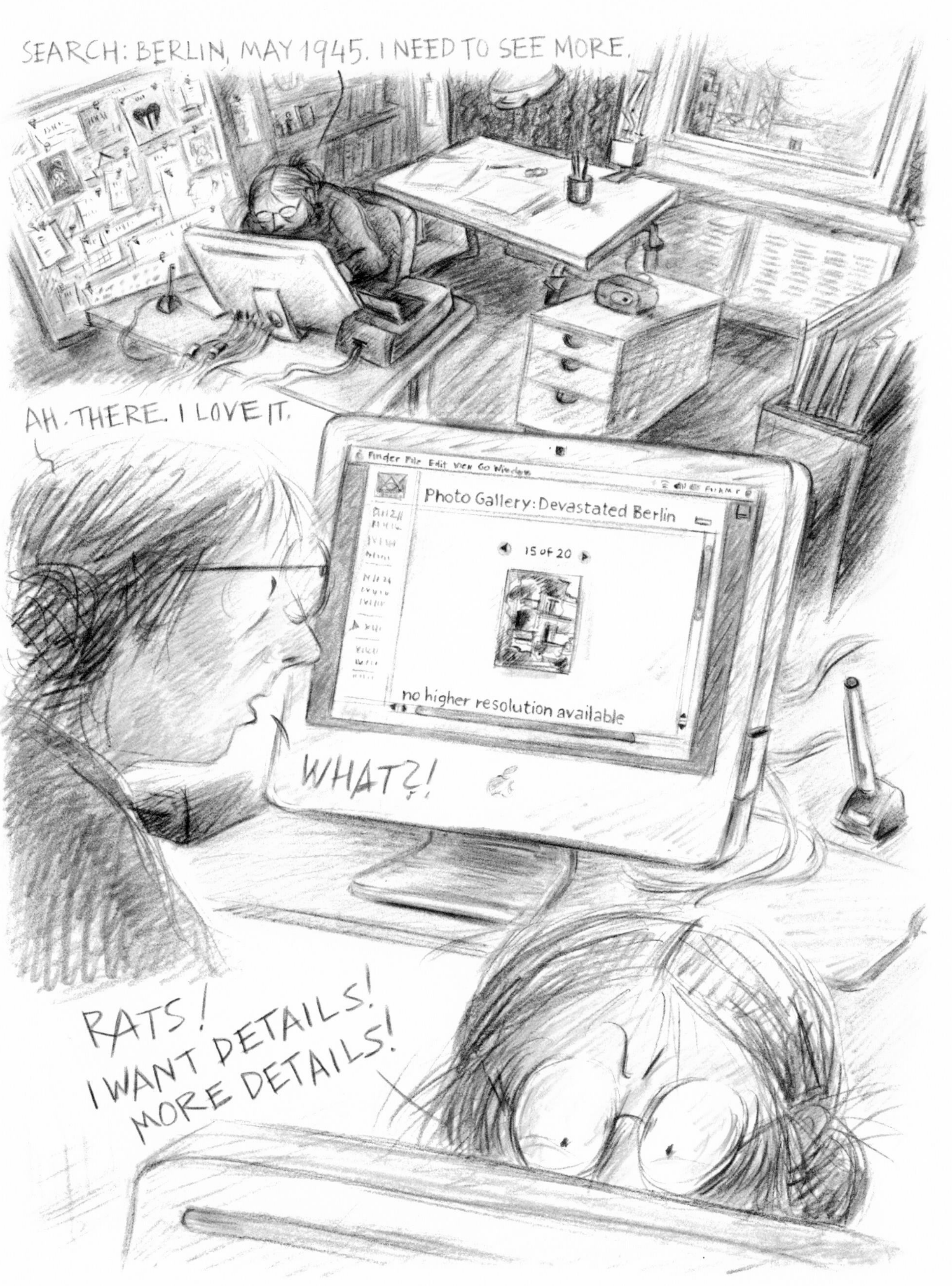
SEARCH: BERLIN, MAY 1945. I NEED TO SEE MORE.
AH. THERE. I LOVE IT.
Finder File Edit View Go Window
Photo Gallery: Devastated Berlin
15 of 20
no higher resolution available
WHAT?!
RATS!
I WANT DETAILS!
MORE DETAILS!

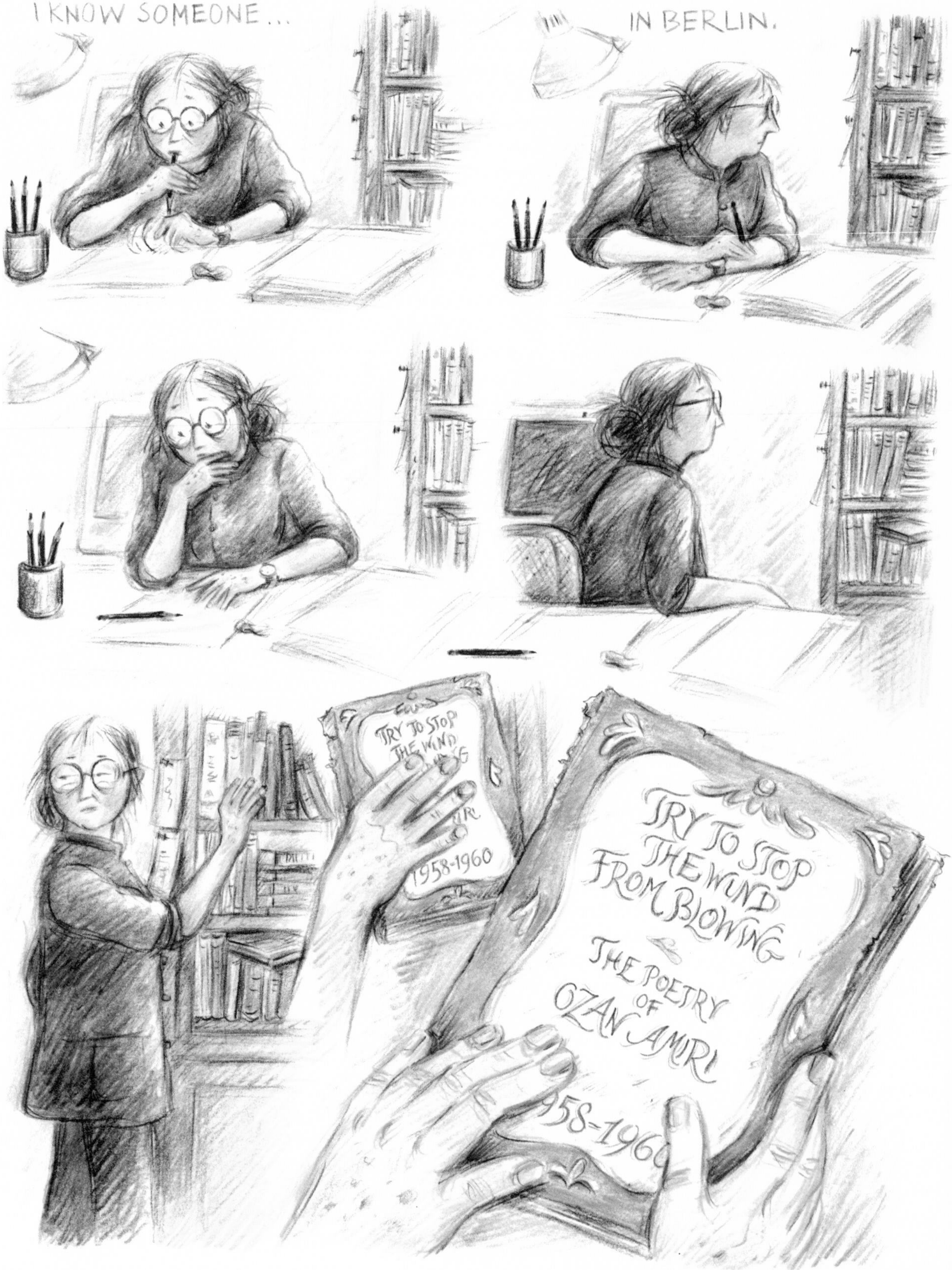
I KNOW SOMEONE...
IN BERLIN.
TRY TO STOP THE WIND
1958-1960
TRY TO STOP THE WIND FROM BLOWING
THE POETRY OF OZAN AMIRI

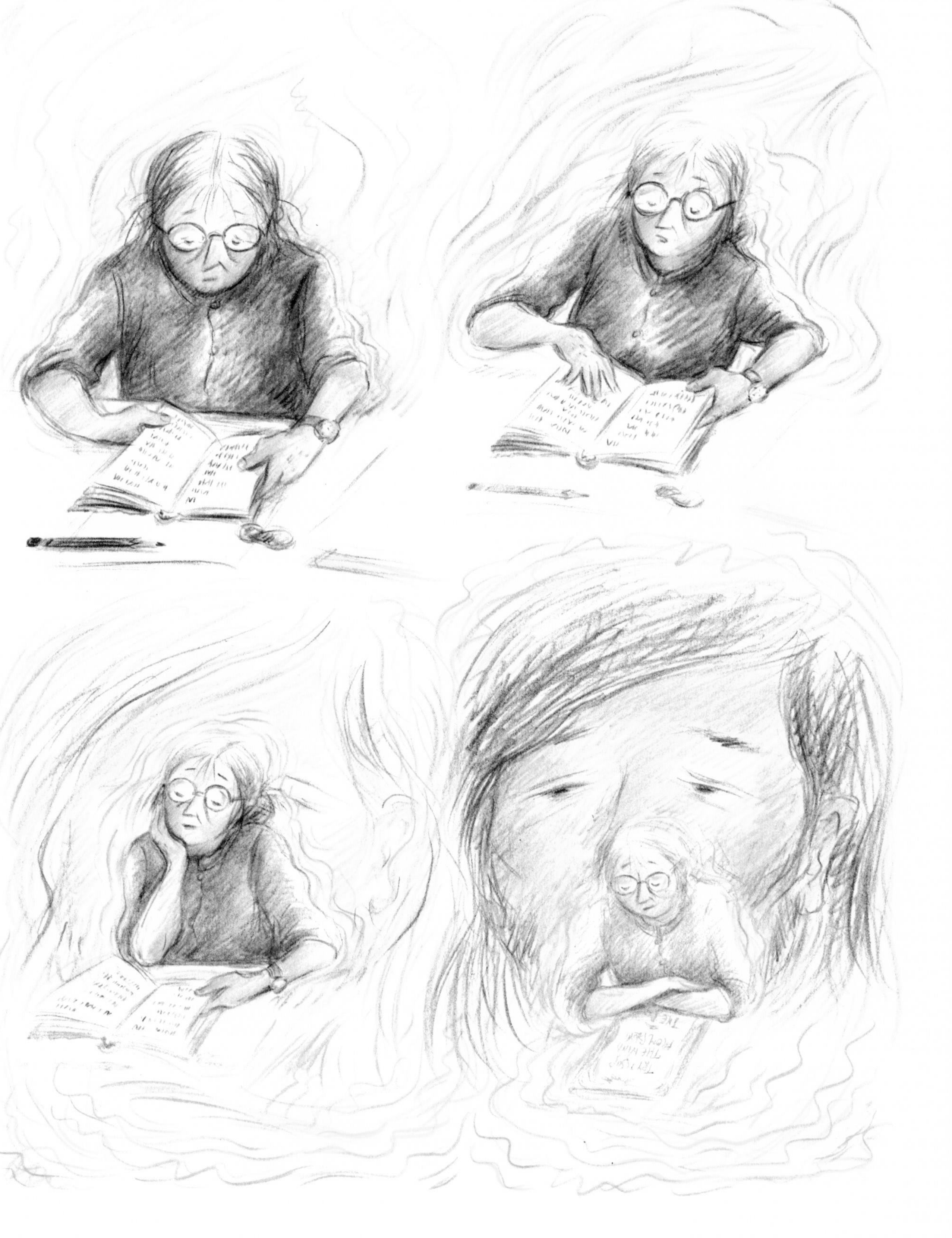

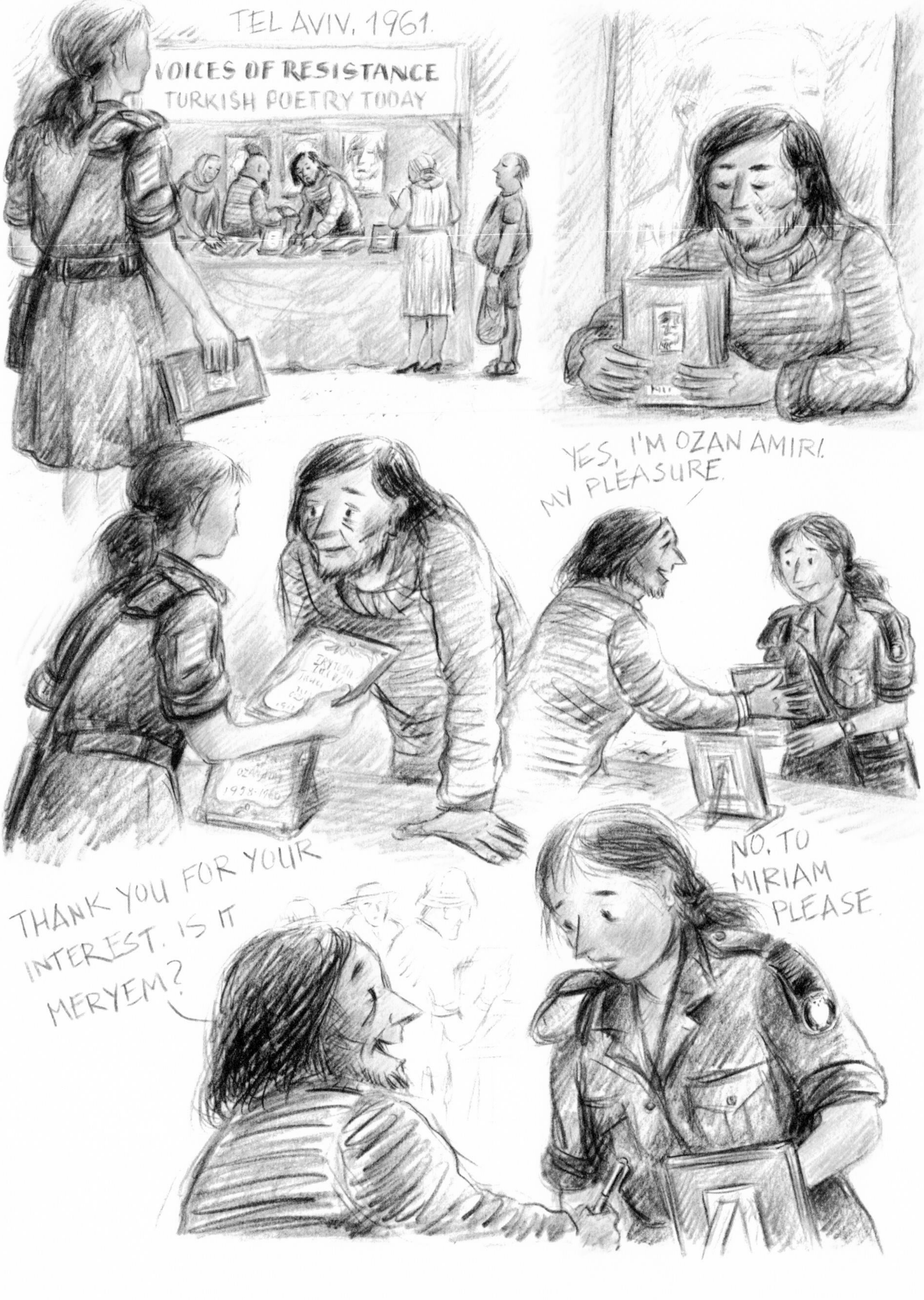
TEL AVIV, 1961.
VOICES OF RESISTANCE
TURKISH POETRY TODAY
YES, I'M OZAN AMIRI. MY PLEASURE.
THANK YOU FOR YOUR INTEREST. IS IT MERYEM?
NO. TO MIRIAM PLEASE.

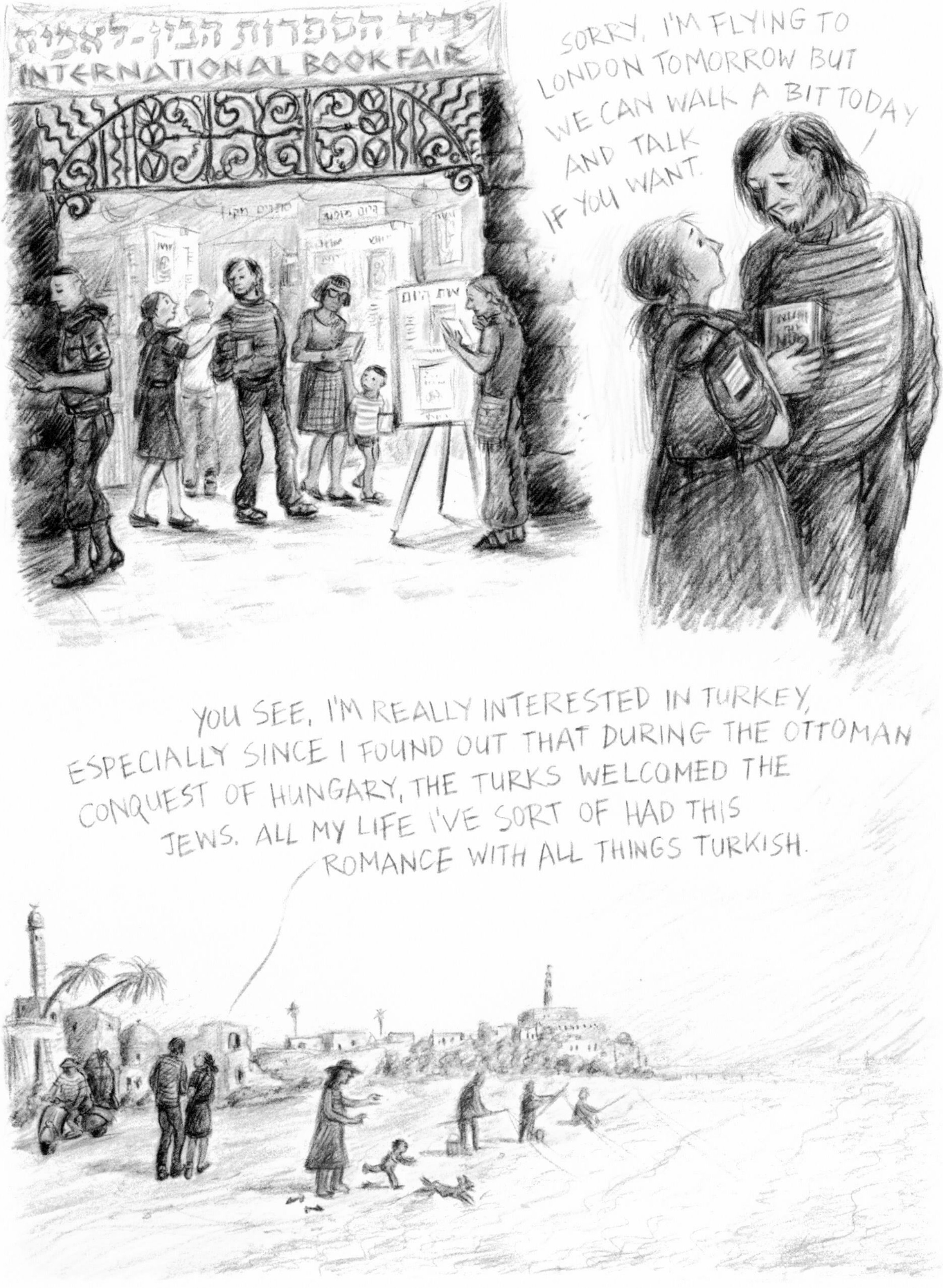
INTERNATIONAL BOOK FAIR
SORRY, I'M FLYING TO LONDON TOMORROW BUT WE CAN WALK A BIT TODAY AND TALK IF YOU WANT.
YOU SEE, I'M REALLY INTERESTED IN TURKEY, ESPECIALLY SINCE I FOUND OUT THAT DURING THE OTTOMAN CONQUEST OF HUNGARY, THE TURKS WELCOMED THE JEWS. ALL MY LIFE I'VE SORT OF HAD THIS ROMANCE WITH ALL THINGS TURKISH.

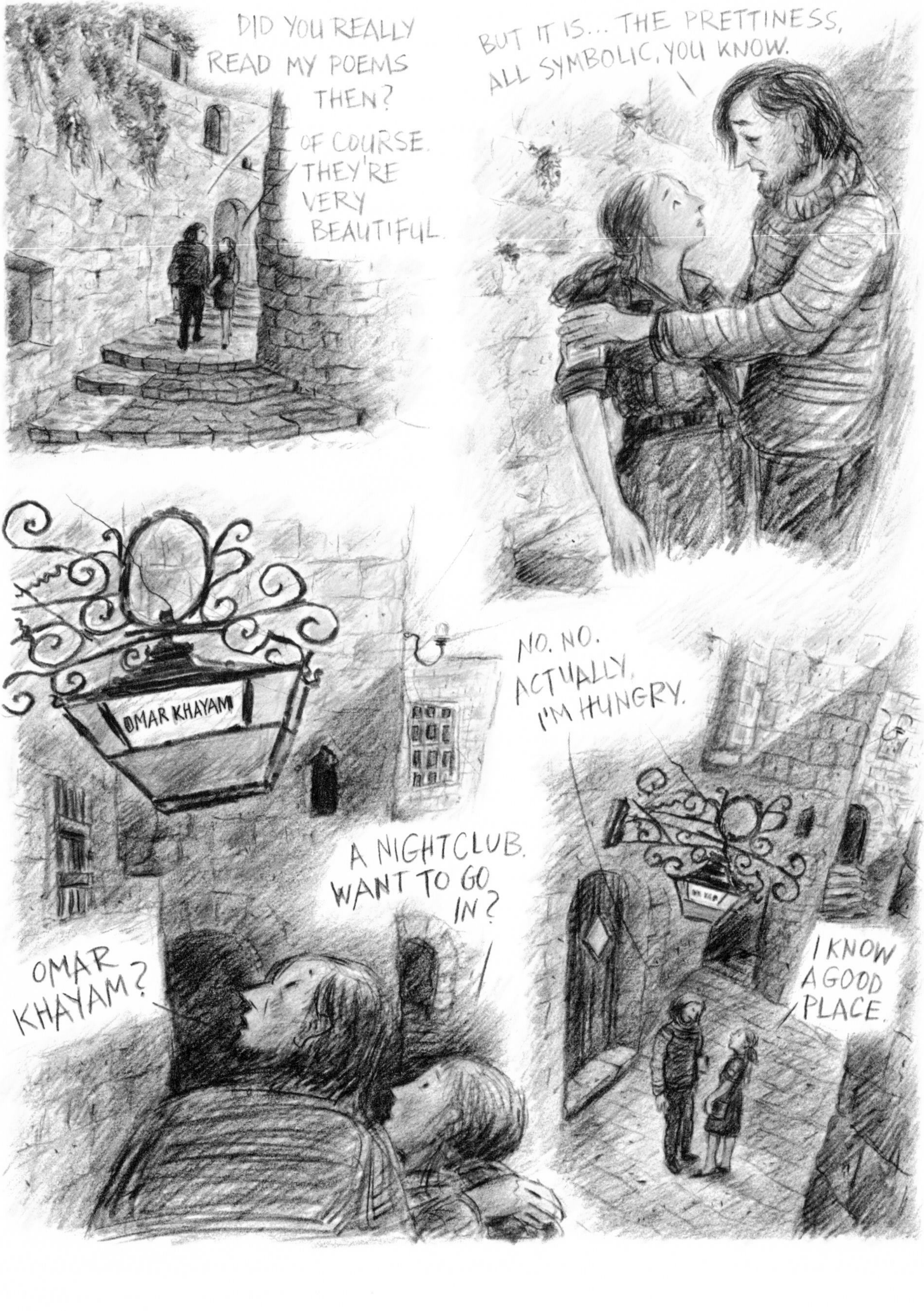
DID YOU REALLY READ MY POEMS THEN?
OF COURSE. THEY'RE VERY BEAUTIFUL.
BUT IT IS... THE PRETTINESS, ALL SYMBOLIC, YOU KNOW.
OMAR KHAYAM
OMAR KHAYAM?
A NIGHTCLUB. WANT TO GO IN?
NO. NO. ACTUALLY, I'M HUNGRY.
I KNOW A GOOD PLACE.

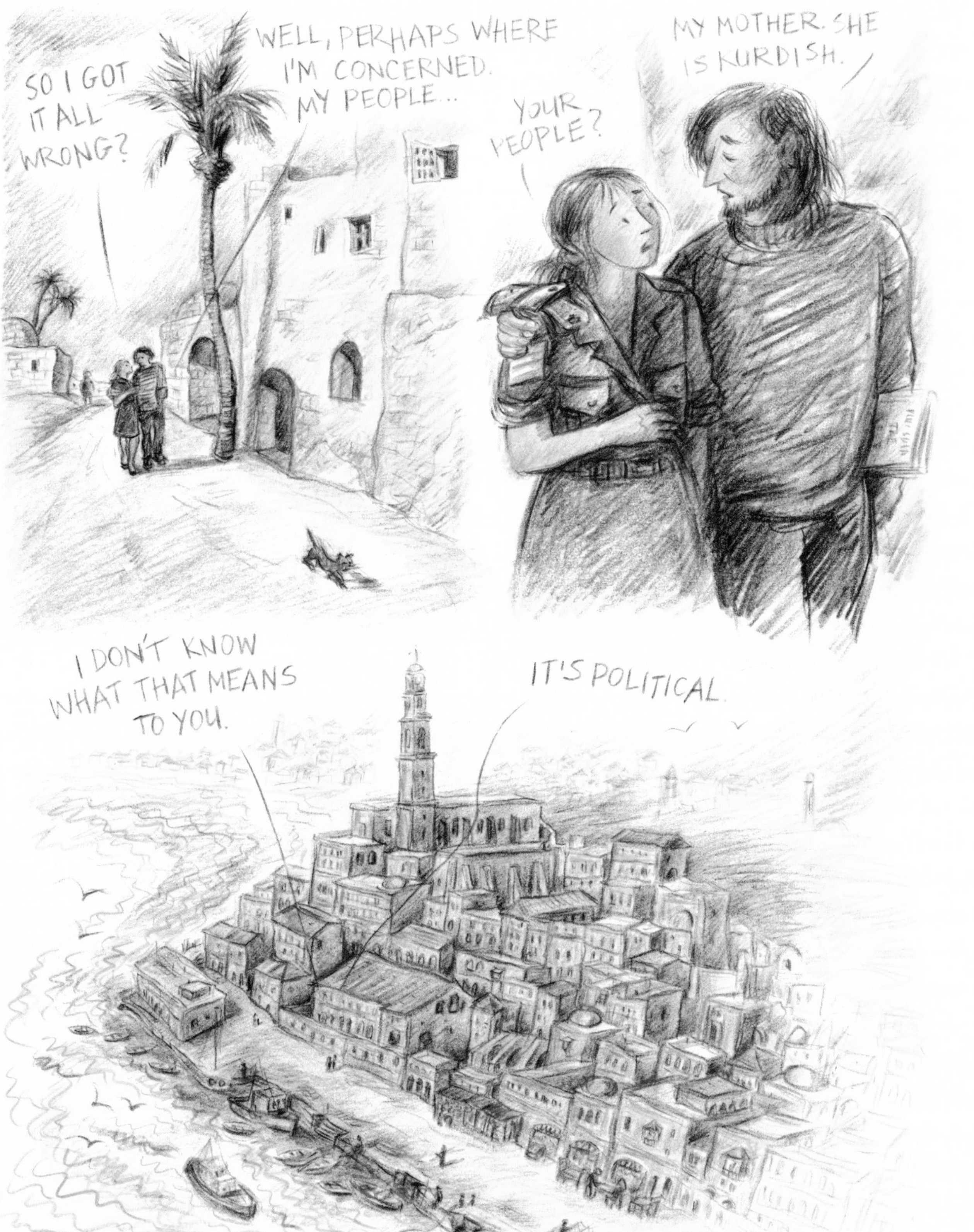
SO I GOT IT ALL WRONG?
WELL, PERHAPS WHERE I'M CONCERNED. MY PEOPLE...
YOUR PEOPLE?
MY MOTHER. SHE IS KURDISH.
I DON'T KNOW WHAT THAT MEANS TO YOU.
IT'S POLITICAL.

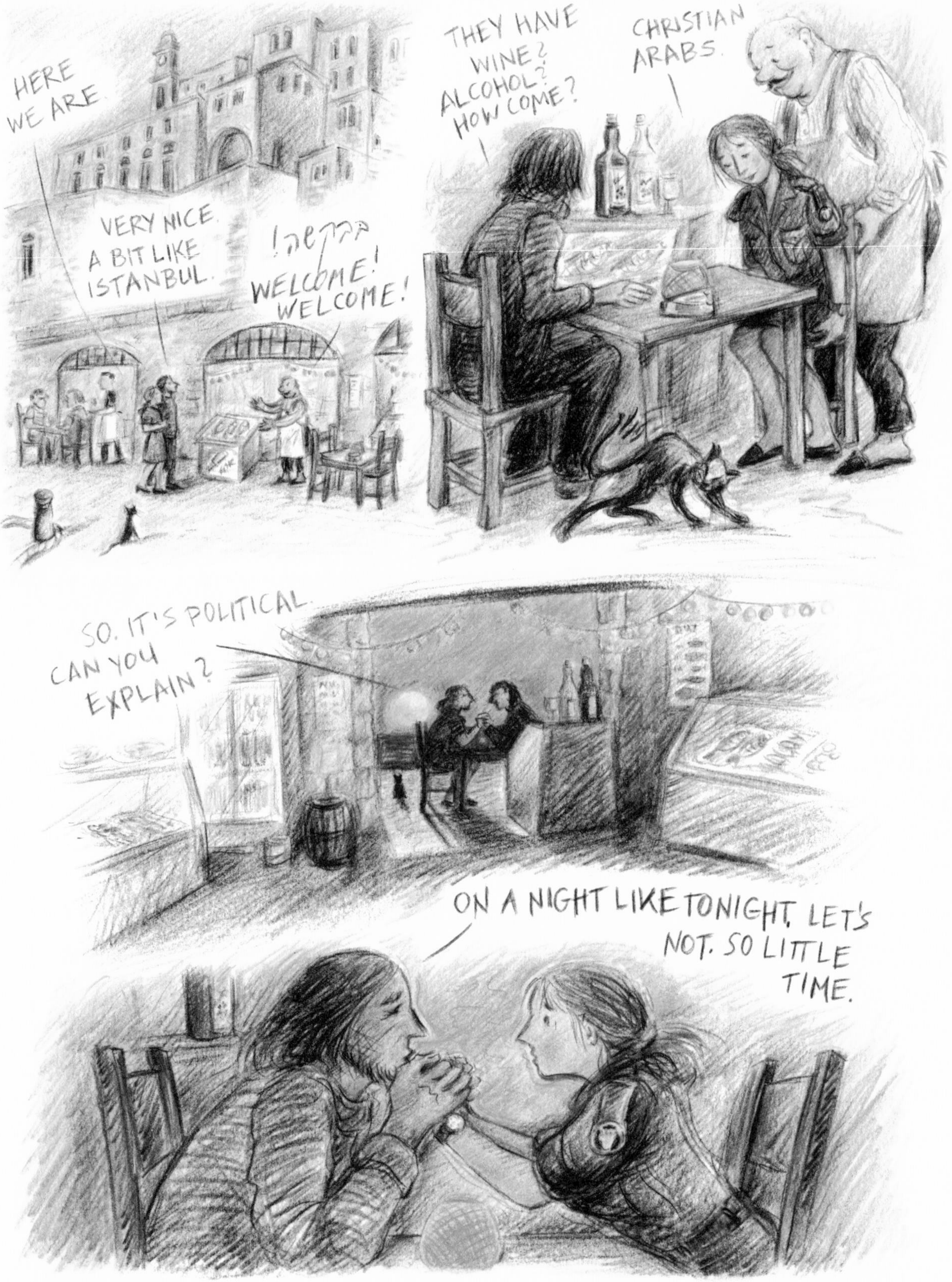
HERE WE ARE.
VERY NICE. A BIT LIKE ISTANBUL.
בבקשה! WELCOME! WELCOME!
THEY HAVE WINE? ALCOHOL? HOW COME?
CHRISTIAN ARABS.
SO. IT'S POLITICAL. CAN YOU EXPLAIN?
ON A NIGHT LIKE TONIGHT, LET'S NOT. SO LITTLE TIME.

בבקשה : PLEASE (HEBREW)

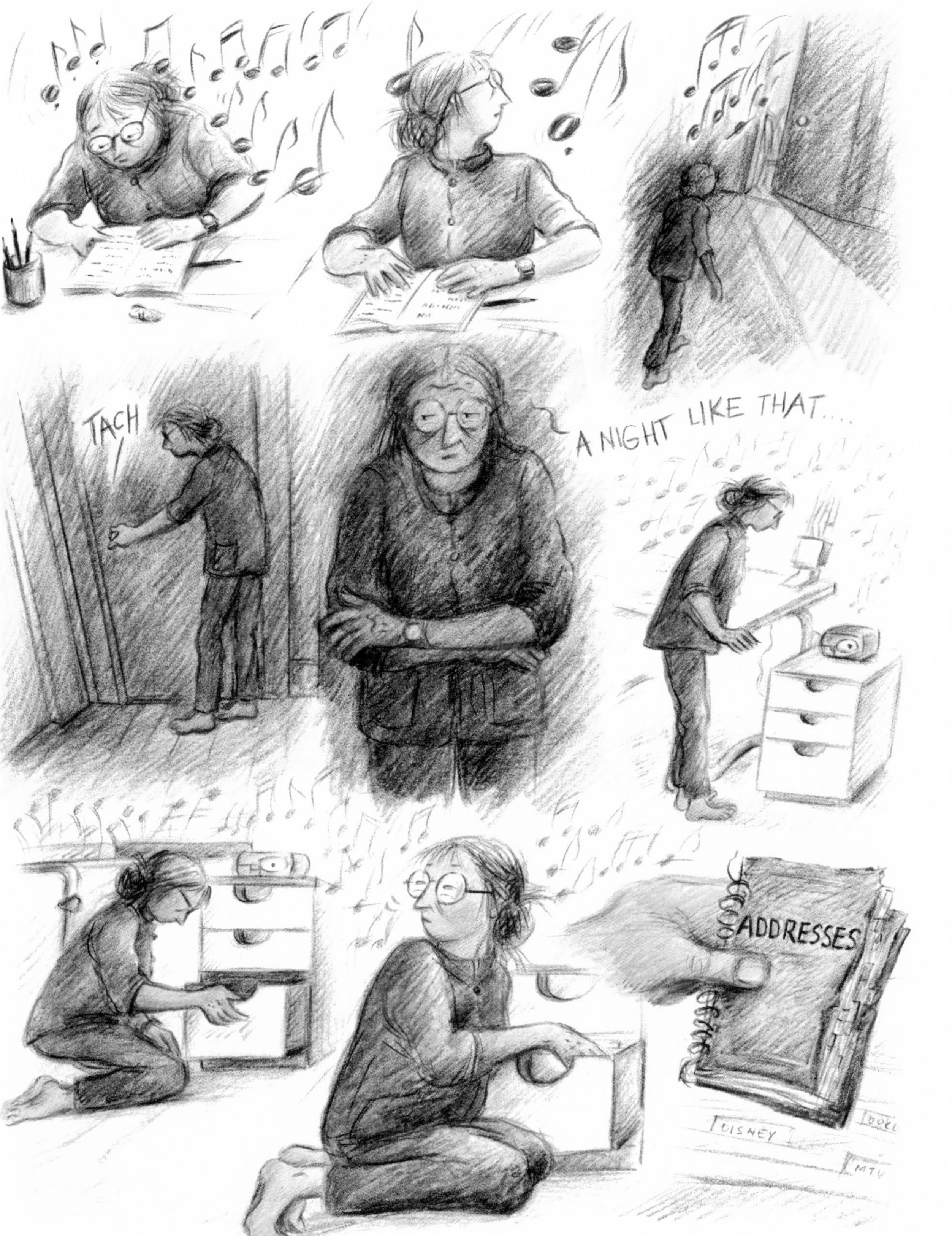
TACH
A NIGHT LIKE THAT....
ADDRESSES
DISNEY
MTV

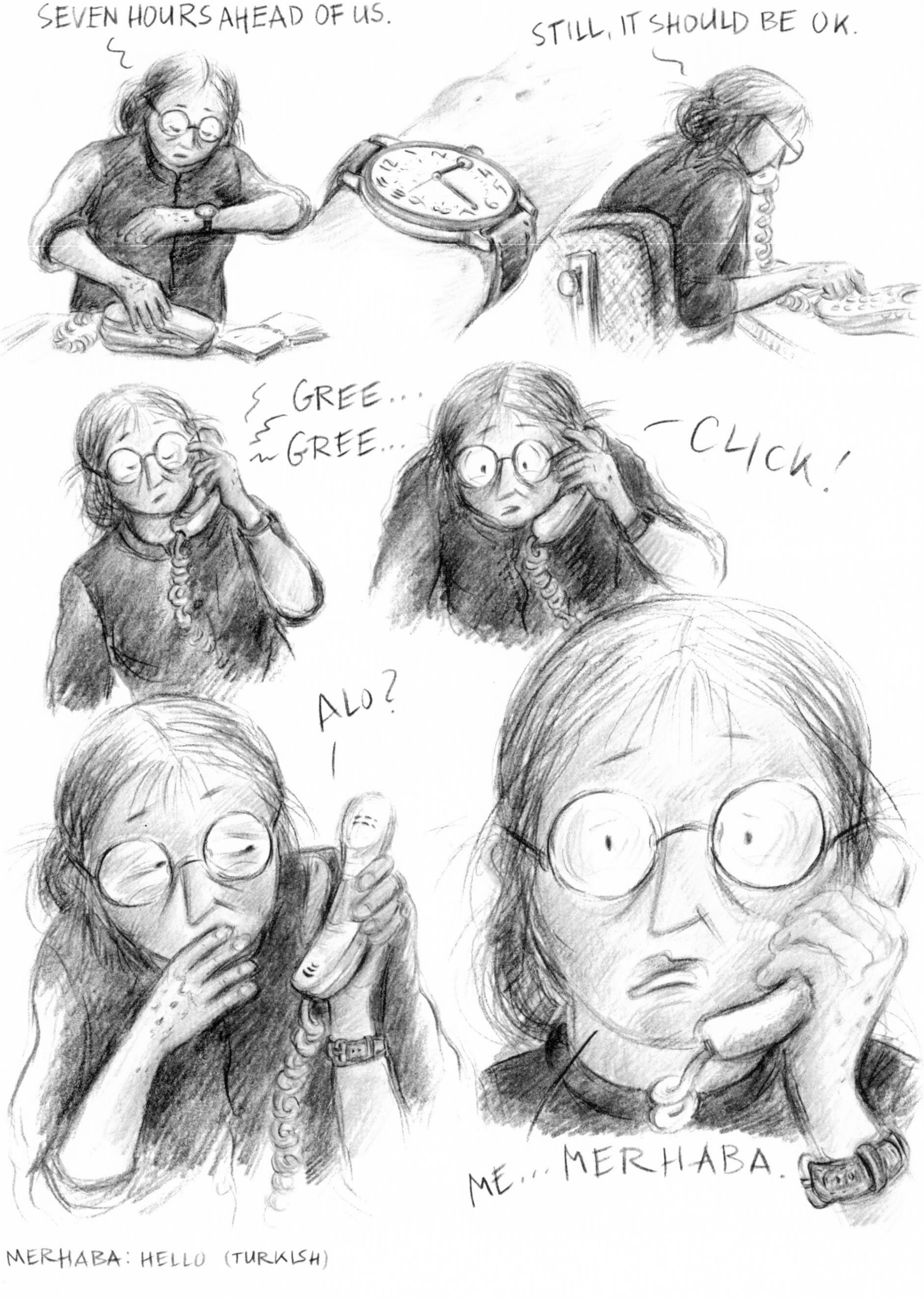
SEVEN HOURS AHEAD OF US.
STILL, IT SHOULD BE OK.
GREE...
GREE...
CLICK!
ALO?
ME... MERHABA.

MERHABA: HELLO (TURKISH)

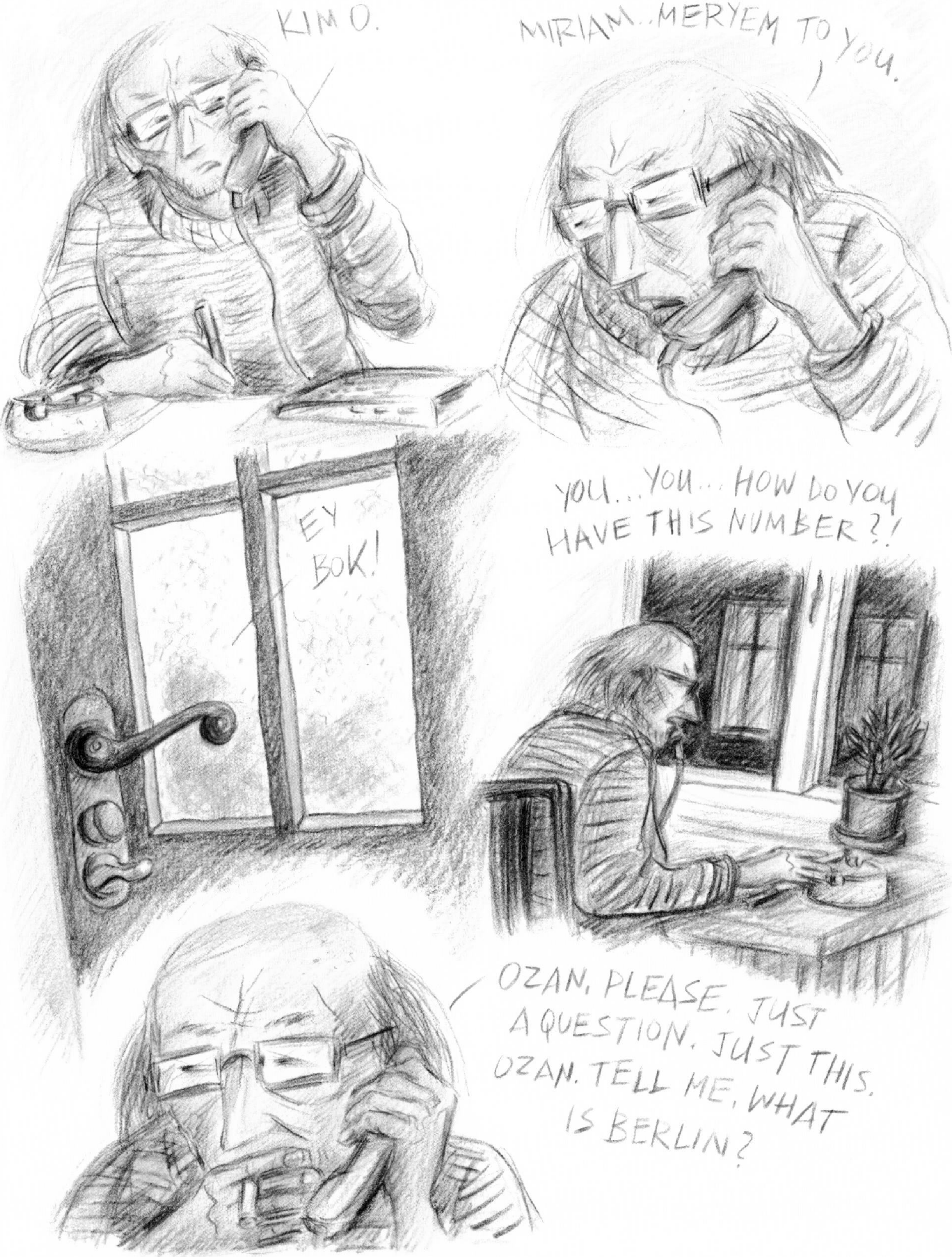
KIM O.
MIRIAM..MERYEM TO YOU.
EY BOK!
YOU...YOU... HOW DO YOU HAVE THIS NUMBER?!
OZAN, PLEASE. JUST A QUESTION. JUST THIS. OZAN. TELL ME, WHAT IS BERLIN?

KIM O: WHO IS IT? EI BOK!: SHIT! (TURKISH)

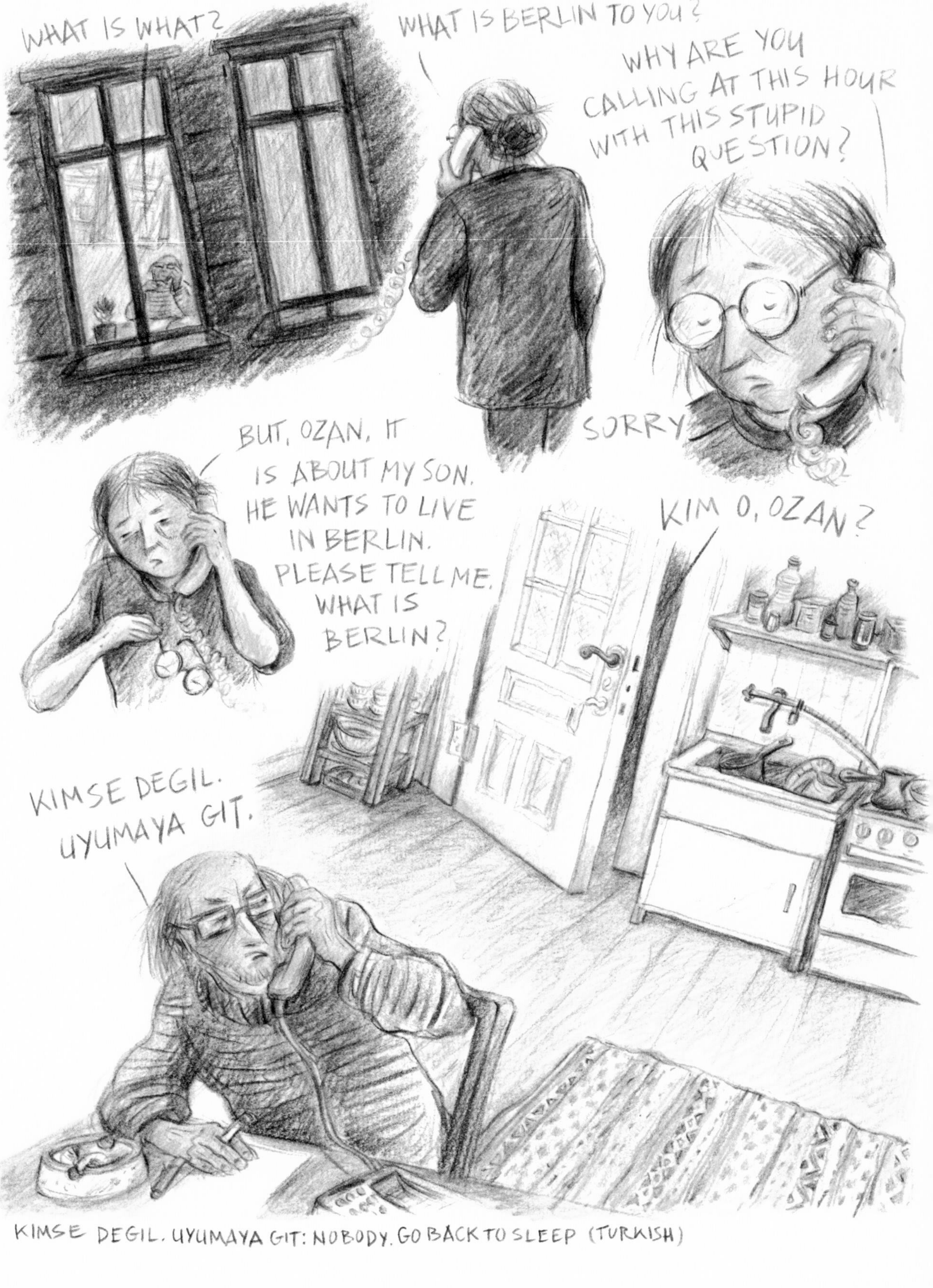
WHAT IS WHAT?
WHAT IS BERLIN TO YOU?
WHY ARE YOU CALLING AT THIS HOUR WITH THIS STUPID QUESTION?
SORRY
BUT, OZAN, IT IS ABOUT MY SON. HE WANTS TO LIVE IN BERLIN. PLEASE TELL ME. WHAT IS BERLIN?
KIM O, OZAN?
KIMSE DEGIL. UYUMAYA GIT.

KIMSE DEGIL. UYUMAYA GIT: NOBODY. GO BACK TO SLEEP (TURKISH)

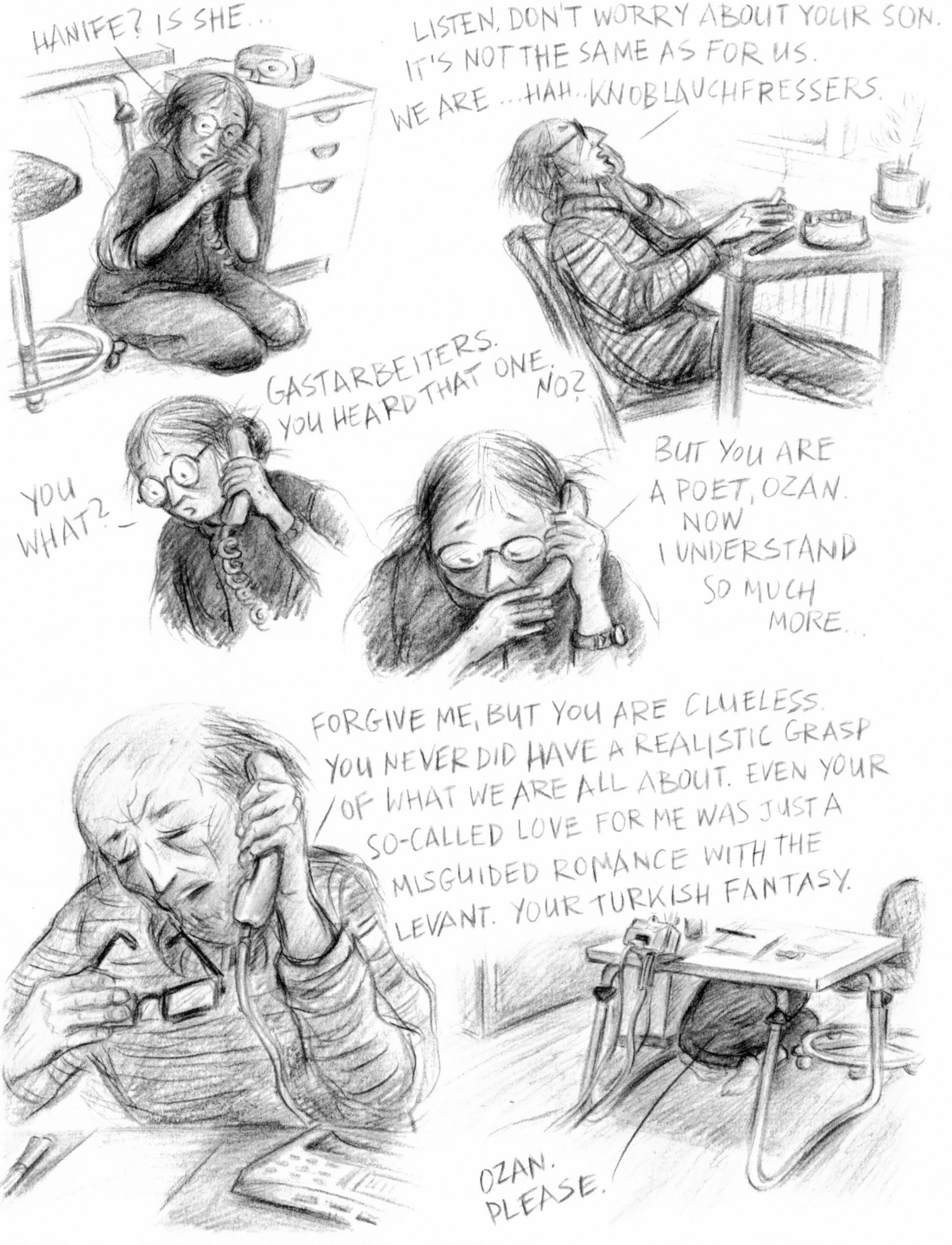
HANIFE? IS SHE...
LISTEN, DON'T WORRY ABOUT YOUR SON. IT'S NOT THE SAME AS FOR US. WE ARE... HAH.. KNOBLAUCHFRESSERS.
GASTARBEITERS. YOU HEARD THAT ONE, NO?
YOU WHAT?
BUT YOU ARE A POET, OZAN. NOW I UNDERSTAND SO MUCH MORE...
FORGIVE ME, BUT YOU ARE CLUELESS. YOU NEVER DID HAVE A REALISTIC GRASP OF WHAT WE ARE ALL ABOUT. EVEN YOUR SO-CALLED LOVE FOR ME WAS JUST A MISGUIDED ROMANCE WITH THE LEVANT. YOUR TURKISH FANTASY.
OZAN. PLEASE.

KNOBLAUCHFRESSER: GARLIC EATERS. GASTARBEITERS: GUEST WORKERS. (GERMAN)

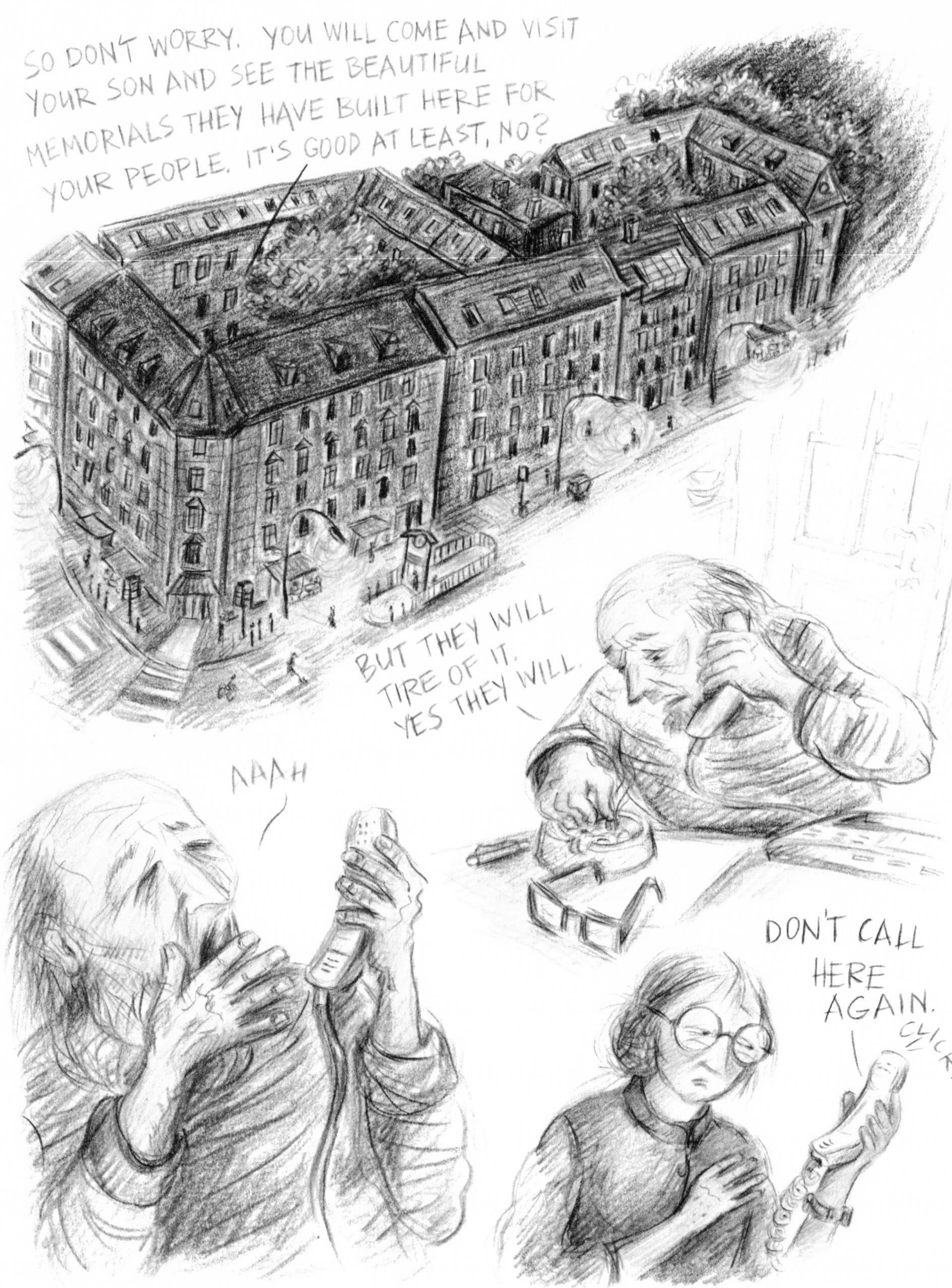
SO DON'T WORRY. YOU WILL COME AND VISIT YOUR SON AND SEE THE BEAUTIFUL MEMORIALS THEY HAVE BUILT HERE FOR YOUR PEOPLE. IT'S GOOD AT LEAST, NO?
BUT THEY WILL TIRE OF IT. YES THEY WILL.
AAAH
DON'T CALL HERE AGAIN.
CLICK

IN JANUARY THE SUN RISES AT ABOUT 6:45AM. IT ARCHES FROM BEHIND THE YESHIVA UNIVERSITY CAMPUS.

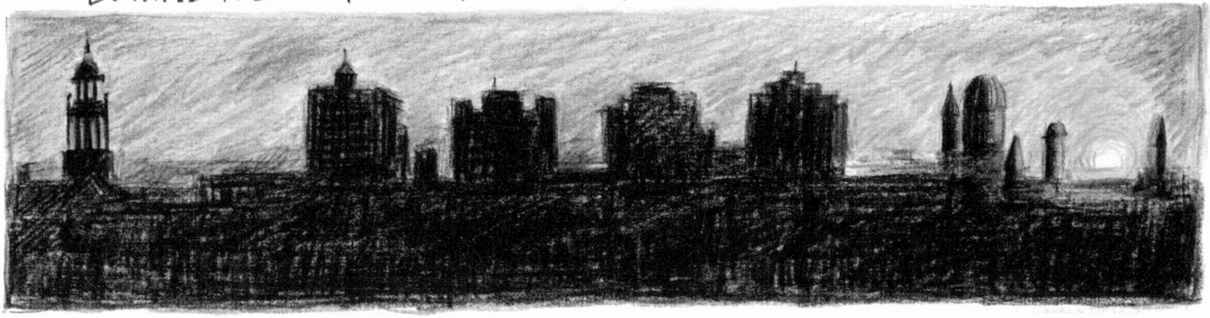

BY MARCH IT MOVES OVER TO THE GEORGE WASHINGTON HIGH SCHOOL.

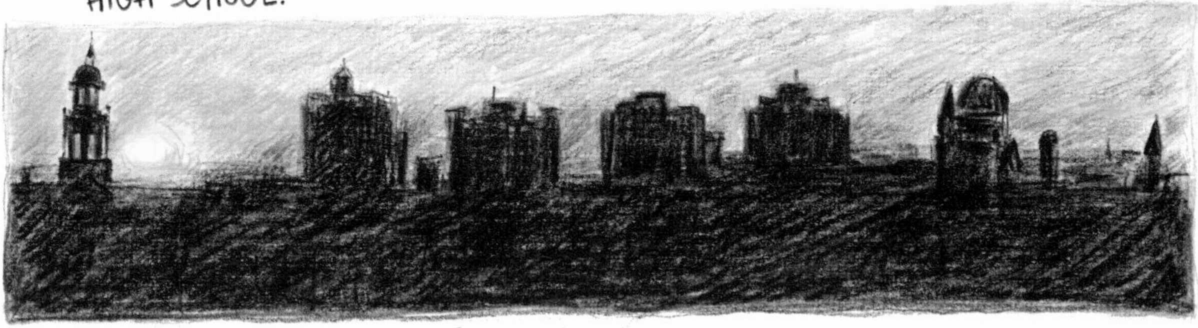

SUNSETS ARE ON THE JERSEY SIDE.

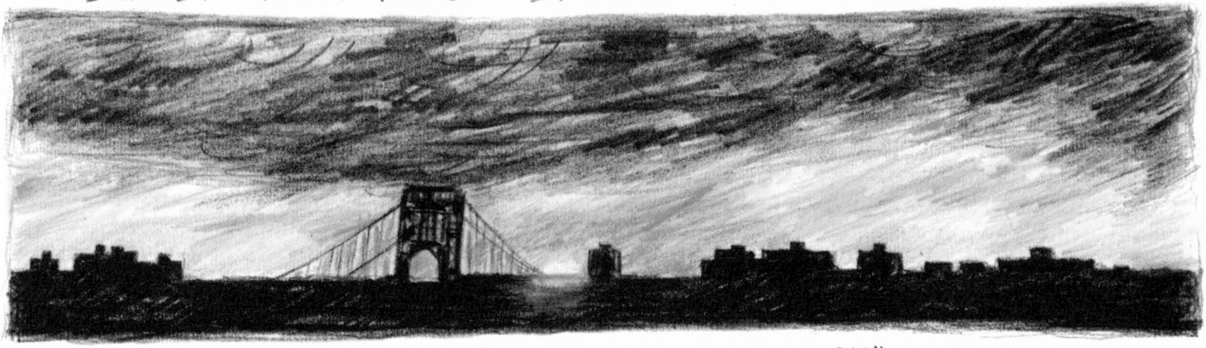

THIS GIVES THE HIDEOUS "BUILDINGS BY THE BRIDGE" A RARE MOMENT OF MAGNIFICENCE.

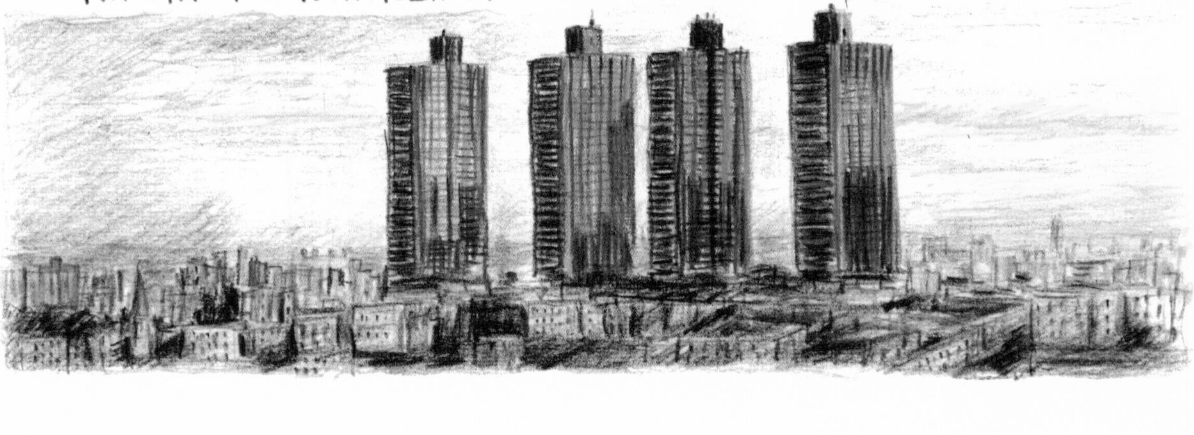

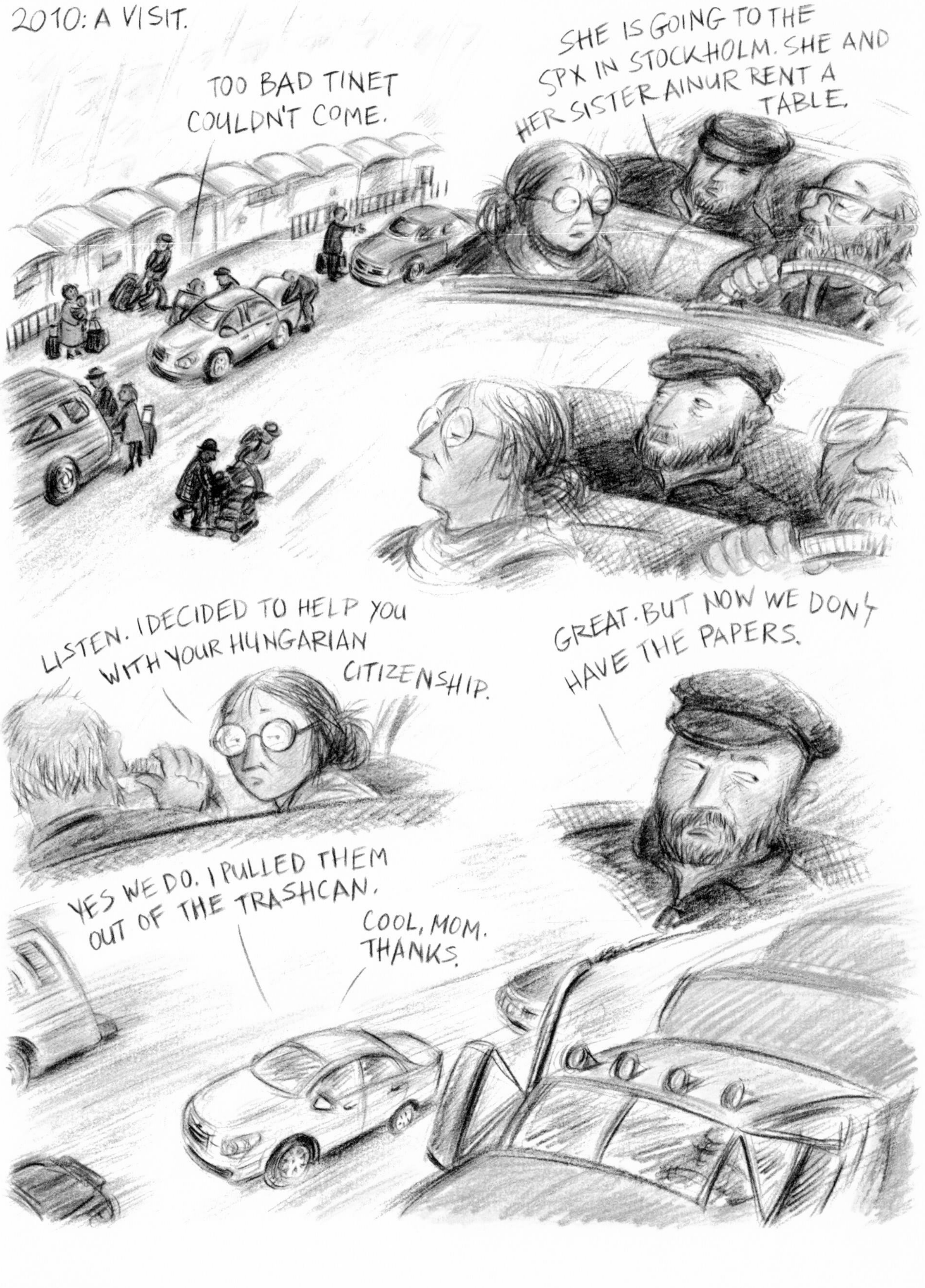
2010: A VISIT.
TOO BAD TINET COULDN'T COME.
SHE IS GOING TO THE SPX IN STOCKHOLM. SHE AND HER SISTER AINUR RENT A TABLE.
LISTEN. I DECIDED TO HELP YOU WITH YOUR HUNGARIAN CITIZENSHIP.
GREAT. BUT NOW WE DON'T HAVE THE PAPERS.
YES WE DO. I PULLED THEM OUT OF THE TRASHCAN.
COOL, MOM. THANKS.

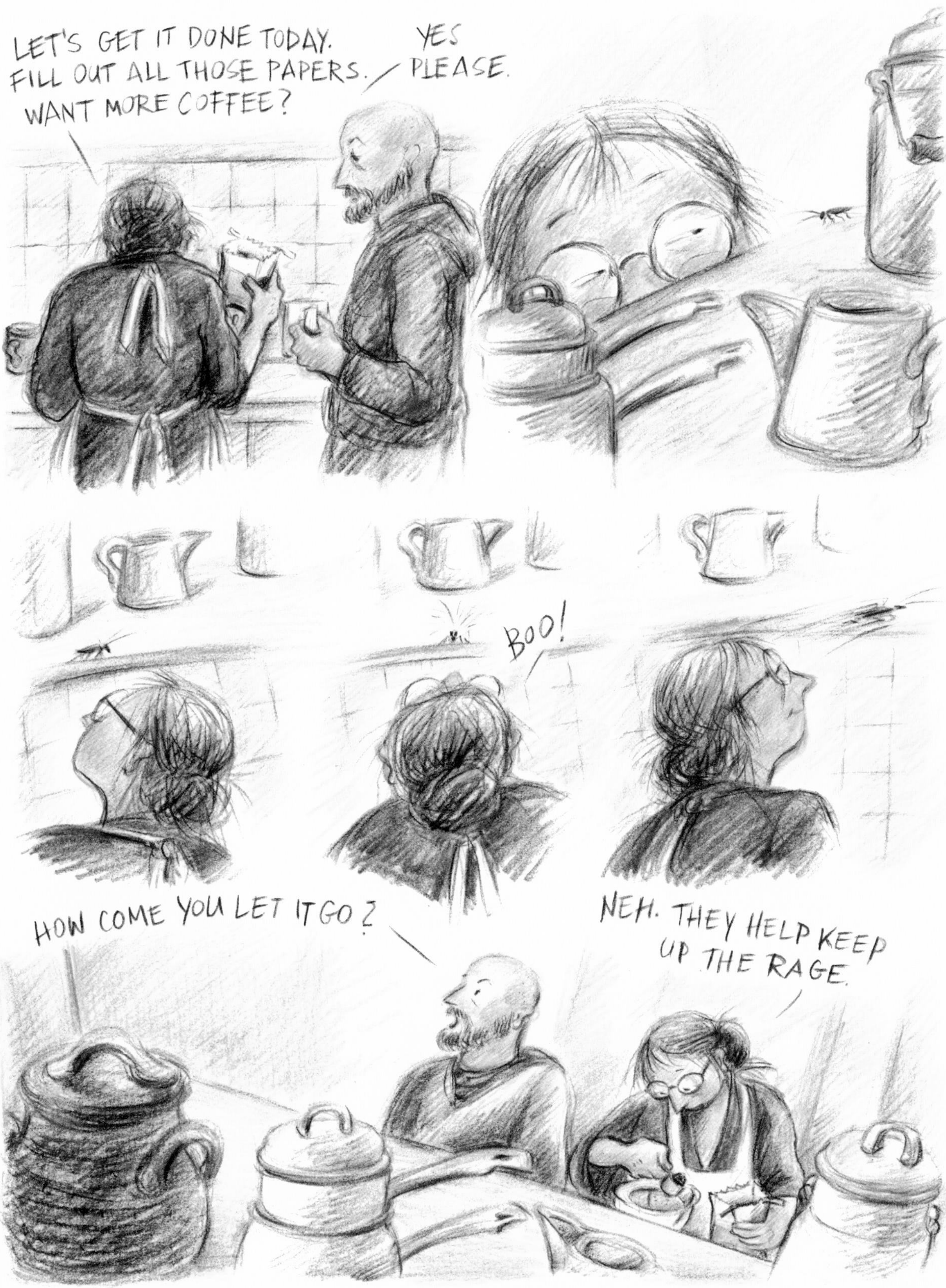
LET'S GET IT DONE TODAY. FILL OUT ALL THOSE PAPERS. WANT MORE COFFEE?
YES PLEASE.
BOO!
HOW COME YOU LET IT GO?
NEH. THEY HELP KEEP UP THE RAGE.

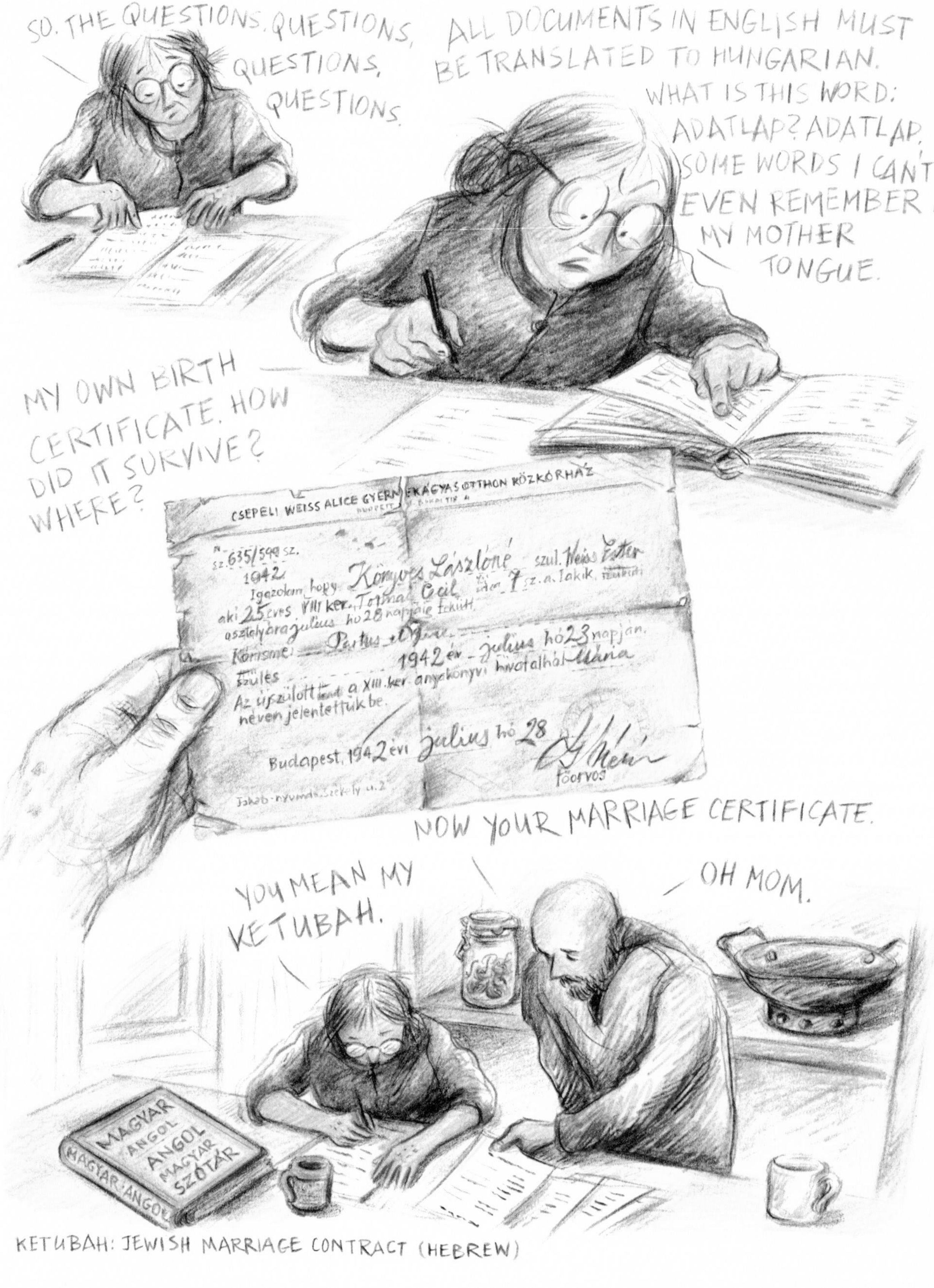
SO. THE QUESTIONS. QUESTIONS, QUESTIONS, QUESTIONS.
ALL DOCUMENTS IN ENGLISH MUST BE TRANSLATED TO HUNGARIAN.
WHAT IS THIS WORD: ADATLAP? ADATLAP. SOME WORDS I CAN'T EVEN REMEMBER IN MY MOTHER TONGUE.
MY OWN BIRTH CERTIFICATE. HOW DID IT SURVIVE? WHERE?
CSEPELI WEISS ALICE GYERMEKÁGYAS OTTHON KÖZKÓRHÁZ
sz. 635/599 sz.
1942
Igazolom hogy Könyves Lászlóné szul. Weiss Eszter
aki 25 éves VIII ker. Tormay Cécil utca 7 sz. a. lakik,
osztályára julius hó 28 napjáig fekütt.
Kórisme: Partus
Szülés 1942 év julius hó 23 napján.
Az újszülöttet a XIII. ker. anyakönyvi hivatalnál Mária
néven jelentettük be.
Budapest, 1942 évi julius hó 28
főorvos
NOW YOUR MARRIAGE CERTIFICATE.
YOU MEAN MY KETUBAH.
OH MOM.
MAGYAR ANGOL
ANGOL MAGYAR SZÓTÁR
MAGYAR-ANGOL

KETUBAH: JEWISH MARRIAGE CONTRACT (HEBREW)

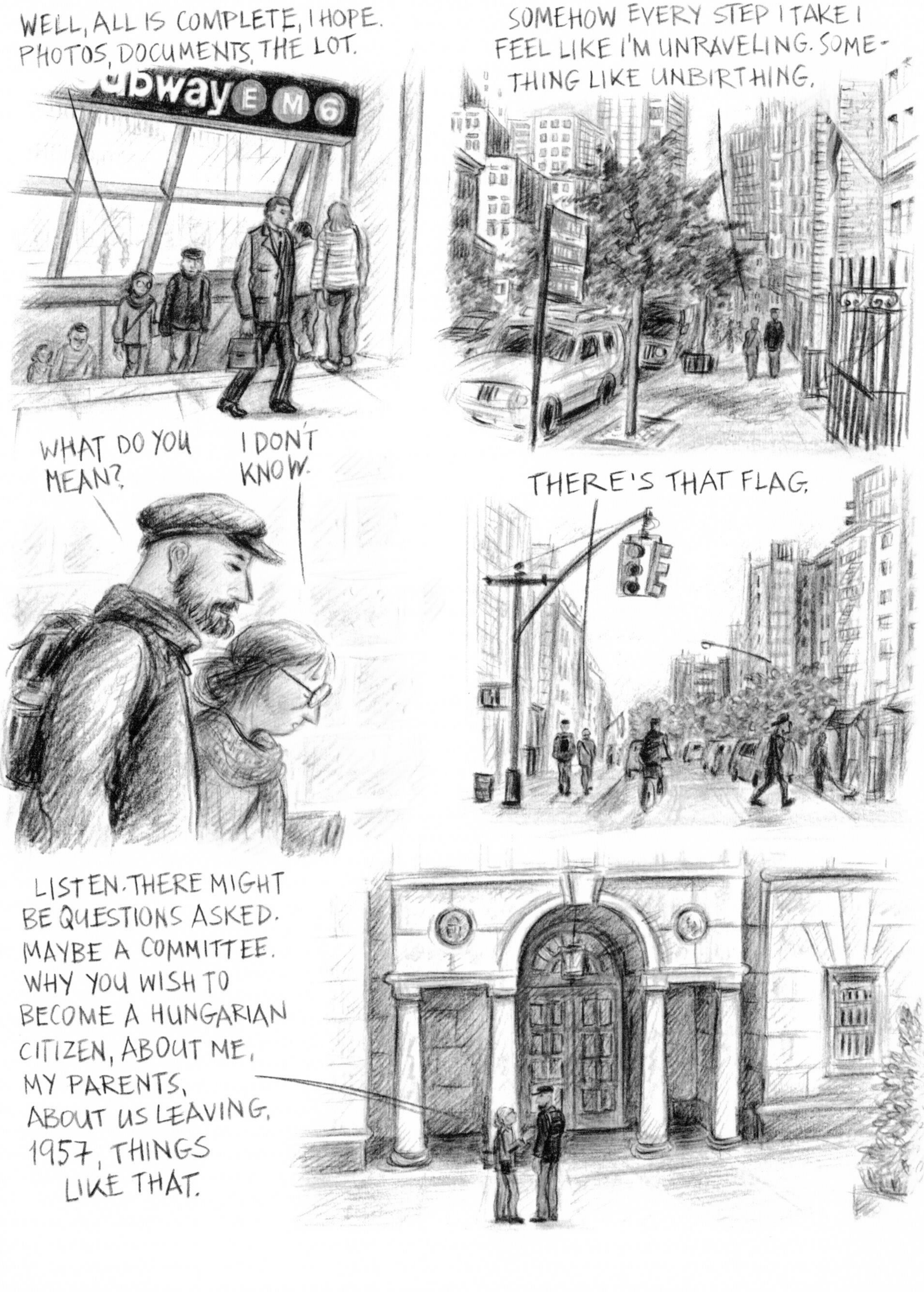

WELL, ALL IS COMPLETE, I HOPE. PHOTOS, DOCUMENTS, THE LOT.
Subway E M 6
SOMEHOW EVERY STEP I TAKE I FEEL LIKE I'M UNRAVELING. SOMETHING LIKE UNBIRTHING.
WHAT DO YOU MEAN?
I DON'T KNOW.
THERE'S THAT FLAG.
LISTEN. THERE MIGHT BE QUESTIONS ASKED. MAYBE A COMMITTEE. WHY YOU WISH TO BECOME A HUNGARIAN CITIZEN, ABOUT ME, MY PARENTS, ABOUT US LEAVING. 1957, THINGS LIKE THAT.

AND THIS IS YOUR SON?

IS THIS YOUR BIRTH CERTIFICATE? IT DOESN'T LOOK RIGHT.

EXCUSE ME!? JUST LOOK AT THE DATE! WE HAD TO BURN EVERYTHING! BUT THIS IS REAL! IT IS A MIRACLE THAT THIS EXISTS AT ALL!

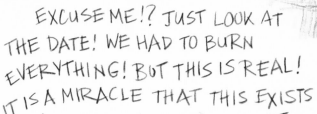

OK. OK. EVERYTHING SEEMS TO BE HERE. I'LL JUST MAKE COPIES. SIT AND WAIT PLEASE.

PHEW. THAT FELT GOOD.

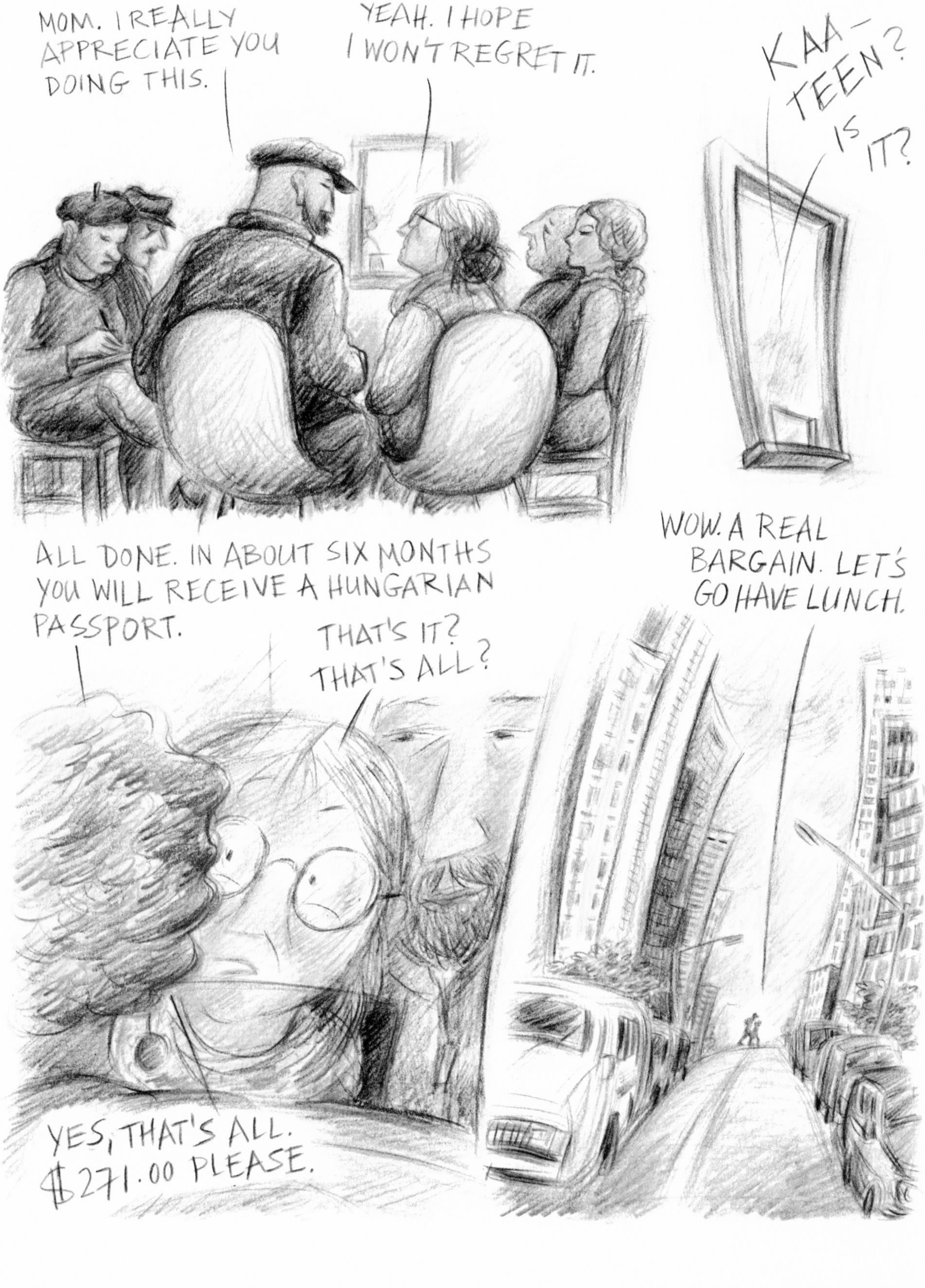
MOM. I REALLY APPRECIATE YOU DOING THIS.
YEAH. I HOPE I WON'T REGRET IT.
KAA-TEEN? IS IT?
ALL DONE. IN ABOUT SIX MONTHS YOU WILL RECEIVE A HUNGARIAN PASSPORT.
THAT'S IT? THAT'S ALL?
YES, THAT'S ALL. $271.00 PLEASE.
WOW. A REAL BARGAIN. LET'S GO HAVE LUNCH.

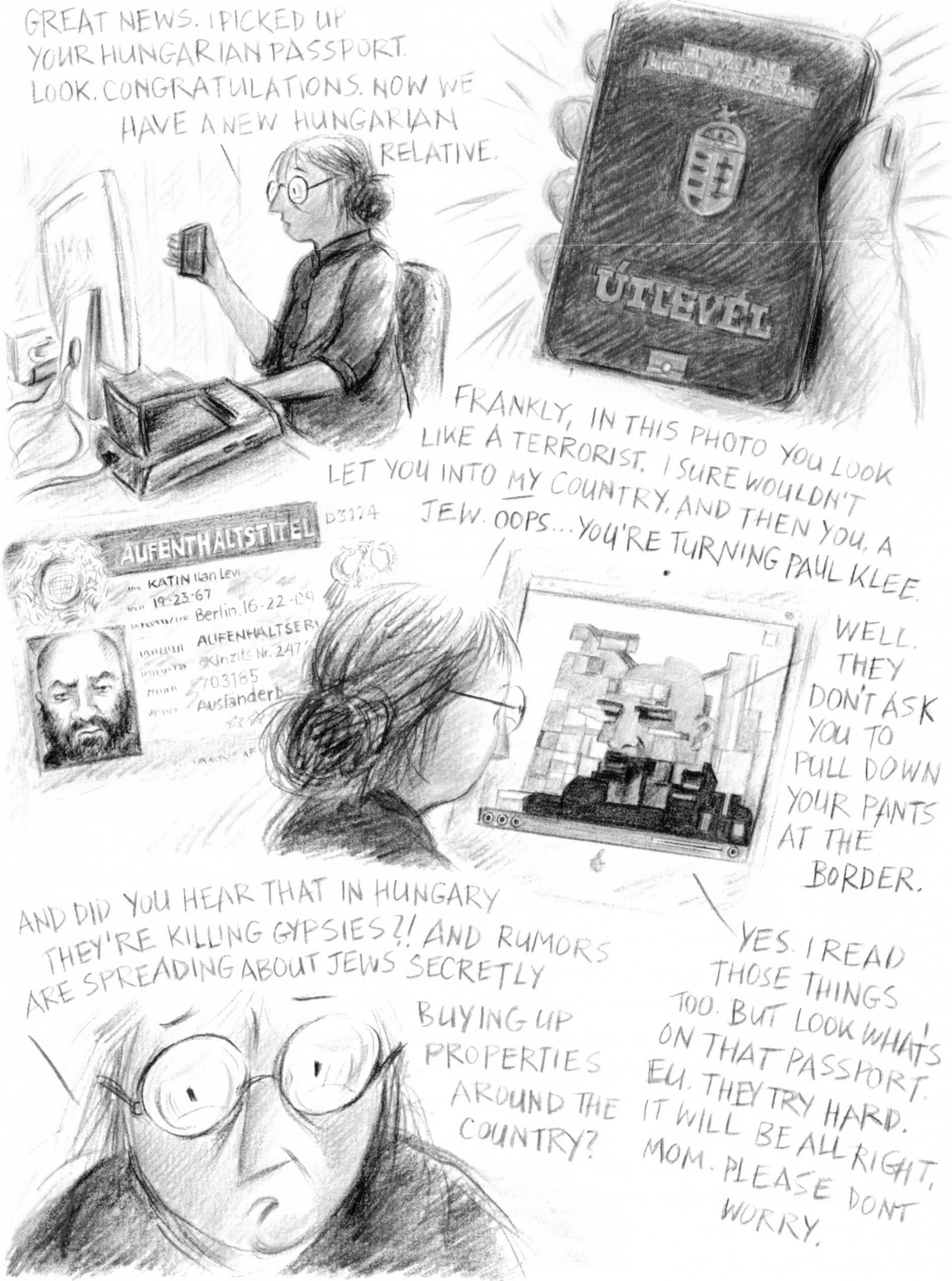

GREAT NEWS. I PICKED UP YOUR HUNGARIAN PASSPORT. LOOK. CONGRATULATIONS. NOW WE HAVE A NEW HUNGARIAN RELATIVE.
ÚTLEVÉL
FRANKLY, IN THIS PHOTO YOU LOOK LIKE A TERRORIST. I SURE WOULDN'T LET YOU INTO MY COUNTRY. AND THEN YOU, A JEW. OOPS... YOU'RE TURNING PAUL KLEE.
AUFENTHALTSTITEL
D3174
KATIN Ilan Levi
19-23-67
Berlin 16-22-09
WELL. THEY DON'T ASK YOU TO PULL DOWN YOUR PANTS AT THE BORDER.
AND DID YOU HEAR THAT IN HUNGARY THEY'RE KILLING GYPSIES?! AND RUMORS ARE SPREADING ABOUT JEWS SECRETLY BUYING UP PROPERTIES AROUND THE COUNTRY?
YES. I READ THOSE THINGS TOO. BUT LOOK WHAT'S ON THAT PASSPORT. EU. THEY TRY HARD. IT WILL BE ALL RIGHT, MOM. PLEASE DONT WORRY.

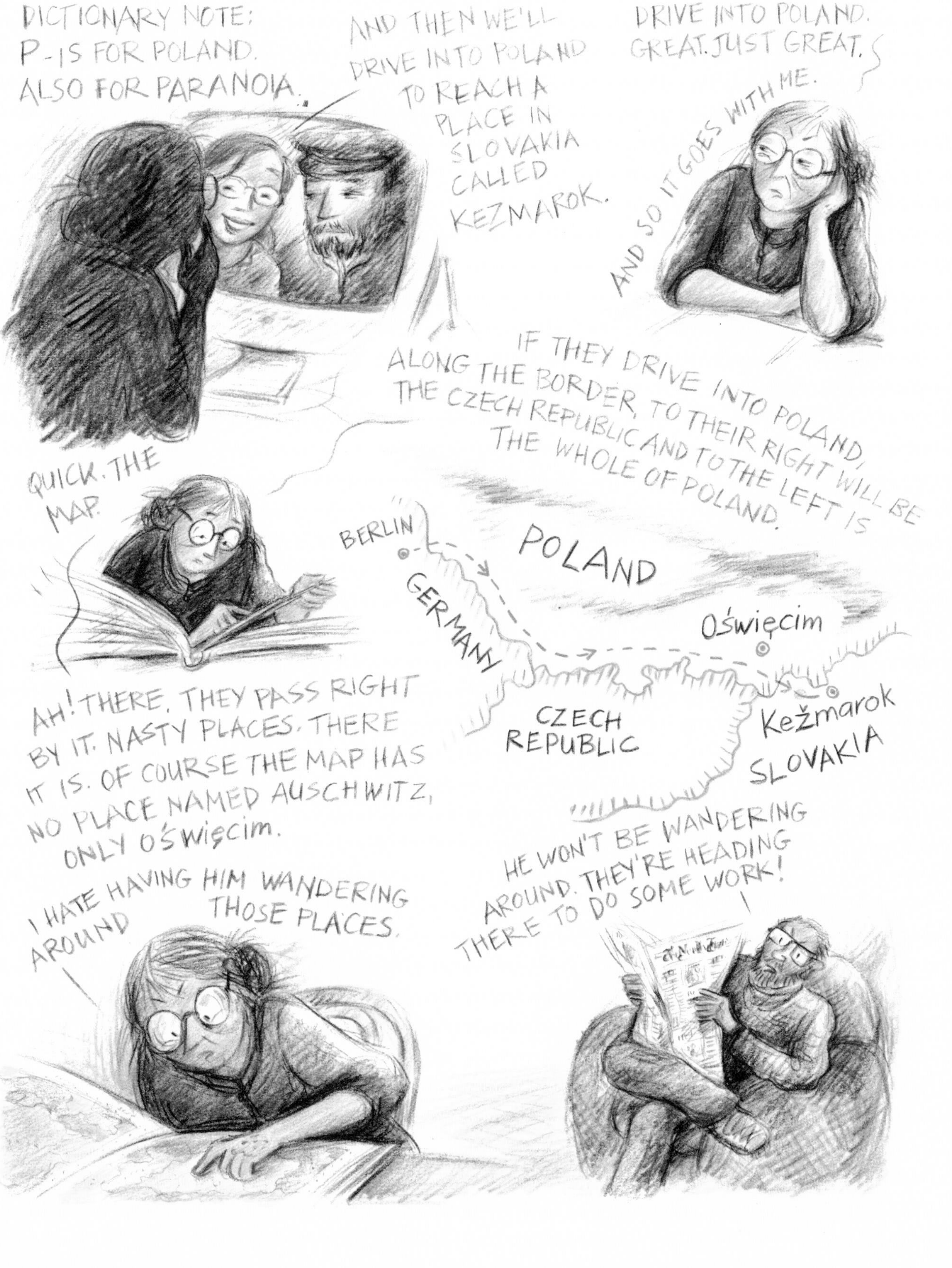
DICTIONARY NOTE: P - IS FOR POLAND. ALSO FOR PARANOIA.
AND THEN WE'LL DRIVE INTO POLAND TO REACH A PLACE IN SLOVAKIA CALLED KEZMAROK.
DRIVE INTO POLAND. GREAT. JUST GREAT.
AND SO IT GOES WITH ME.
IF THEY DRIVE INTO POLAND, ALONG THE BORDER, TO THEIR RIGHT WILL BE THE CZECH REPUBLIC AND TO THE LEFT IS THE WHOLE OF POLAND.
QUICK. THE MAP.
BERLIN
POLAND
GERMANY
Oświęcim
CZECH REPUBLIC
Kežmarok
SLOVAKIA
AH! THERE. THEY PASS RIGHT BY IT. NASTY PLACES. THERE IT IS. OF COURSE THE MAP HAS NO PLACE NAMED AUSCHWITZ, ONLY OŚWIĘCIM.
I HATE HAVING HIM WANDERING AROUND THOSE PLACES.
HE WON'T BE WANDERING AROUND. THEY'RE HEADING THERE TO DO SOME WORK!

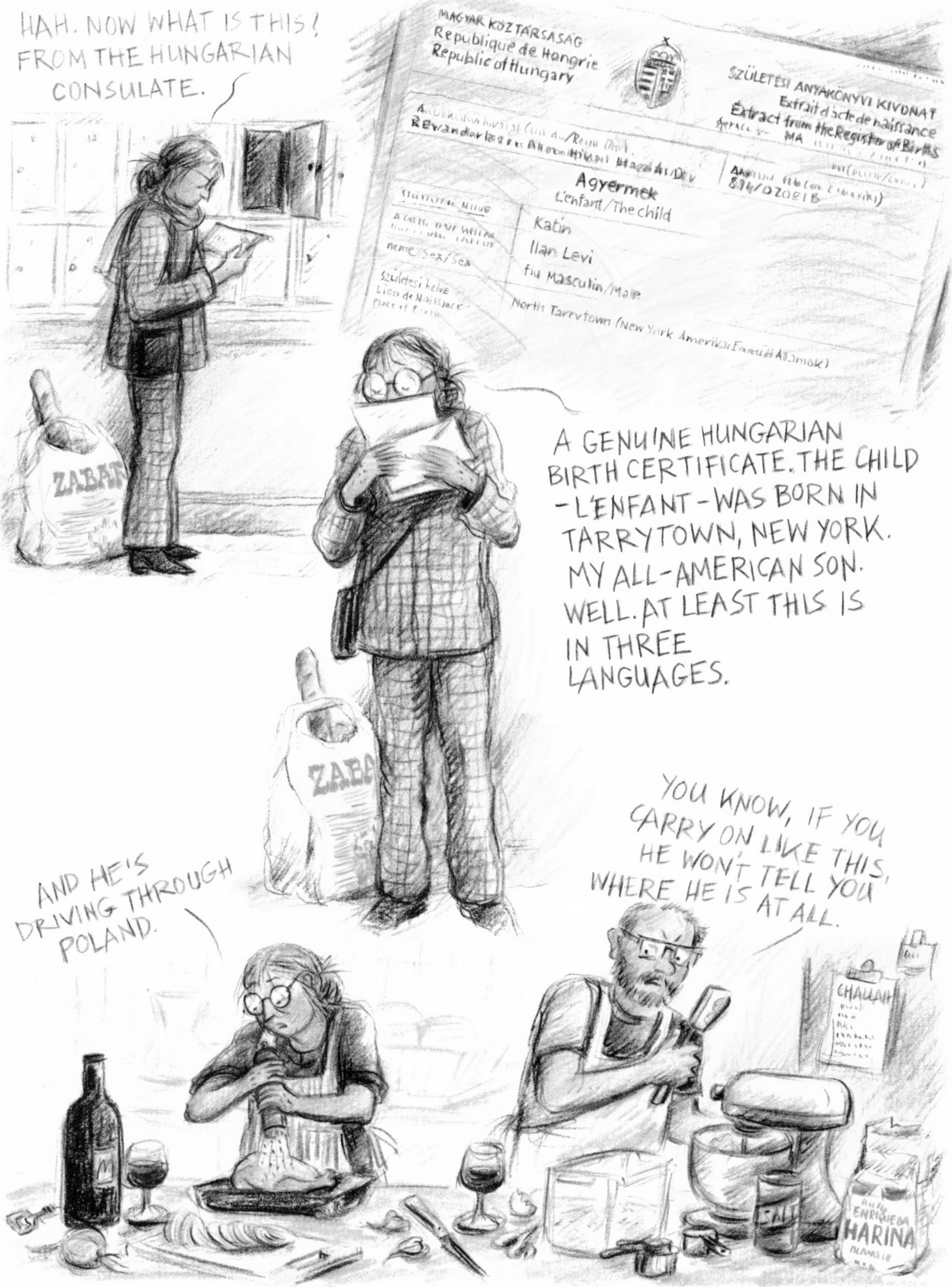
HAH. NOW WHAT IS THIS? FROM THE HUNGARIAN CONSULATE.
MAGYAR KÖZTÁRSASÁG
Republique de Hongrie
Republic of Hungary
SZÜLETÉSI ANYAKÖNYVI KIVONAT
Extrait d'acte de naissance
Extract from the Register of Births
MA
894/02081B
Agyermek
L'enfant/The child
Katin
Ilan Levi
neme Sex/Sex
fiu Masculin/Male
Születési helve
Lieu de Naissance
Place of Birth
North Tarrytown (New York Amerikai Egyesült Államok)
ZABAR
A GENUINE HUNGARIAN BIRTH CERTIFICATE. THE CHILD - L'ENFANT - WAS BORN IN TARRYTOWN, NEW YORK. MY ALL-AMERICAN SON. WELL. AT LEAST THIS IS IN THREE LANGUAGES.
ZABA
AND HE'S DRIVING THROUGH POLAND.
YOU KNOW, IF YOU CARRY ON LIKE THIS, HE WON'T TELL YOU WHERE HE IS AT ALL.
CHALLAH
HARINA

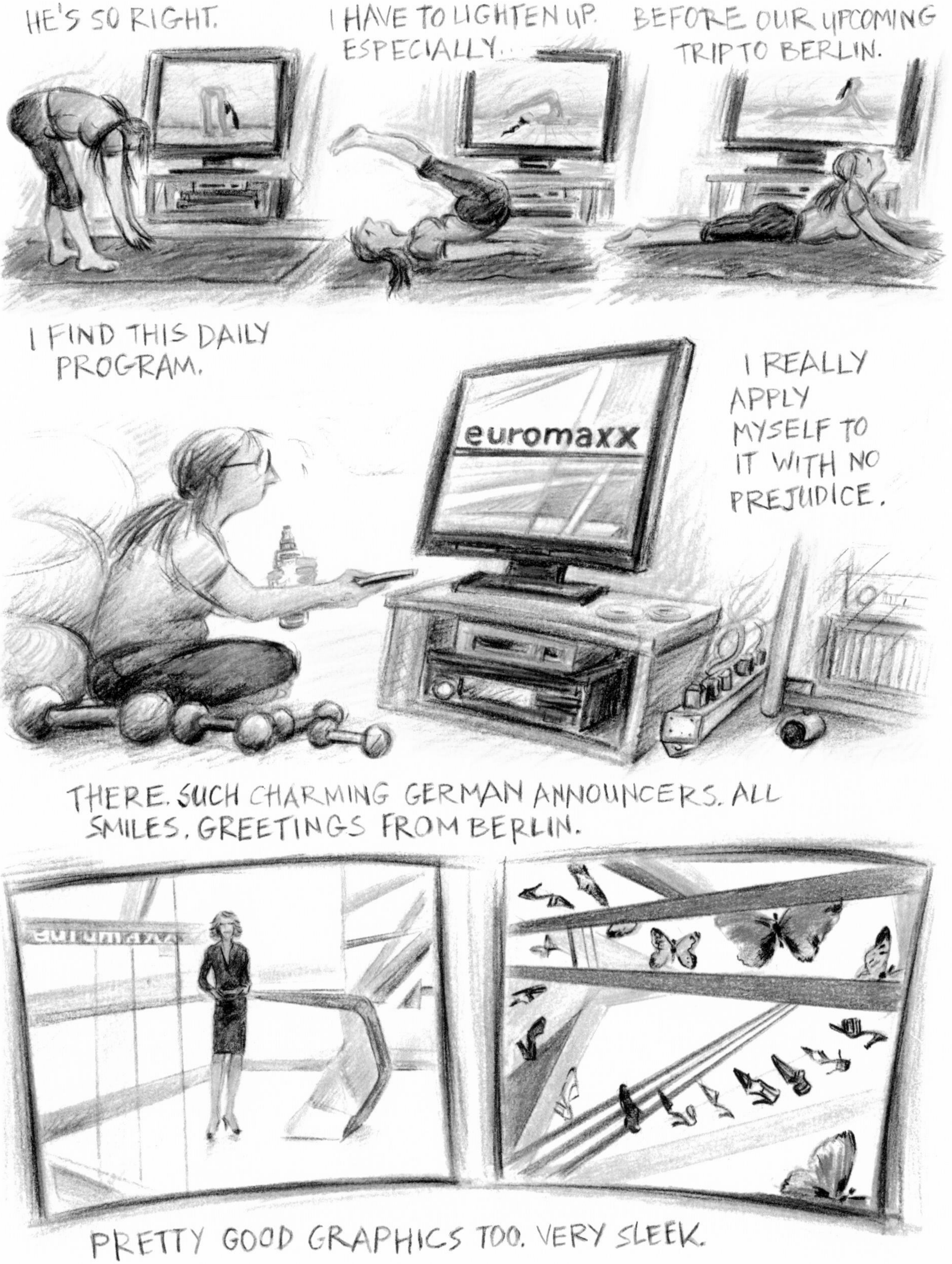
HE'S SO RIGHT.
I HAVE TO LIGHTEN UP. ESPECIALLY...
BEFORE OUR UPCOMING TRIP TO BERLIN.
I FIND THIS DAILY PROGRAM.
euromaxx
I REALLY APPLY MYSELF TO IT WITH NO PREJUDICE.
THERE. SUCH CHARMING GERMAN ANNOUNCERS. ALL SMILES. GREETINGS FROM BERLIN.
PRETTY GOOD GRAPHICS TOO. VERY SLEEK.

WELL. IT LOOKS CHEERFUL ENOUGH. I CAN GO WITH THAT. I BECOME DEVOTED TO THIS PROGRAM. I HAVE NO IDEA WHAT IS FUN OVER THERE.

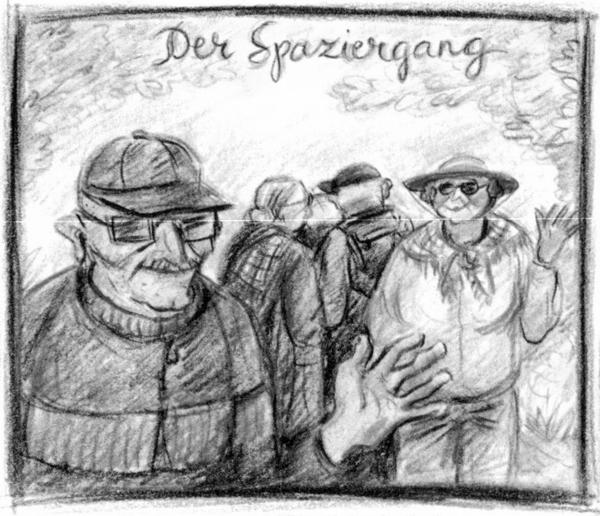
Der Spaziergang

HERE ARE SOME NICE GERMAN RETIREES, DEVOTED TO WALKING. HOW OLD ARE THOSE... OLD ENOUGH... OK... STOP IT RIGHT NOW.

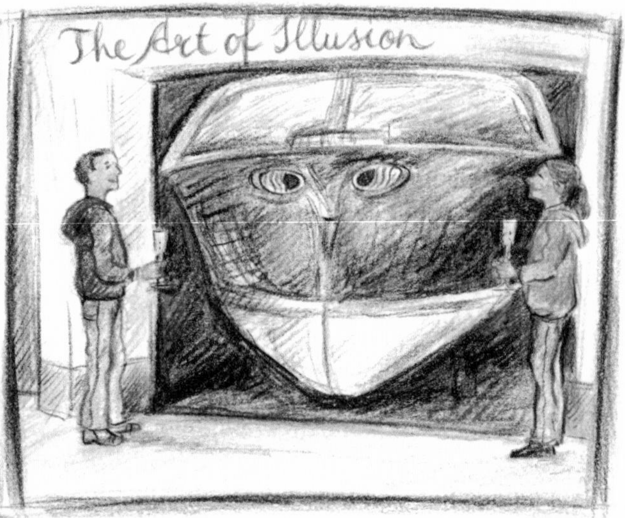
The Art of Illusion

THE SASSENBACH AD AGENCY IN COLOGNE CAN PRODUCE A GIANT POSTER TO COVER YOUR DULL GARAGE DOOR WITH A DESIGN OF YOUR CHOICE.

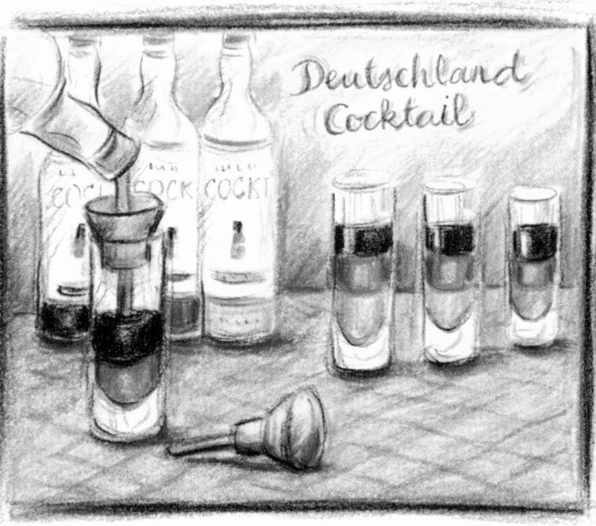
Deutschland Cocktail

THIS IS FROM YOUTUBE. HERE WE CAN LEARN HOW TO CONCOCT A DEUTSCHLAND COCKTAIL. THIS COULD BE VERY USEFUL SOMETIME IN THE FUTURE.

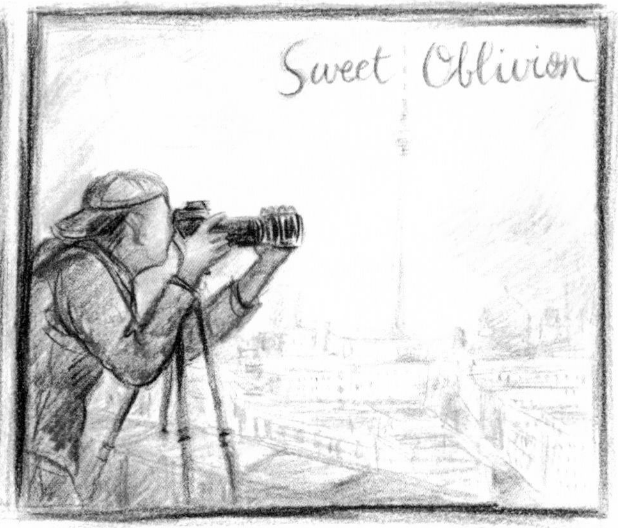
Sweet Oblivion

THIS PHOTOGRAPHER EXCLUSIVELY TAKES OUT-OF-FOCUS PICTURES OF BERLIN. THAT'S IT! THAT'S WHAT I NEED! TO SEE BERLIN OUT OF FOCUS.

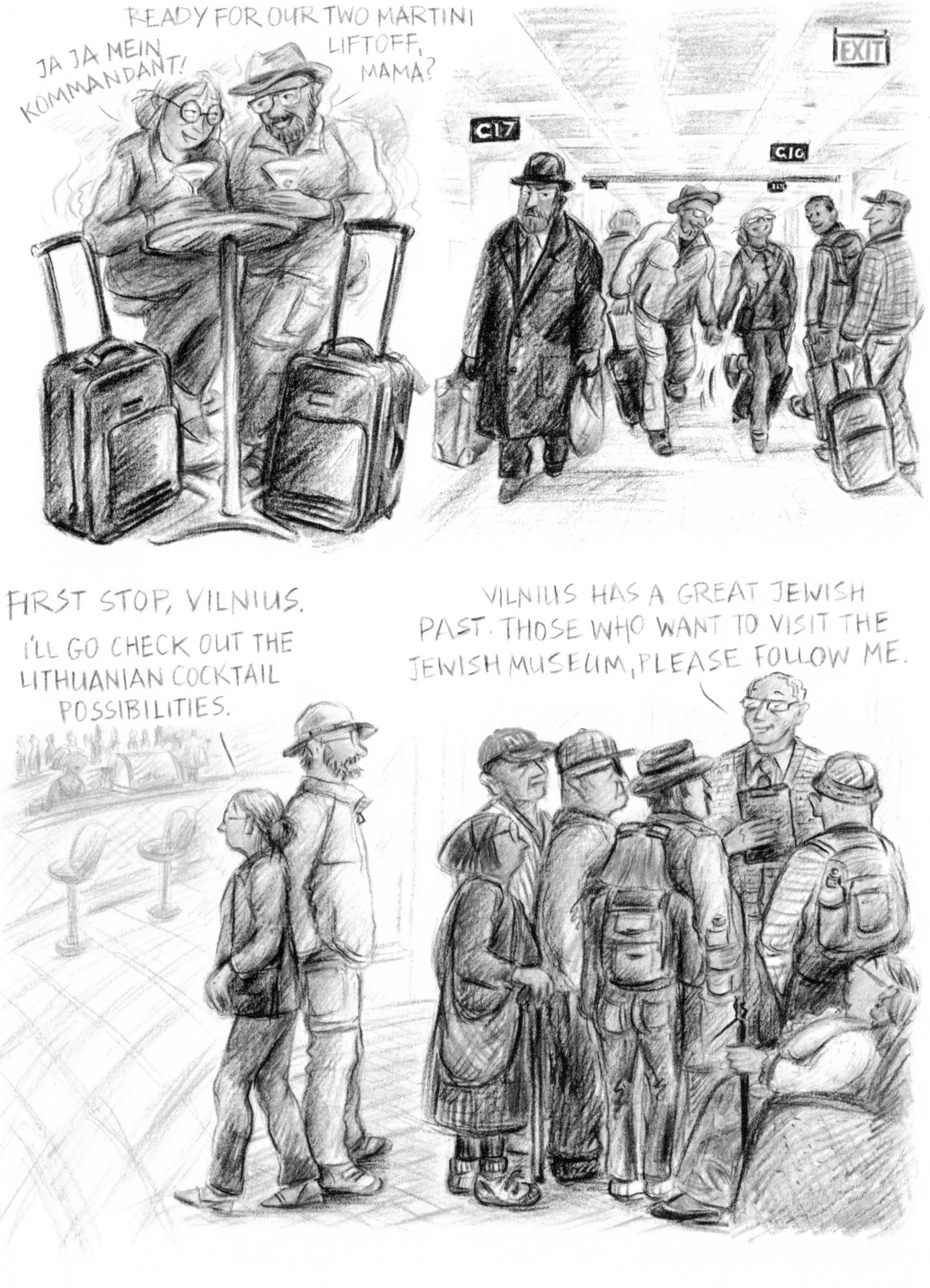
READY FOR OUR TWO MARTINI LIFTOFF, MAMA?
JA JA MEIN KOMMANDANT!
EXIT
C17
C16
FIRST STOP, VILNIUS.
I'LL GO CHECK OUT THE LITHUANIAN COCKTAIL POSSIBILITIES.
VILNIUS HAS A GREAT JEWISH PAST. THOSE WHO WANT TO VISIT THE JEWISH MUSEUM, PLEASE FOLLOW ME.

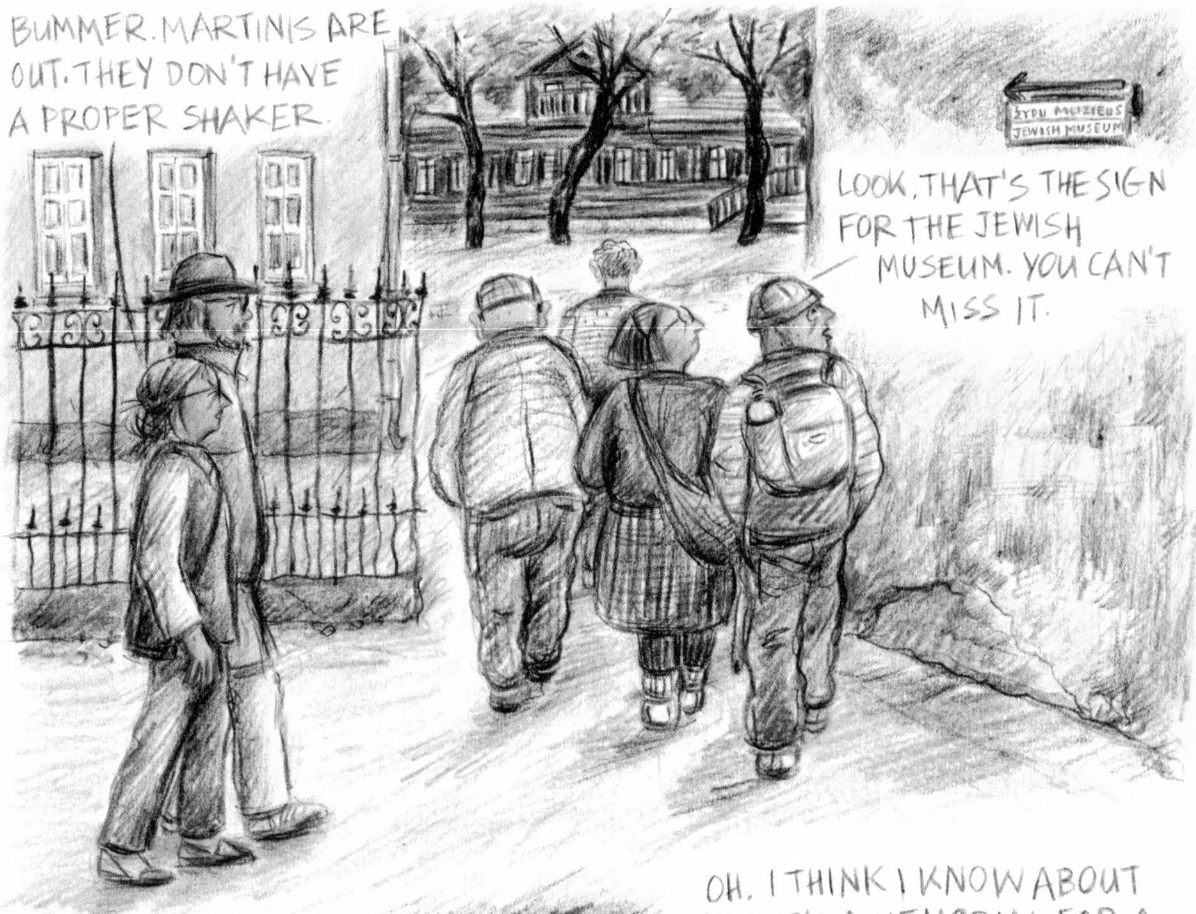
BUMMER. MARTINIS ARE OUT. THEY DON'T HAVE A PROPER SHAKER.
JEWISH MUSEUM
LOOK, THAT'S THE SIGN FOR THE JEWISH MUSEUM. YOU CAN'T MISS IT.

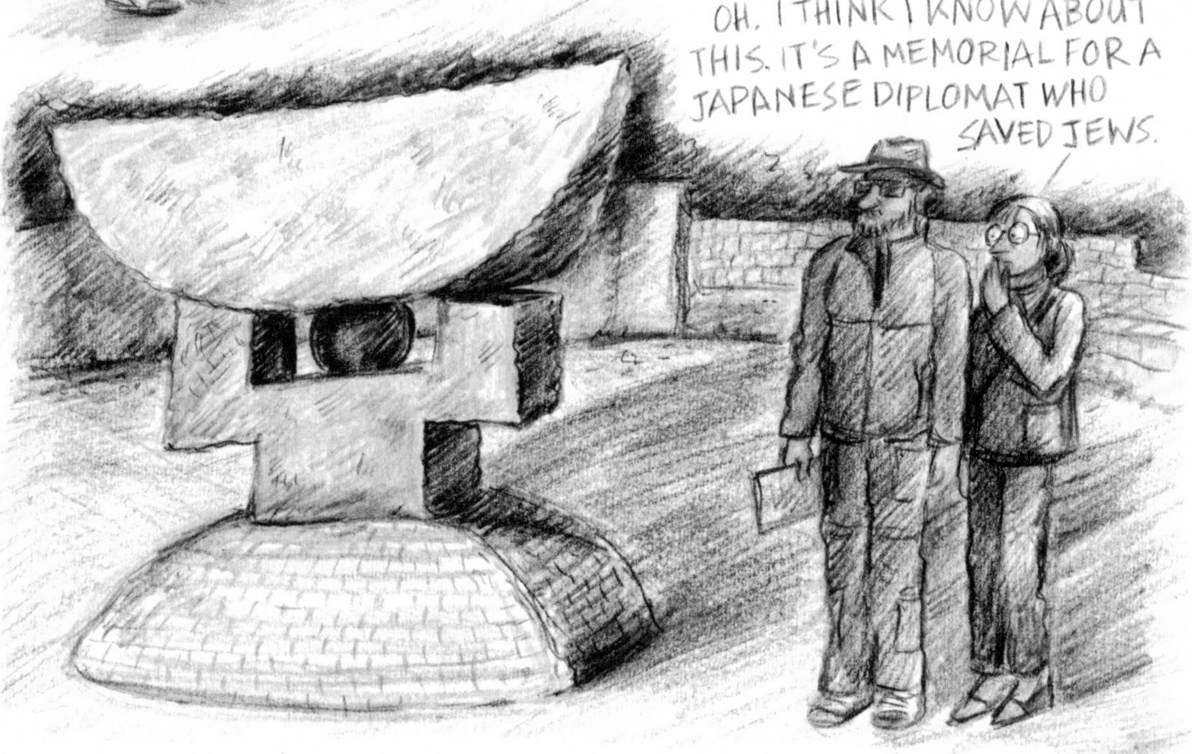
OH. I THINK I KNOW ABOUT THIS. IT'S A MEMORIAL FOR A JAPANESE DIPLOMAT WHO SAVED JEWS.

IN 1940 CHIUNE SUGIHARA WAS THE VICE-CONSUL FOR THE JAPANESE EMPIRE IN LITHUANIA. THE CONSULATE WAS IN KAUNAS.

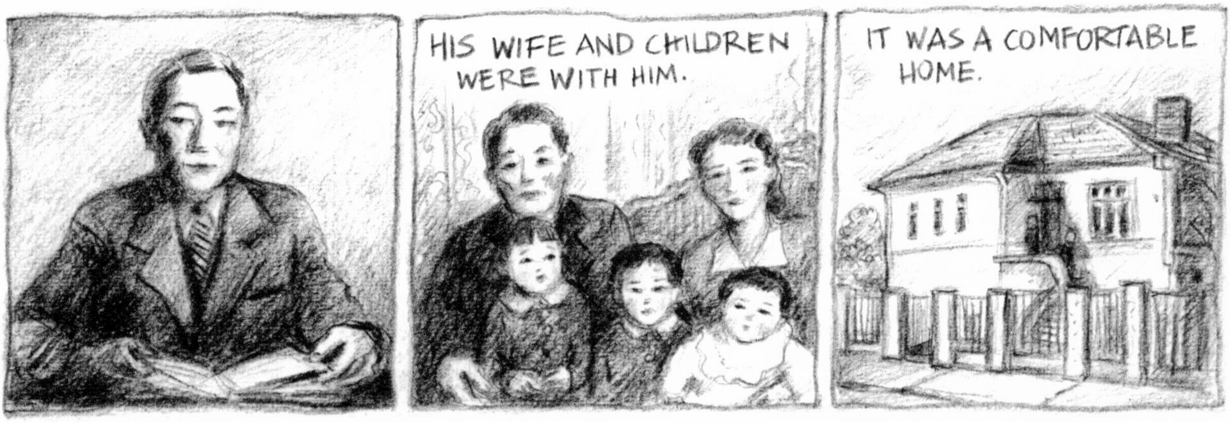
HIS WIFE AND CHILDREN WERE WITH HIM.
IT WAS A COMFORTABLE HOME.

WHEN THE RUSSIANS OCCUPIED LITHUANIA, SUGIHARA WAS SUMMONED BACK TO BERLIN. HE AND HIS FAMILY WERE GETTING READY TO LEAVE.

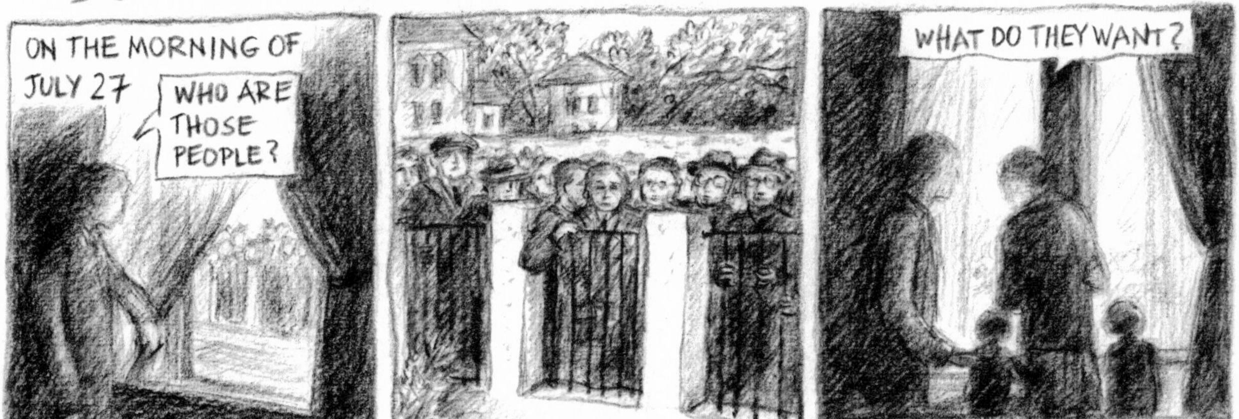
ON THE MORNING OF JULY 27
WHO ARE THOSE PEOPLE?
WHAT DO THEY WANT?

HE ASKED THEM TO SEND IN A DELEGATION TO REPRESENT THEM.

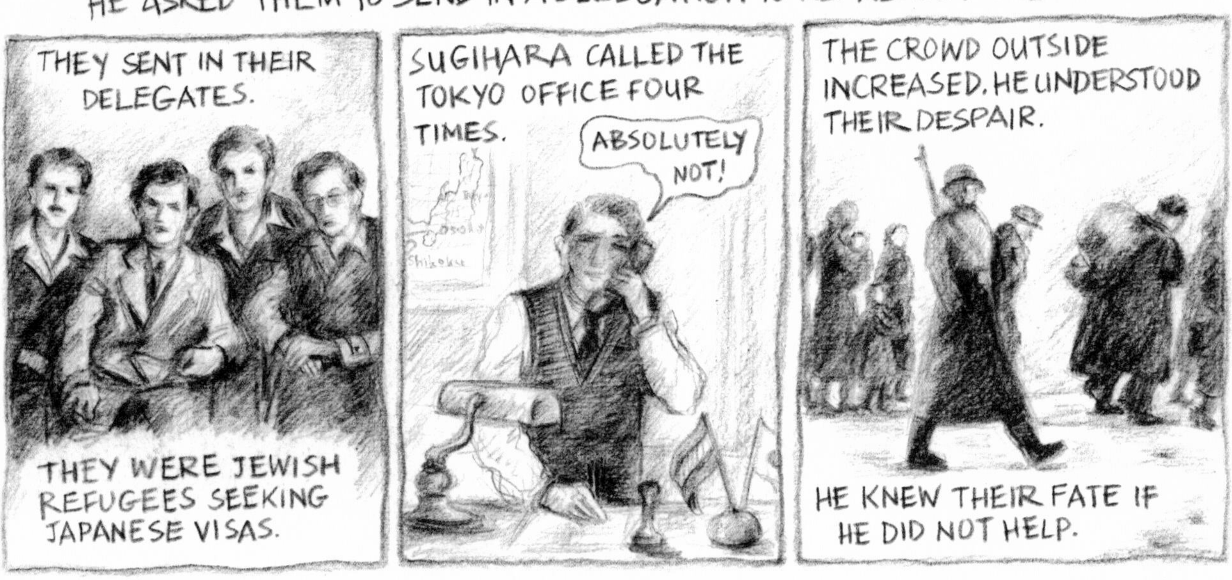
THEY SENT IN THEIR DELEGATES.
THEY WERE JEWISH REFUGEES SEEKING JAPANESE VISAS.
SUGIHARA CALLED THE TOKYO OFFICE FOUR TIMES.
ABSOLUTELY NOT!
THE CROWD OUTSIDE INCREASED. HE UNDERSTOOD THEIR DESPAIR.
HE KNEW THEIR FATE IF HE DID NOT HELP.

SUGIHARA DECIDED TO DEFY HIS GOVERNMENT, TO RISK HIS CAREER AND HIS FUTURE. HIS WIFE, YUKIKO, AGREED. SHE WOULD HELP HIM.

29 DAYS THEY LABORED.

ISSUING UP TO 300 VISAS A DAY.

AT NIGHT YUKIKO MASSAGED HIS HAND.

AT LAST THEY HAD TO LEAVE THE CONSULATE.

ON THE WAY TO THE TRAIN STATION HE WAS STILL ISSUING VISAS.

I AM SORRY THAT I MUST LEAVE!

AT LAST, IN DESPERATION, HE THREW THE OFFICIAL STAMP OUT TO THE CROWD AS HE HADN'T TIME TO STAMP ALL THE VISAS.

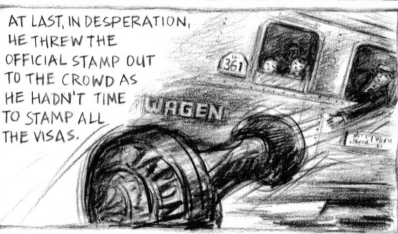

THE MORE THAN 2000 VISAS SAVED 6000 JEWS. SUGIHARA AND HIS FAMILY WERE ARRESTED BY THE SOVIETS AND SPENT EIGHTEEN MONTHS IN A POW CAMP. AFTER HIS RETURN TO JAPAN HE WAS FIRED FROM THE FOREIGN MINISTRY.

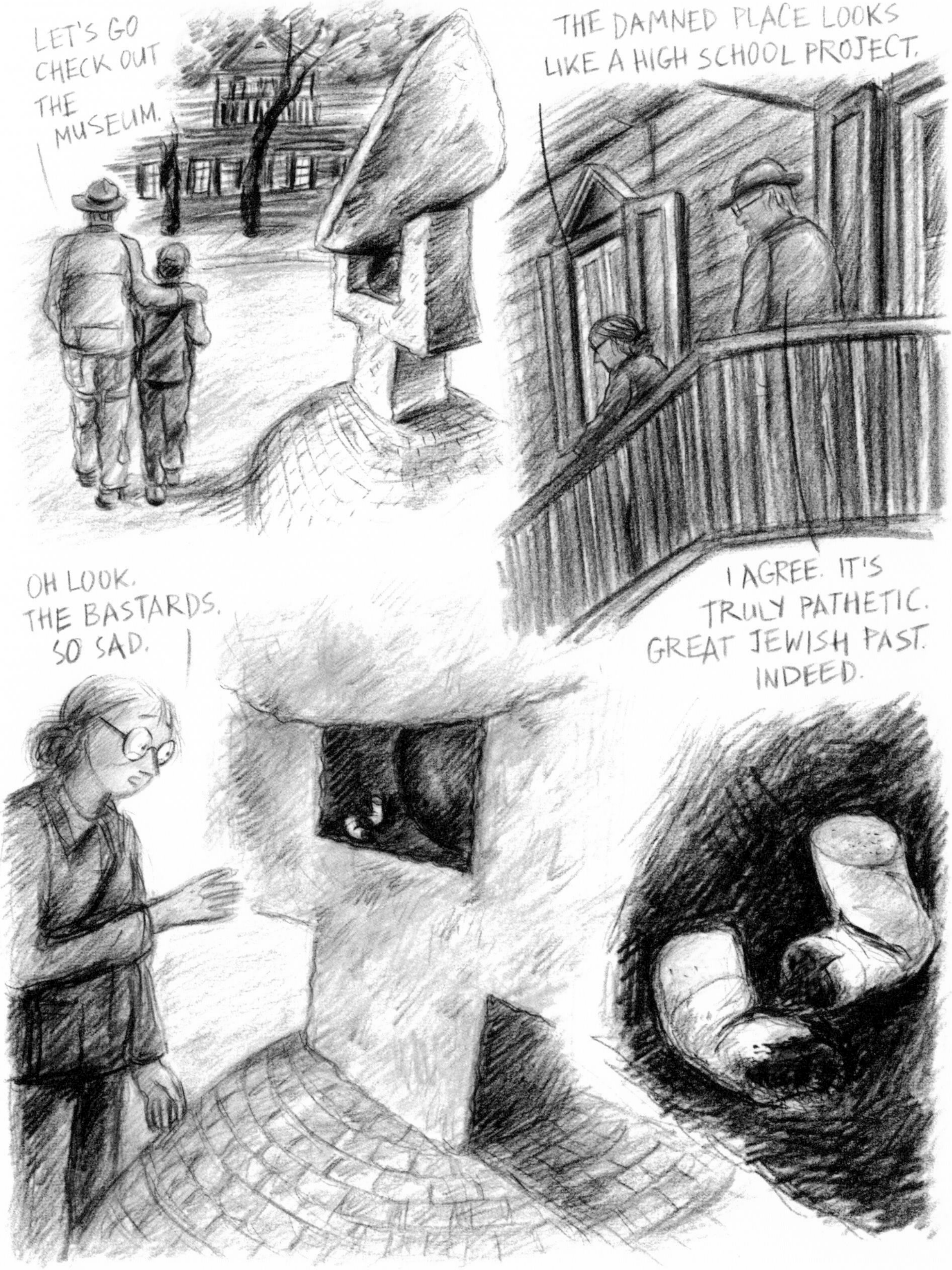
LET'S GO CHECK OUT THE MUSEUM.
THE DAMNED PLACE LOOKS LIKE A HIGH SCHOOL PROJECT.
I AGREE. IT'S TRULY PATHETIC. GREAT JEWISH PAST. INDEED.
OH LOOK. THE BASTARDS. SO SAD.

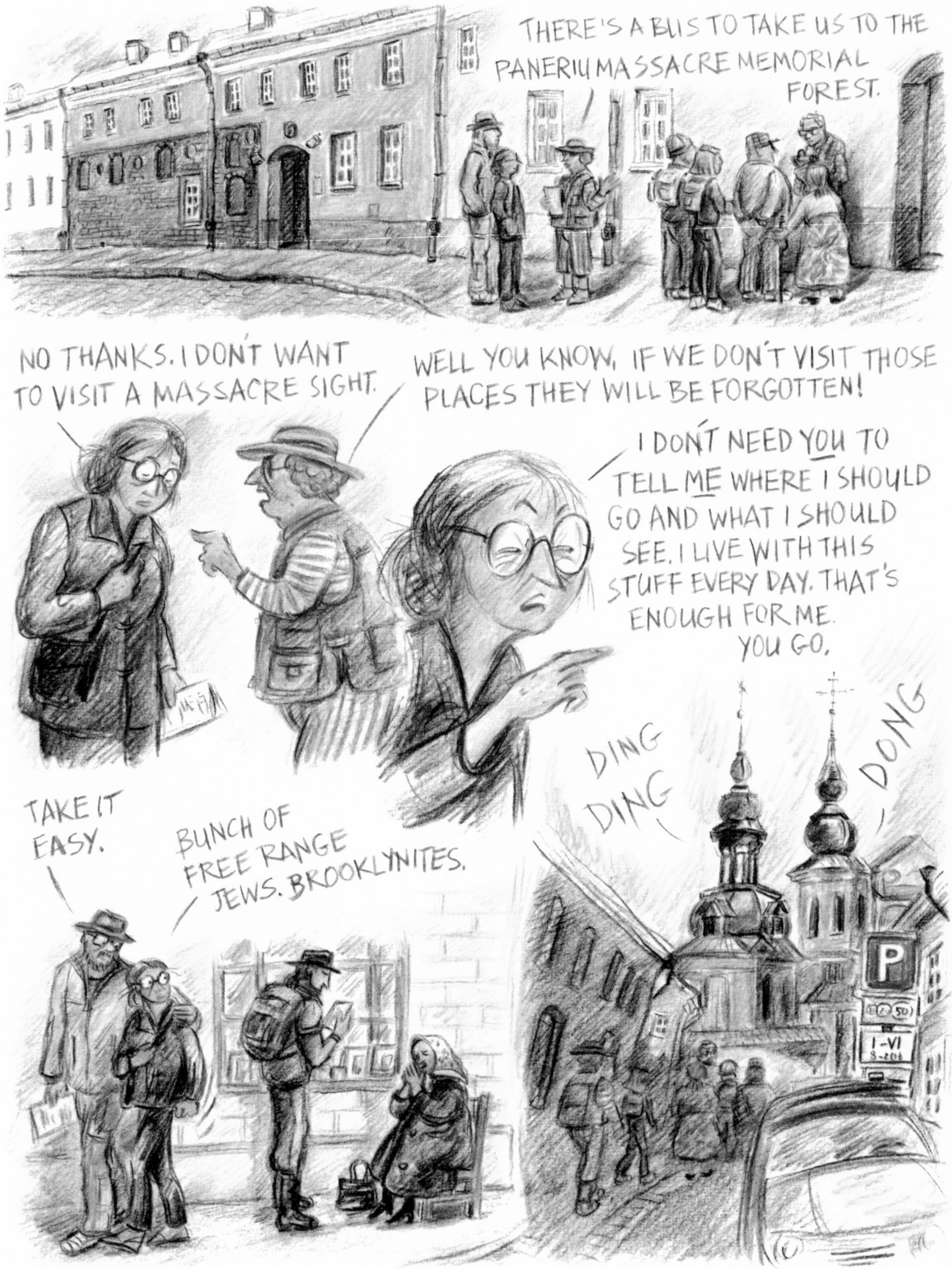
THERE'S A BUS TO TAKE US TO THE PANERIU MASSACRE MEMORIAL FOREST.
NO THANKS. I DON'T WANT TO VISIT A MASSACRE SIGHT.
WELL YOU KNOW, IF WE DON'T VISIT THOSE PLACES THEY WILL BE FORGOTTEN!
I DON'T NEED YOU TO TELL ME WHERE I SHOULD GO AND WHAT I SHOULD SEE. I LIVE WITH THIS STUFF EVERY DAY. THAT'S ENOUGH FOR ME. YOU GO.
TAKE IT EASY.
BUNCH OF FREE RANGE JEWS. BROOKLYNITES.
DING
DING
DONG
P

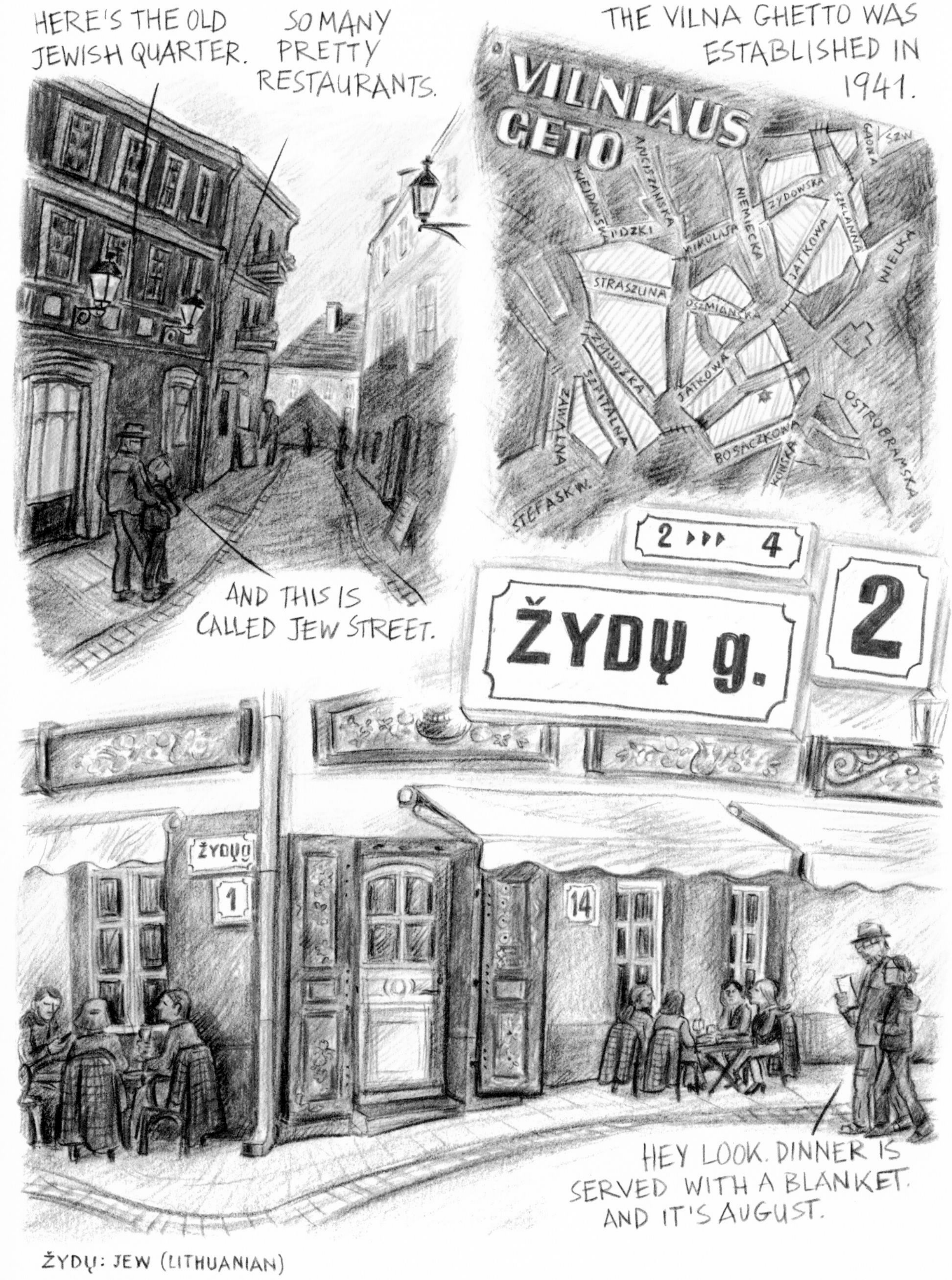
HERE'S THE OLD JEWISH QUARTER.
SO MANY PRETTY RESTAURANTS.
AND THIS IS CALLED JEW STREET.
THE VILNA GHETTO WAS ESTABLISHED IN 1941.
VILNIAUS GETO
STRASZUNA
OSZMIANSKA
NIEMIECKA
ZYDOWSKA
SZKLANNA
JATKOWA
WIELKA
ZAWALNA
SZPITALNA
ZMUDZKA
BOSACZKOWA
OSTROBRAMSKA
2 ▸▸▸ 4
ŽYDŲ g.
2
ŽYDŲ
1
14
HEY LOOK. DINNER IS SERVED WITH A BLANKET. AND IT'S AUGUST.

ŽYDŲ: JEW (LITHUANIAN)

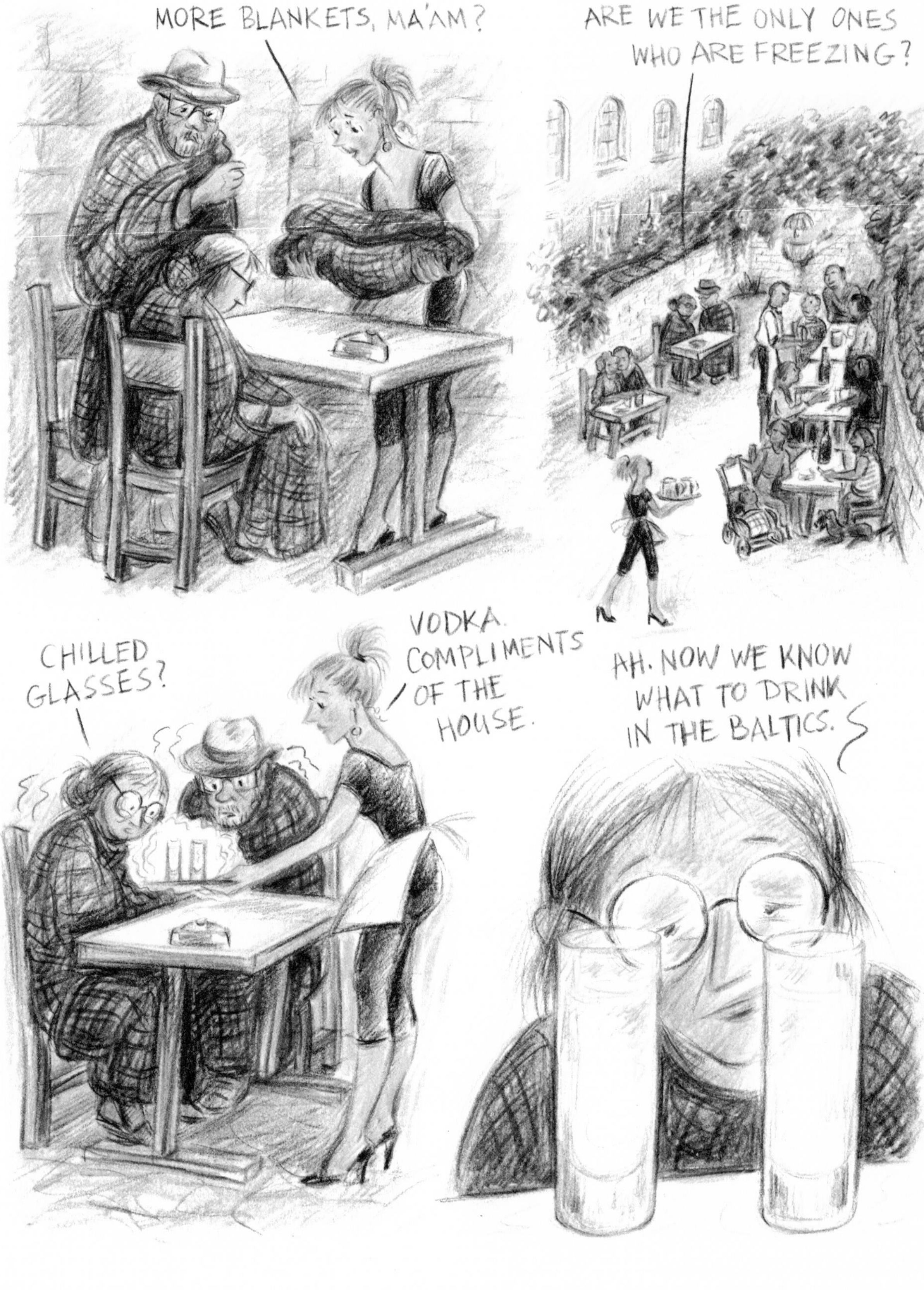
MORE BLANKETS, MA'AM?
ARE WE THE ONLY ONES WHO ARE FREEZING?
CHILLED GLASSES?
VODKA. COMPLIMENTS OF THE HOUSE.
AH. NOW WE KNOW WHAT TO DRINK IN THE BALTICS.

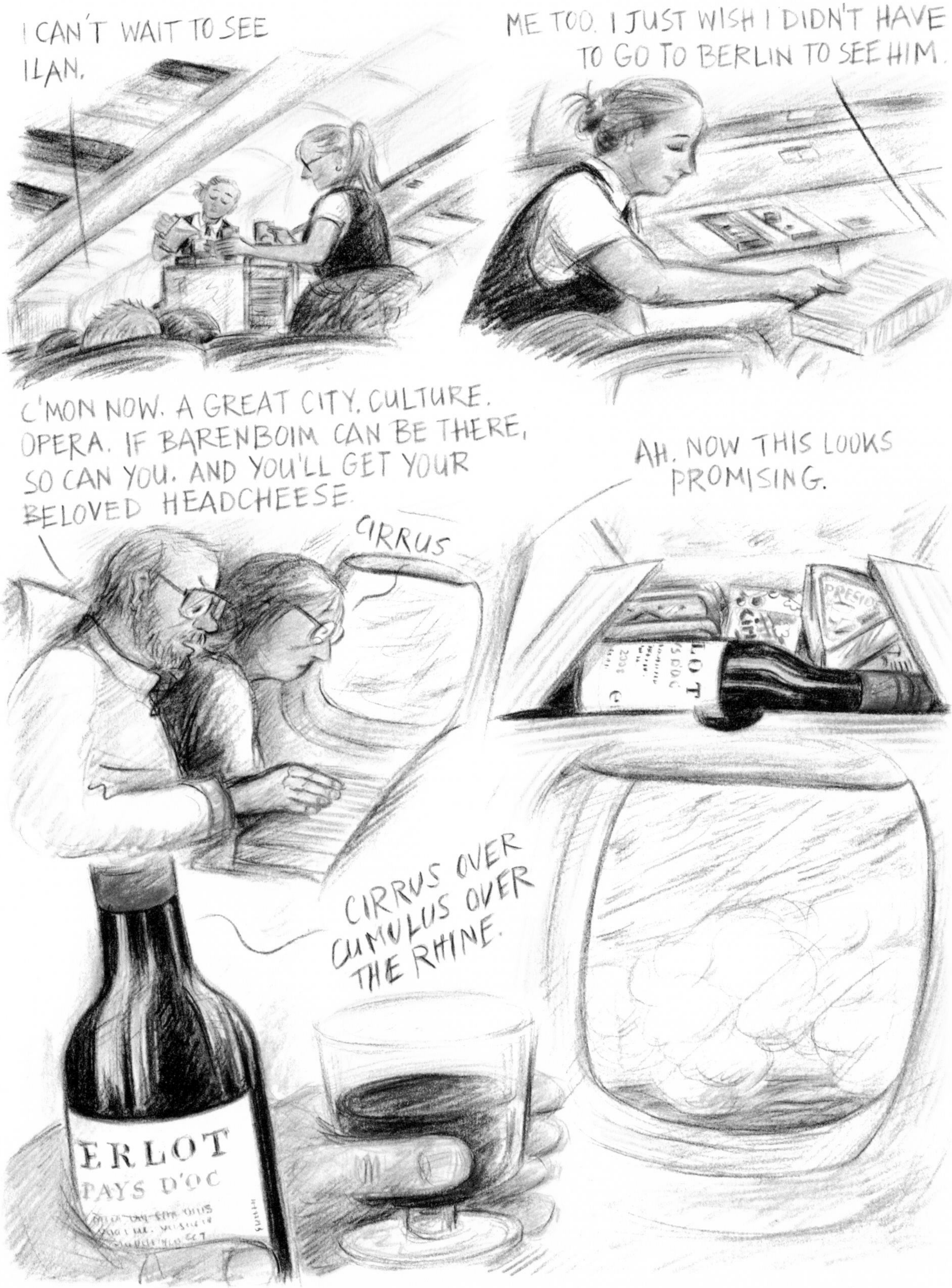
I CAN'T WAIT TO SEE ILAN.
ME TOO. I JUST WISH I DIDN'T HAVE TO GO TO BERLIN TO SEE HIM.
C'MON NOW. A GREAT CITY. CULTURE. OPERA. IF BARENBOIM CAN BE THERE, SO CAN YOU. AND YOU'LL GET YOUR BELOVED HEADCHEESE.
CIRRUS
AH. NOW THIS LOOKS PROMISING.
CIRRUS OVER CUMULUS OVER THE RHINE.
ERLOT
PAYS D'OC

DANIEL BARENBOIM: ARGENTINIAN-ISRAELI-SPANISH-PALESTINIAN PIANIST & CONDUCTOR. CONDUCTOR OF THE BERLIN STATE OPERA AND THE STAATSKAPELLE BERLIN.

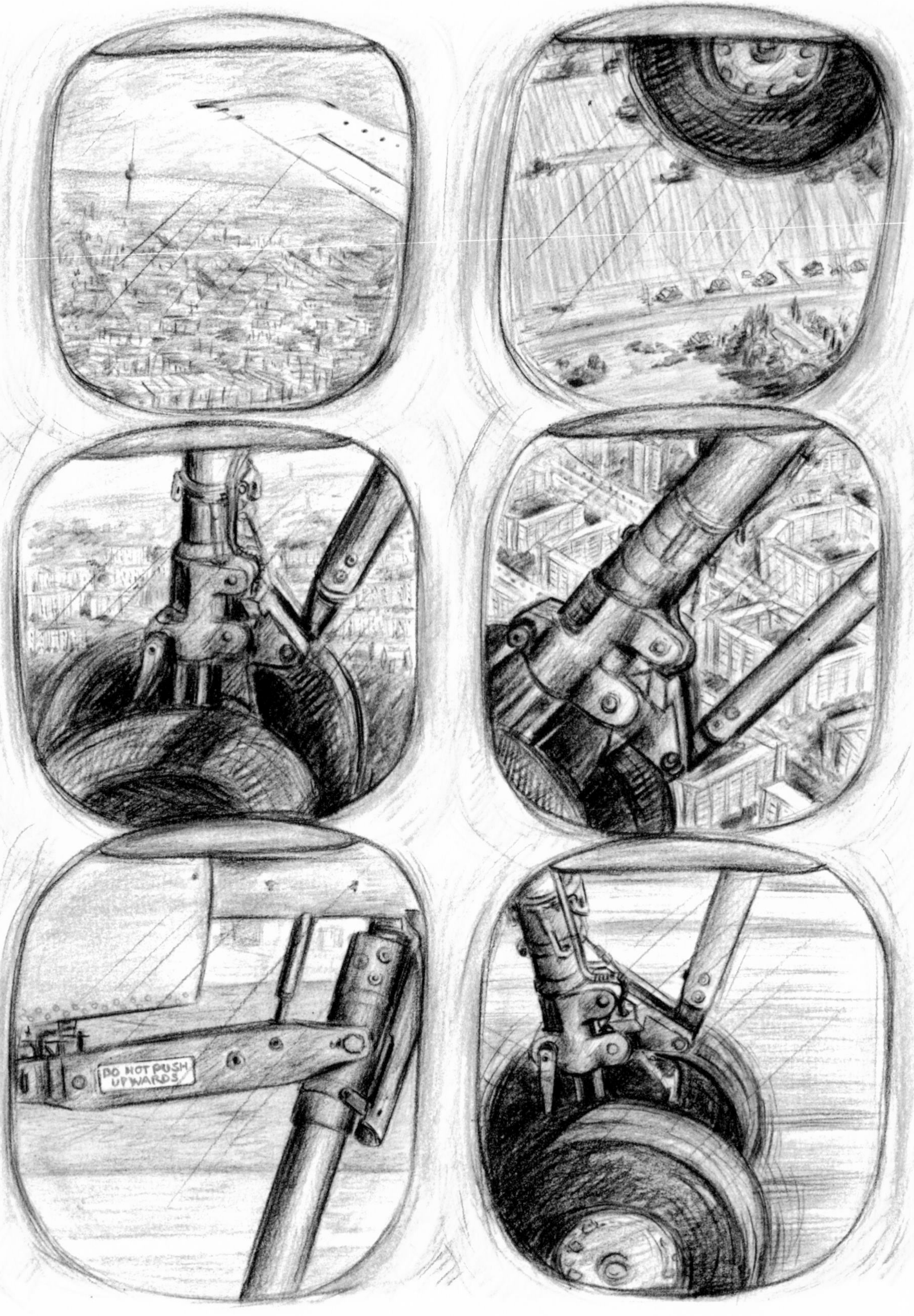
DO NOT PUSH
UPWARDS

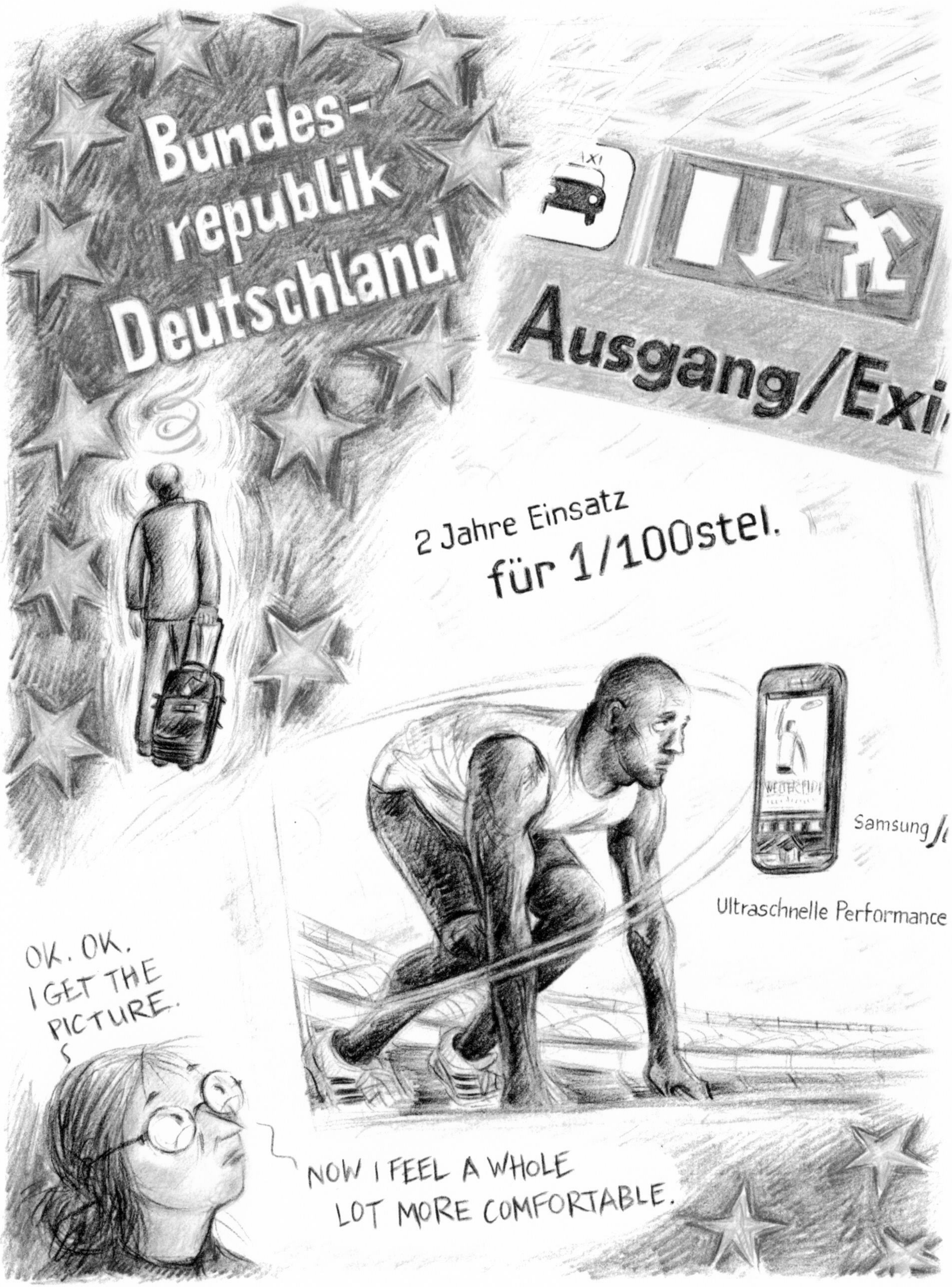

Bundes-
republik
Deutschland
Ausgang/Exi
2 Jahre Einsatz
für 1/100stel.
Samsung
Ultraschnelle Performance
OK. OK.
I GET THE
PICTURE.
NOW I FEEL A WHOLE
LOT MORE COMFORTABLE.

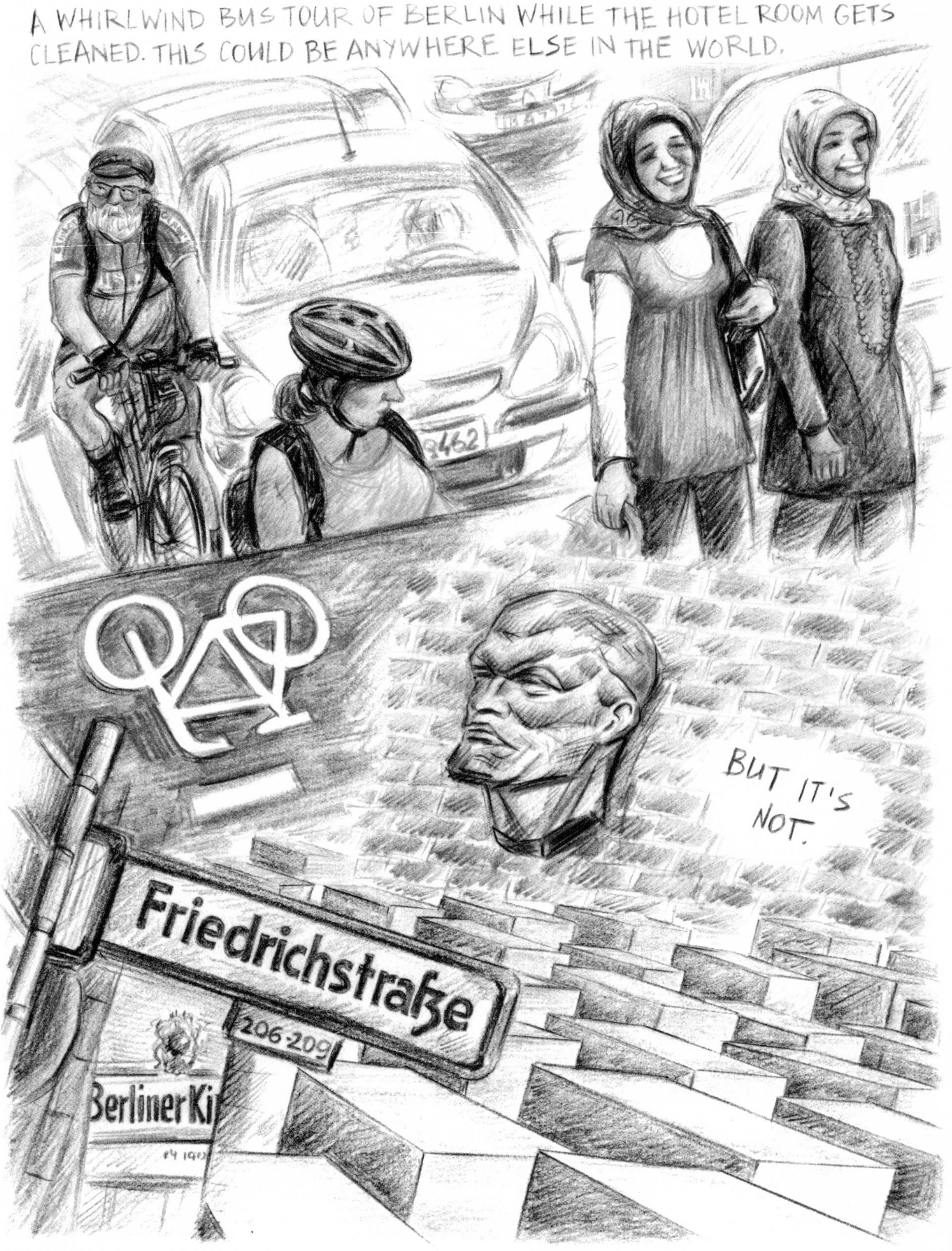
A WHIRLWIND BUS TOUR OF BERLIN WHILE THE HOTEL ROOM GETS CLEANED. THIS COULD BE ANYWHERE ELSE IN THE WORLD.
Friedrichstraße
206-209
BerlinerKi
BUT IT'S NOT.

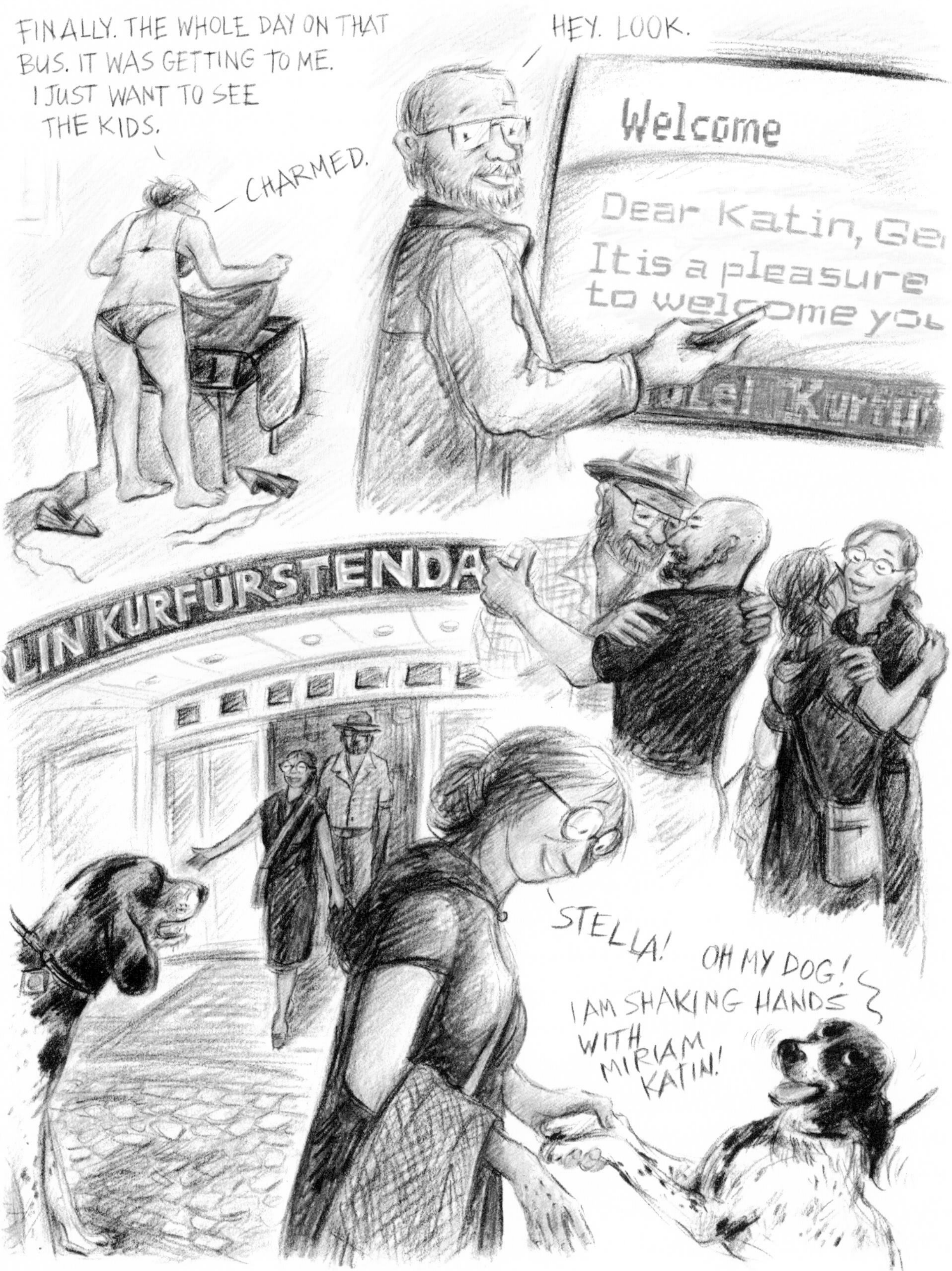
FINALLY. THE WHOLE DAY ON THAT BUS. IT WAS GETTING TO ME. I JUST WANT TO SEE THE KIDS.
CHARMED.
HEY. LOOK.
Welcome
Dear Katin, Ge
It is a pleasure to welcome you
KURFÜRSTENDA
STELLA!
OH MY DOG!
I AM SHAKING HANDS WITH MIRIAM KATIN!

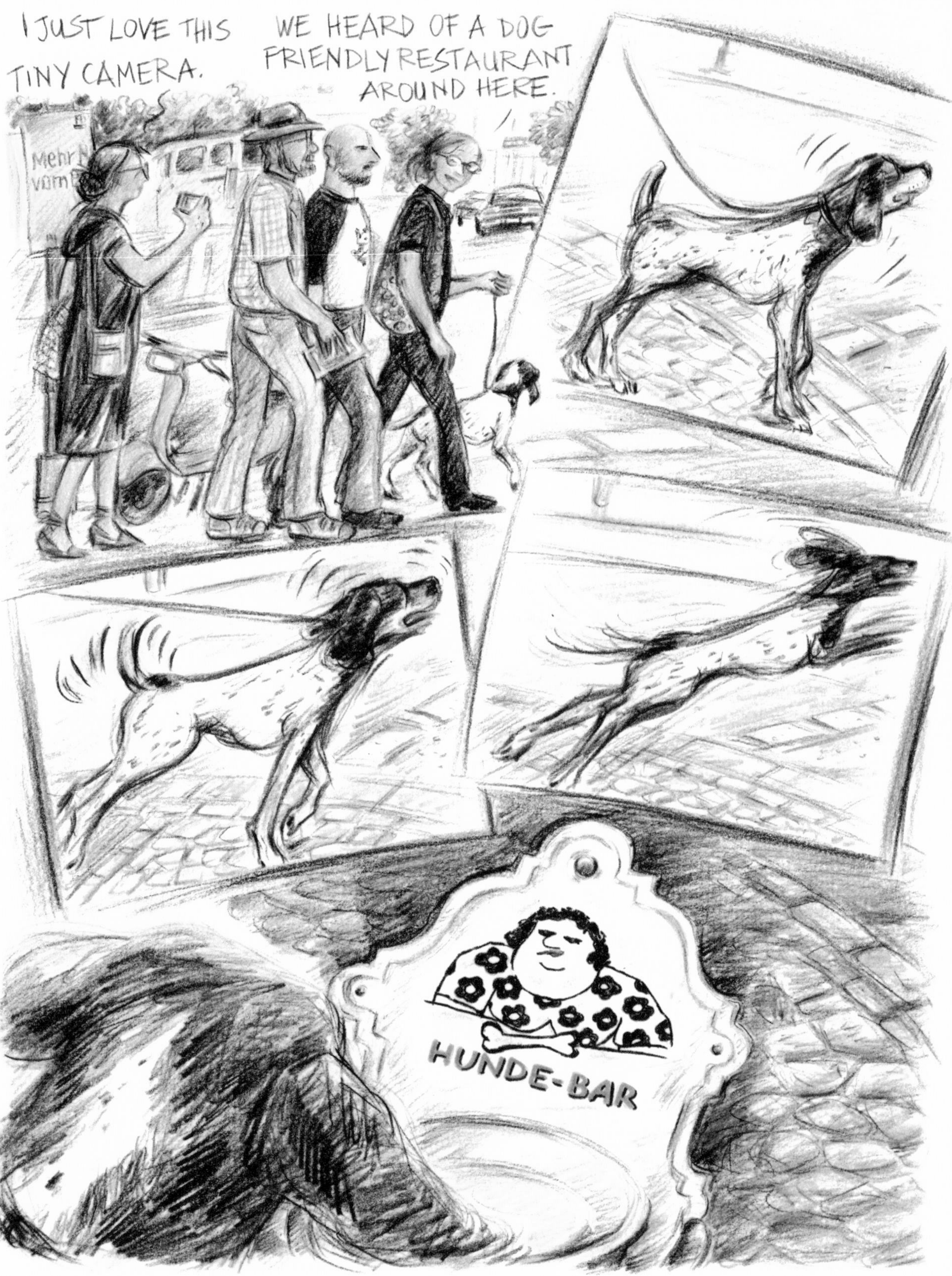
I JUST LOVE THIS TINY CAMERA.
WE HEARD OF A DOG FRIENDLY RESTAURANT AROUND HERE.
HUNDE-BAR

HUND: DOG (GERMAN)

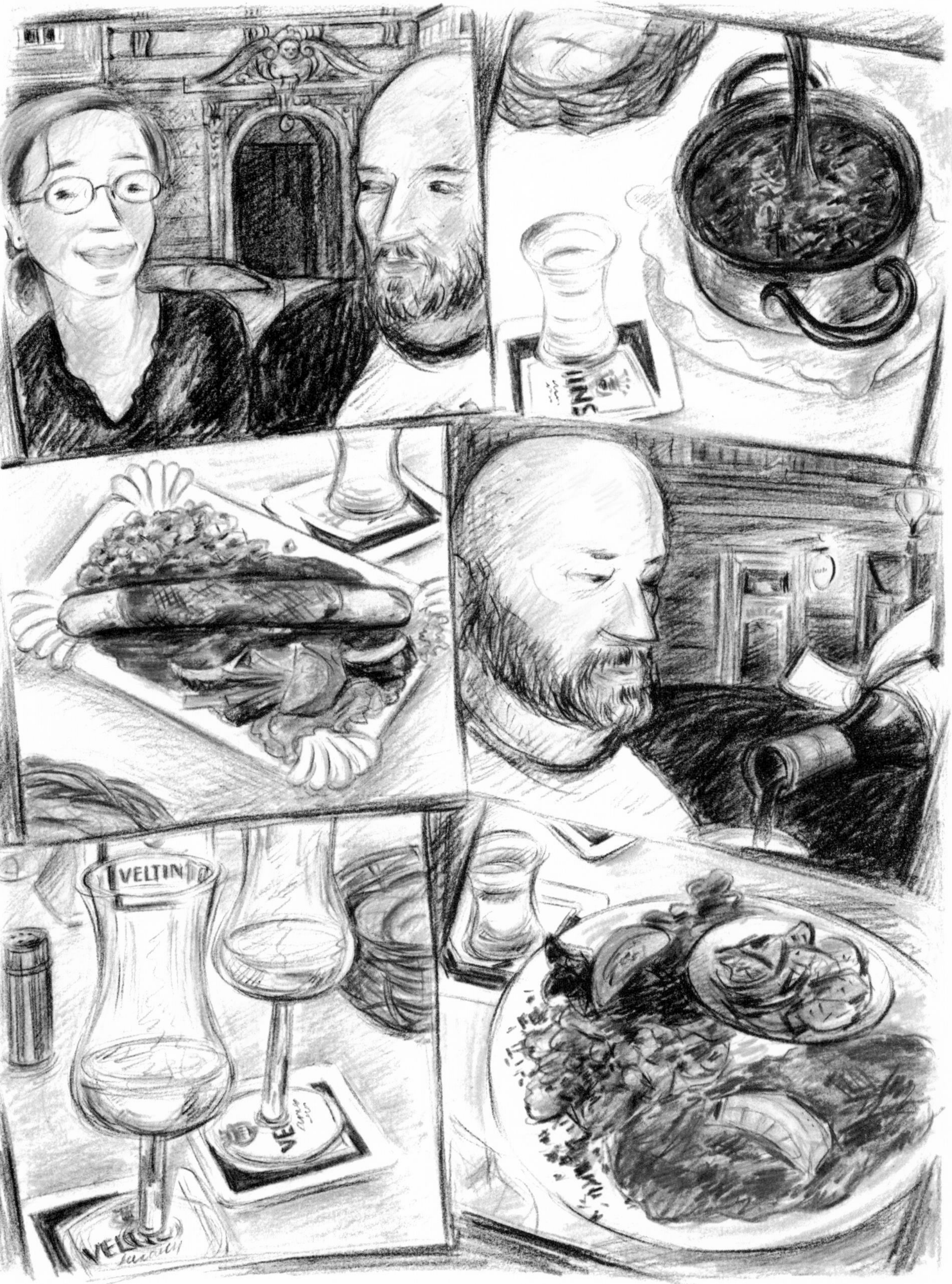
VELTIN

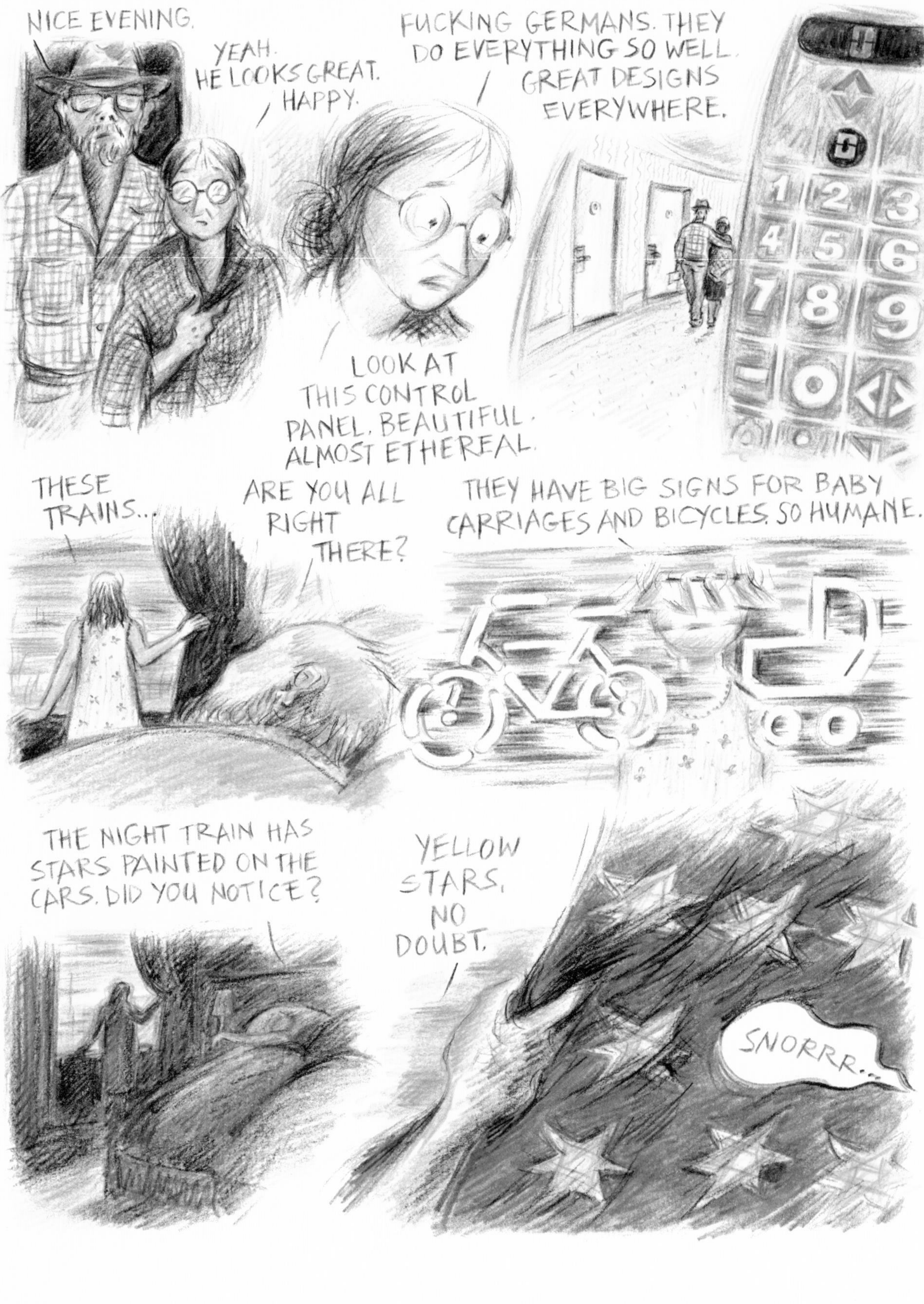
NICE EVENING.
YEAH. HE LOOKS GREAT. HAPPY.
FUCKING GERMANS. THEY DO EVERYTHING SO WELL. GREAT DESIGNS EVERYWHERE.
LOOK AT THIS CONTROL PANEL. BEAUTIFUL. ALMOST ETHEREAL.
THESE TRAINS...
ARE YOU ALL RIGHT THERE?
THEY HAVE BIG SIGNS FOR BABY CARRIAGES AND BICYCLES. SO HUMANE.
THE NIGHT TRAIN HAS STARS PAINTED ON THE CARS. DID YOU NOTICE?
YELLOW STARS, NO DOUBT.
SNORRR...

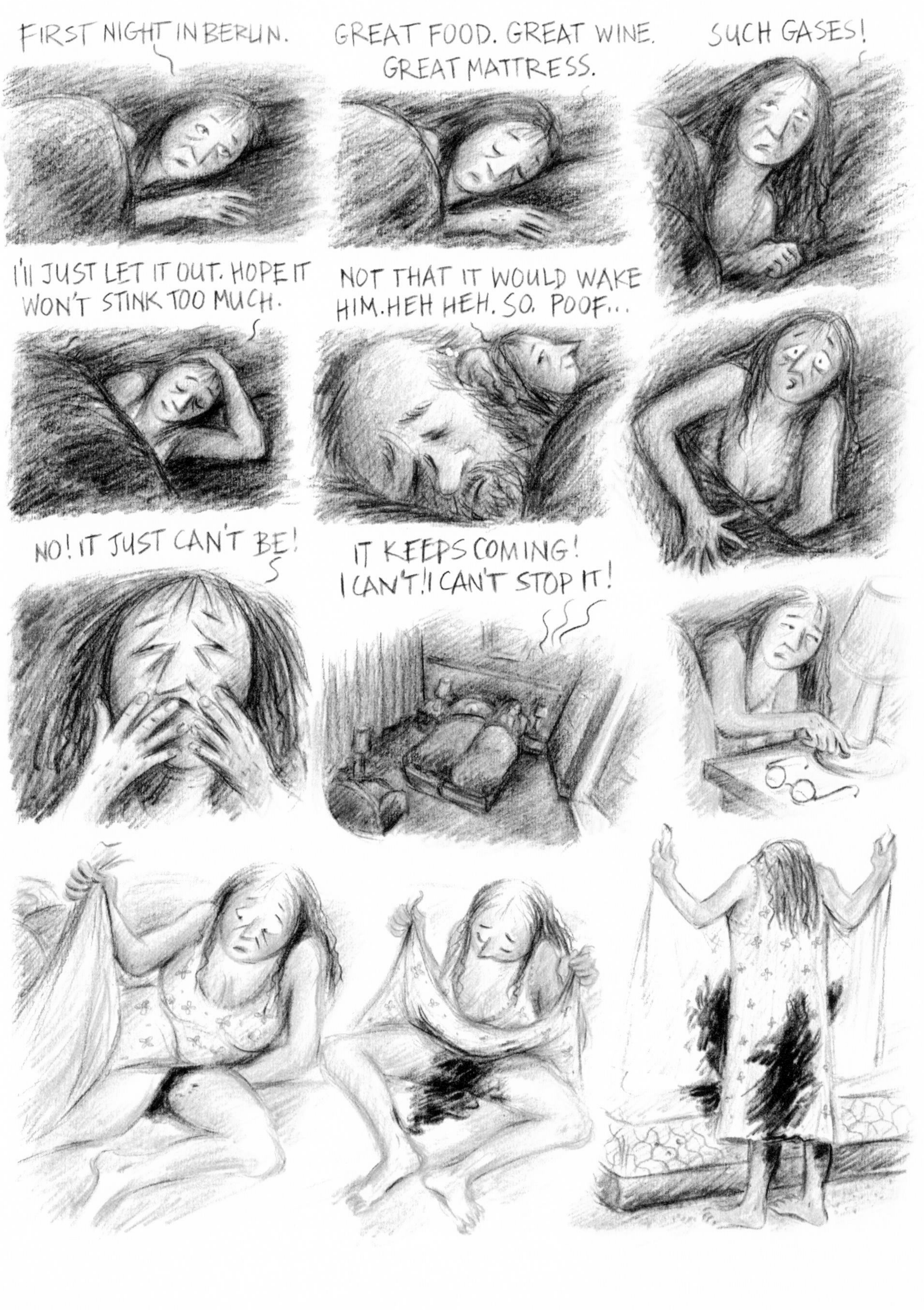
FIRST NIGHT IN BERLIN.
GREAT FOOD. GREAT WINE. GREAT MATTRESS.
SUCH GASES!
I'LL JUST LET IT OUT. HOPE IT WON'T STINK TOO MUCH.
NOT THAT IT WOULD WAKE HIM. HEH HEH. SO. POOF...
NO! IT JUST CAN'T BE!
IT KEEPS COMING! I CAN'T! I CAN'T STOP IT!

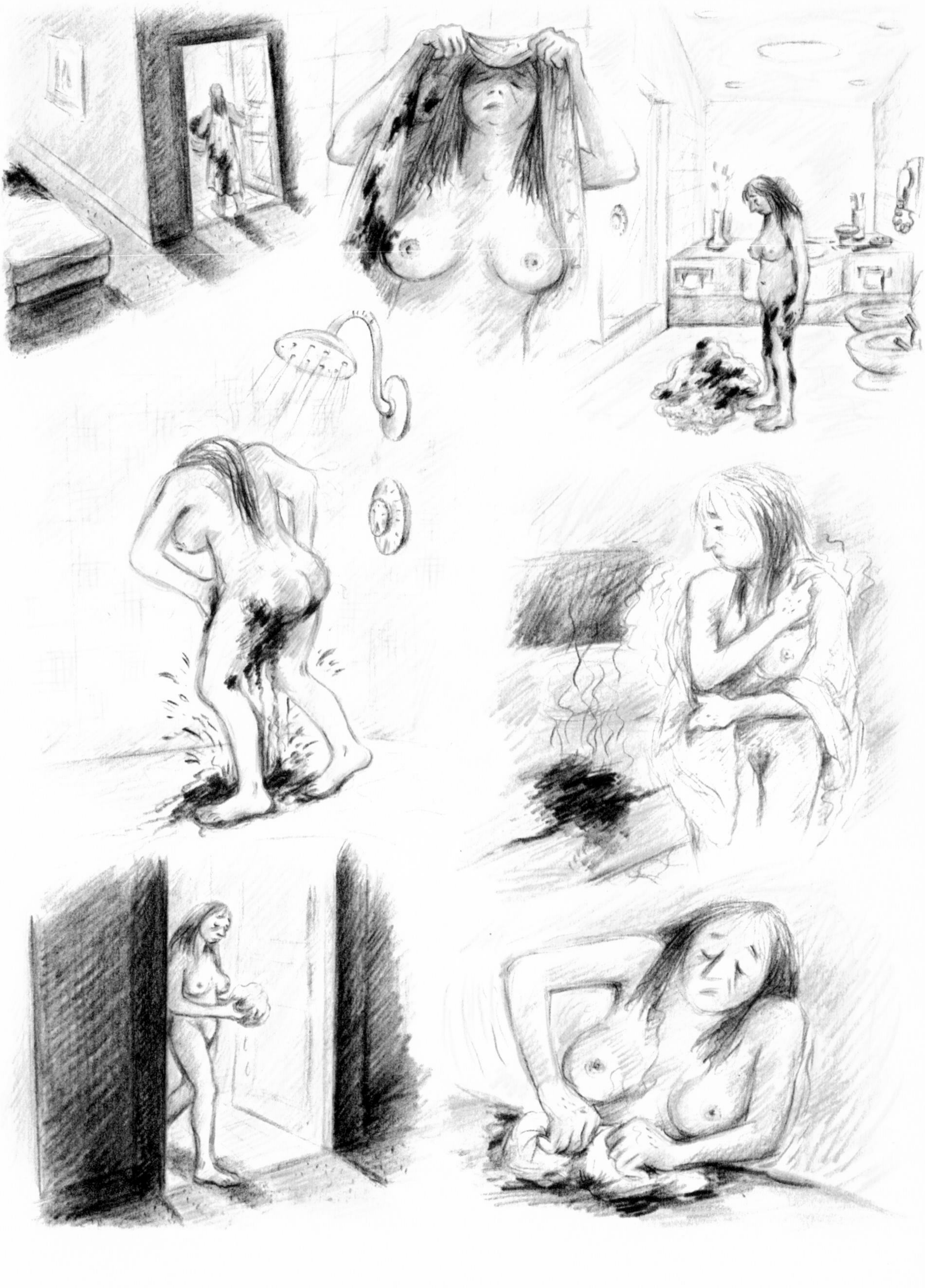

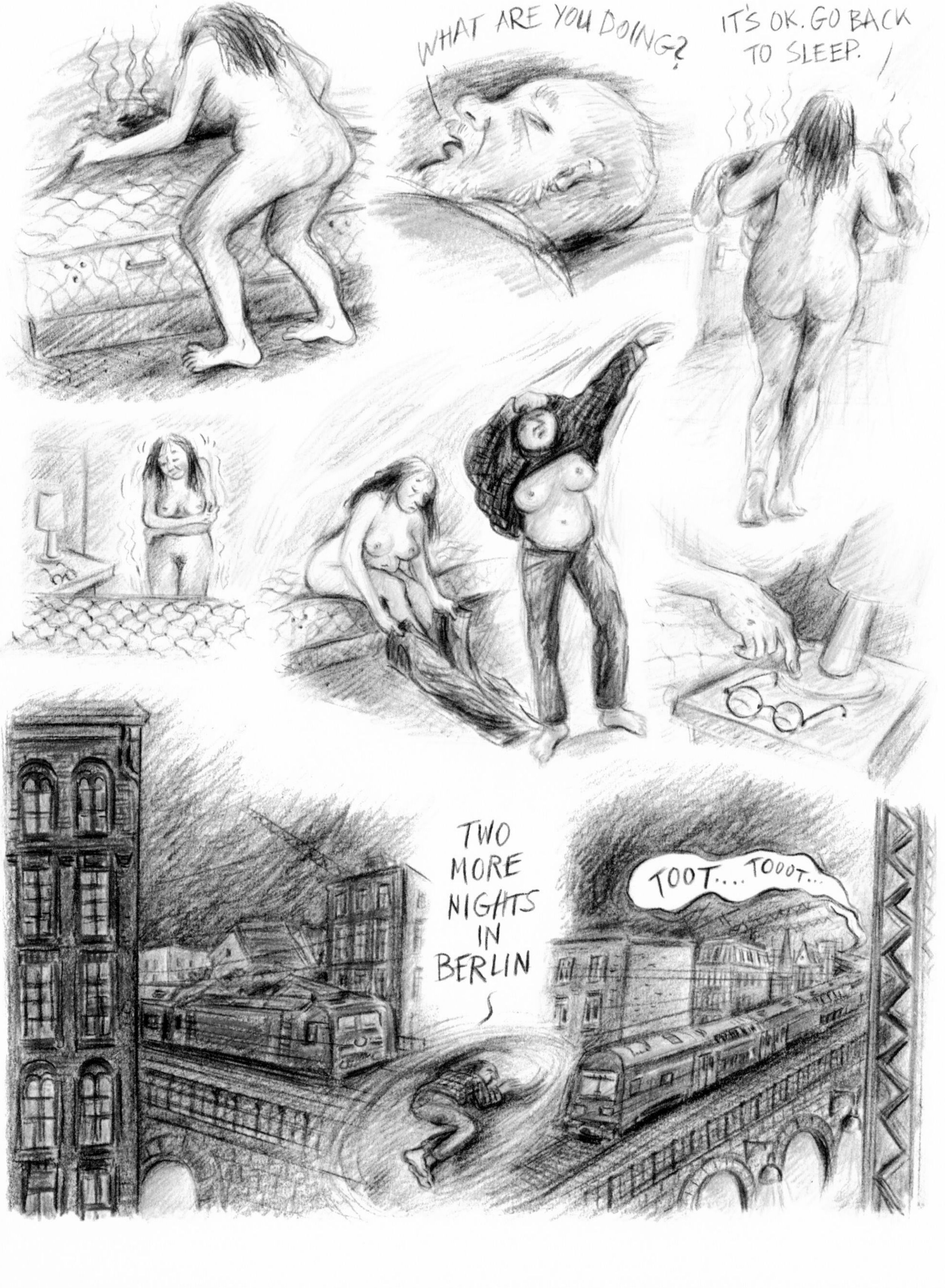
WHAT ARE YOU DOING?
IT'S OK. GO BACK TO SLEEP.
TWO MORE NIGHTS IN BERLIN
TOOT.... TOOOT...

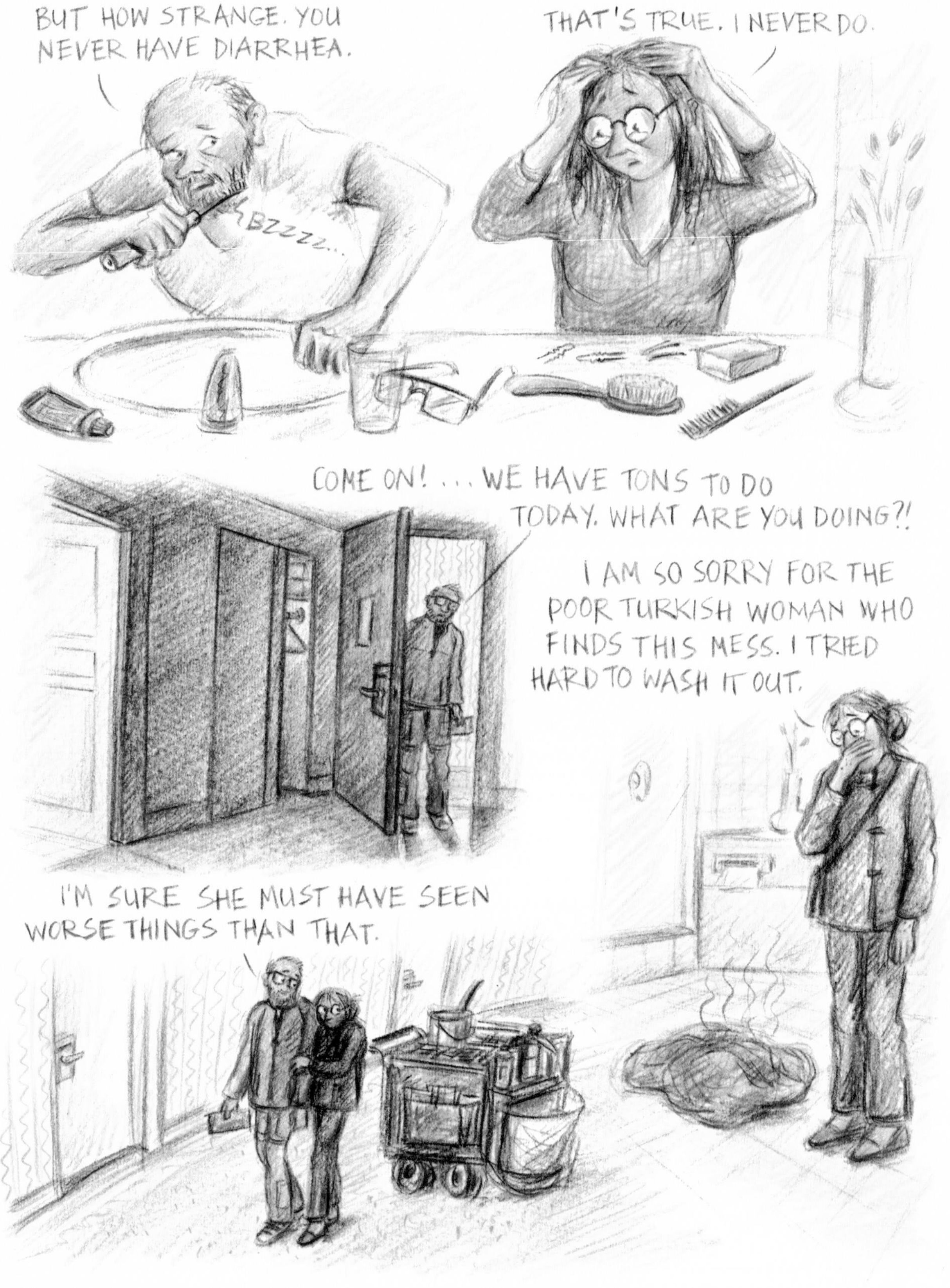
BUT HOW STRANGE. YOU NEVER HAVE DIARRHEA.
BZZZZZ...
THAT'S TRUE. I NEVER DO.
COME ON! ... WE HAVE TONS TO DO TODAY. WHAT ARE YOU DOING?!
I AM SO SORRY FOR THE POOR TURKISH WOMAN WHO FINDS THIS MESS. I TRIED HARD TO WASH IT OUT.
I'M SURE SHE MUST HAVE SEEN WORSE THINGS THAN THAT.

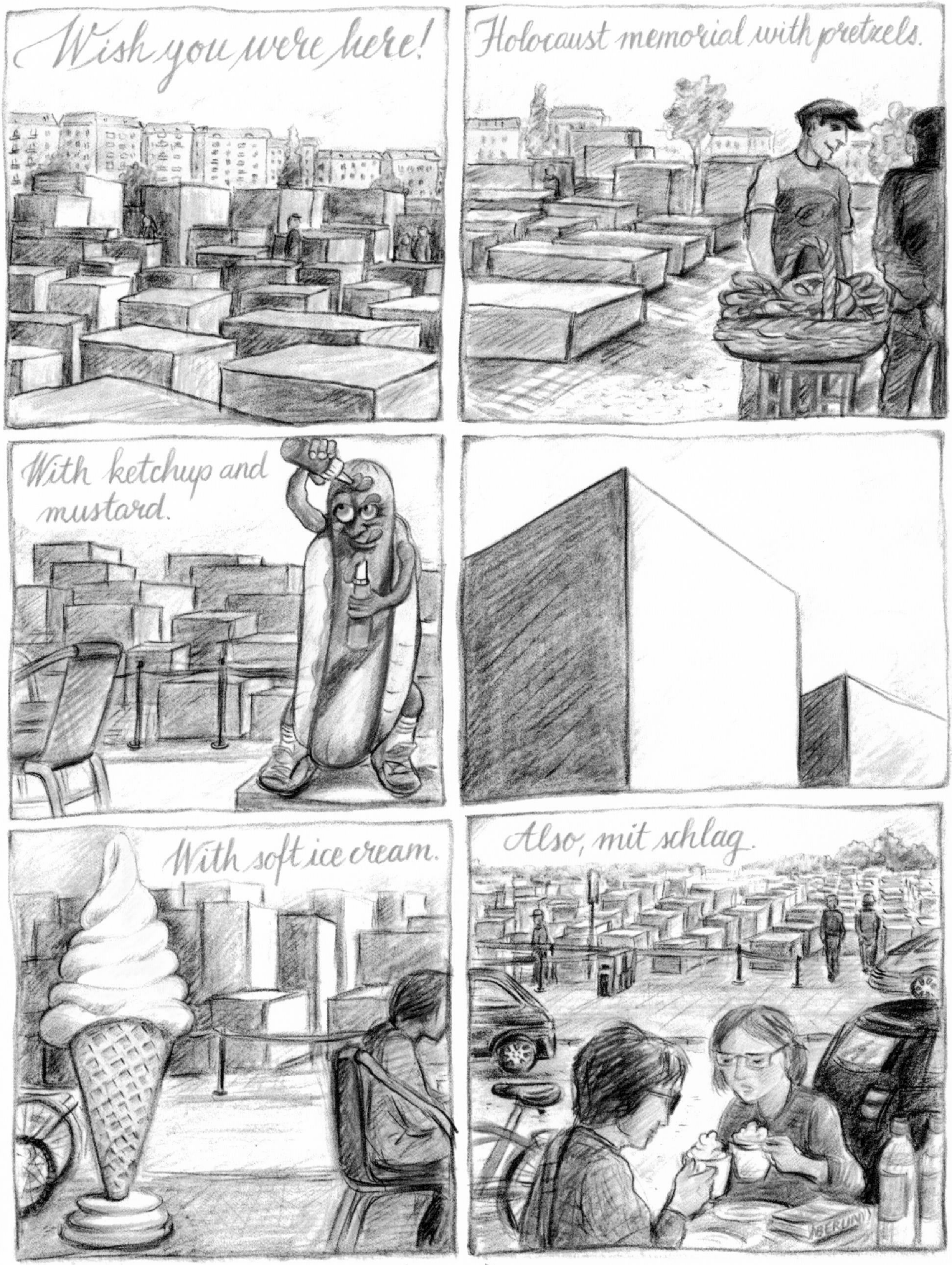
Wish you were here!
Holocaust memorial with pretzels.
With ketchup and mustard.
With soft ice cream.
Also, mit schlag.

MIT SCHLAG: WITH WHIPPED CREAM (GERMAN)

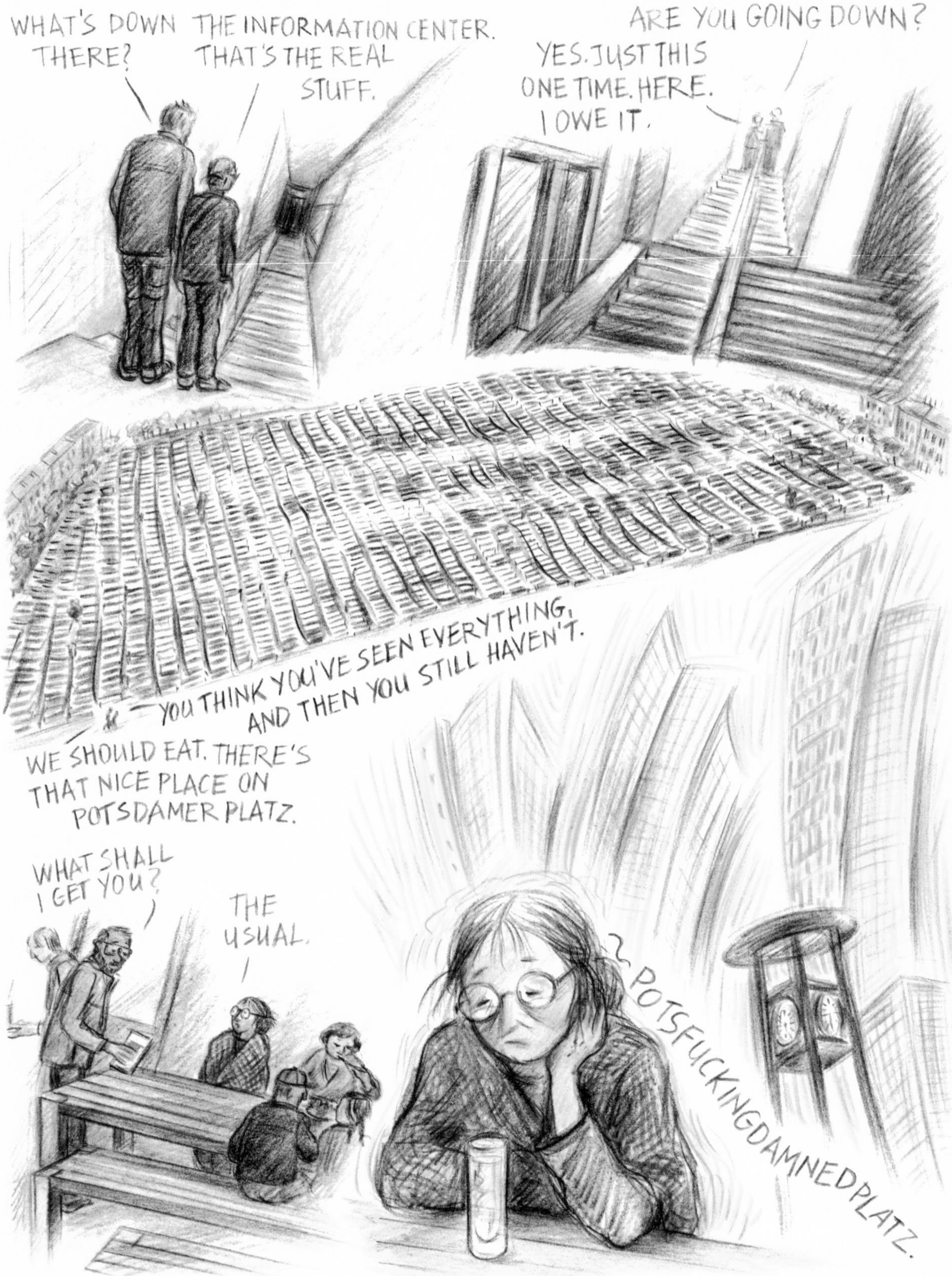
WHAT'S DOWN THERE?
THE INFORMATION CENTER. THAT'S THE REAL STUFF.
ARE YOU GOING DOWN?
YES. JUST THIS ONE TIME. HERE. I OWE IT.
YOU THINK YOU'VE SEEN EVERYTHING, AND THEN YOU STILL HAVEN'T.
WE SHOULD EAT. THERE'S THAT NICE PLACE ON POTSDAMER PLATZ.
WHAT SHALL I GET YOU?
THE USUAL.
POTSFUCKINGDAMNEDPLATZ.

THE FIELD OF STELAE IS A MEMORIAL FOR THE MURDERED JEWS OF EUROPE.

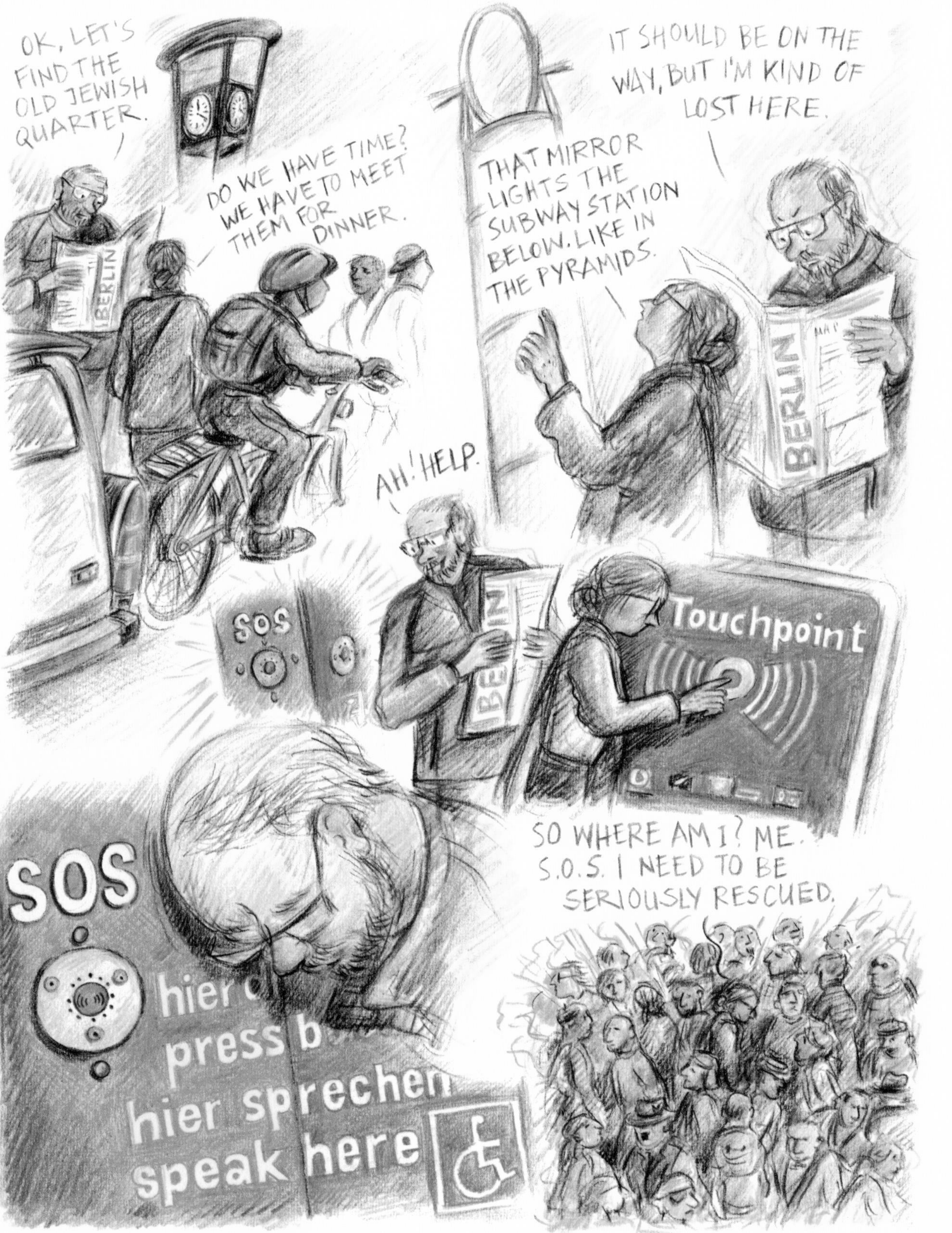

OK, LET'S FIND THE OLD JEWISH QUARTER.
BERLIN
DO WE HAVE TIME? WE HAVE TO MEET THEM FOR DINNER.
THAT MIRROR LIGHTS THE SUBWAY STATION BELOW. LIKE IN THE PYRAMIDS.
IT SHOULD BE ON THE WAY, BUT I'M KIND OF LOST HERE.
BERLIN
AH! HELP.
SOS
Touchpoint
SOS
hier
press b
hier sprechen
speak here
SO WHERE AM I? ME. S.O.S. I NEED TO BE SERIOUSLY RESCUED.

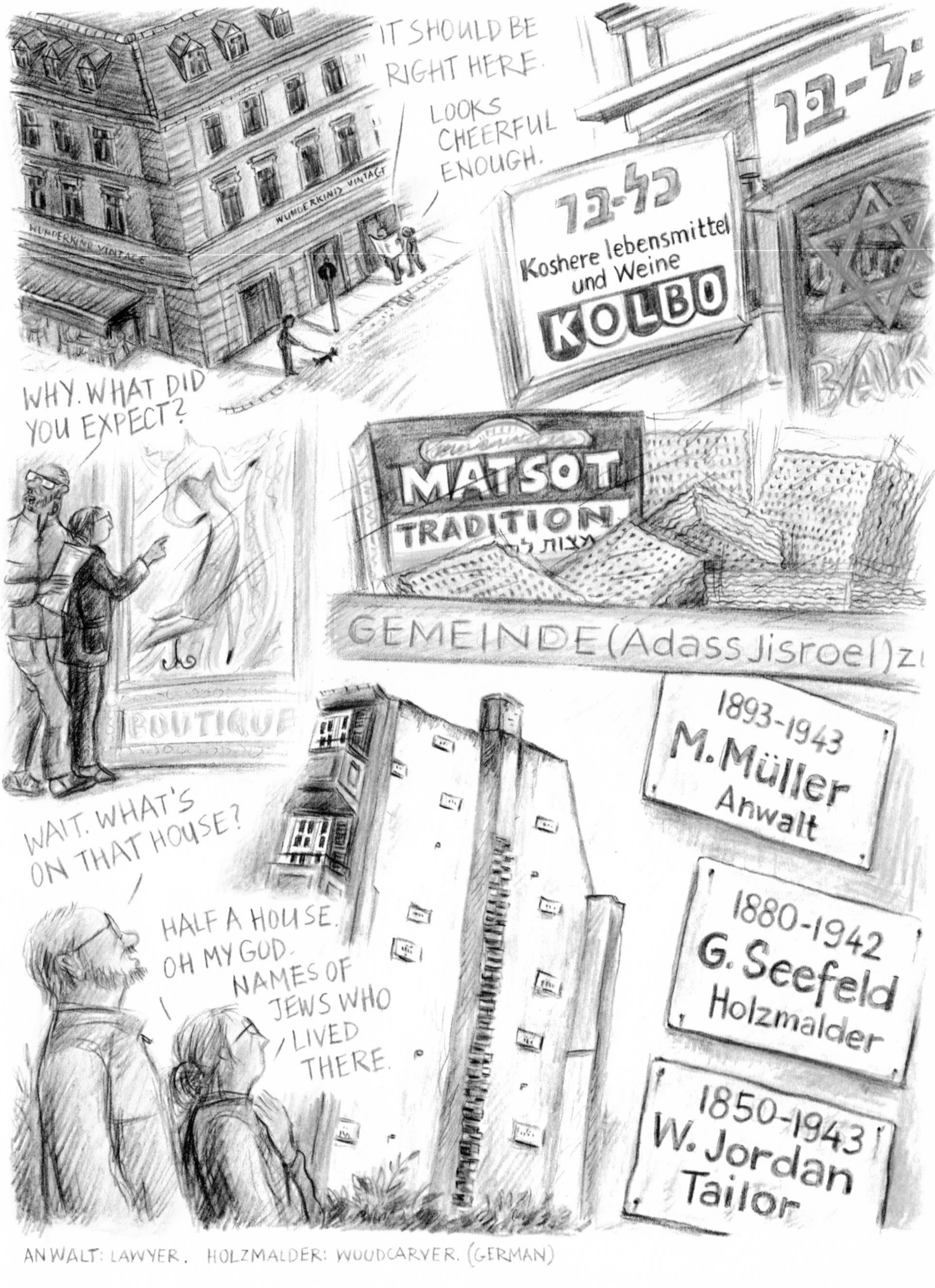
IT SHOULD BE RIGHT HERE.
LOOKS CHEERFUL ENOUGH.
WUNDERKIND VINTAGE
כל-בו
Koshere lebensmittel und Weine
KOLBO
WHY. WHAT DID YOU EXPECT?
MATSOT
TRADITION
GEMEINDE (Adass Jisroel) zu
BOUTIQUE
1893-1943
M. Müller
Anwalt
WAIT. WHAT'S ON THAT HOUSE?
HALF A HOUSE.
OH MY GOD.
NAMES OF JEWS WHO LIVED THERE.
1880-1942
G. Seefeld
Holzmalder
1850-1943
W. Jordan
Tailor
ANWALT: LAWYER. HOLZMALDER: WOODCARVER. (GERMAN)

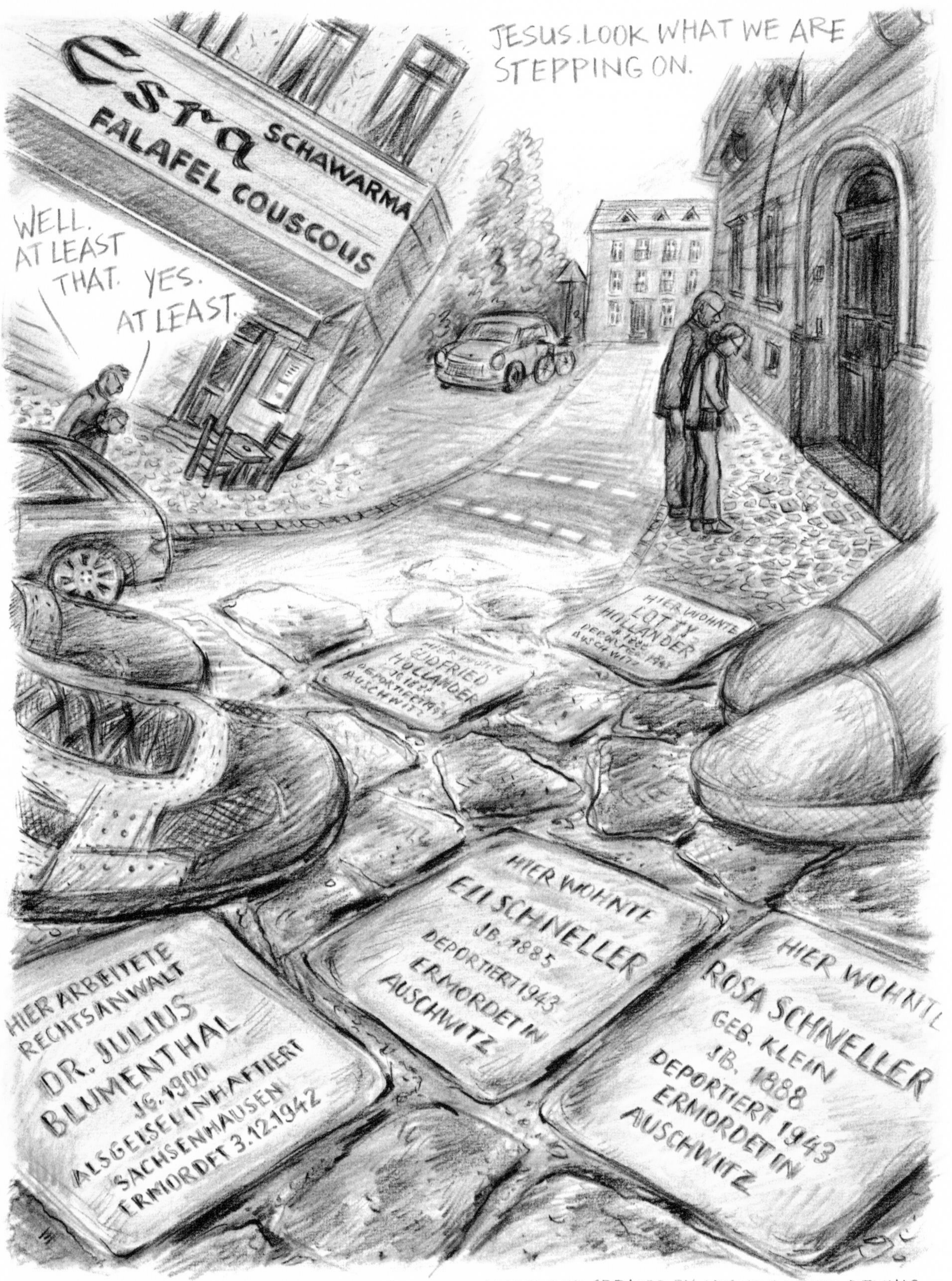
Esra
SCHAWARMA
FALAFEL COUSCOUS
JESUS. LOOK WHAT WE ARE STEPPING ON.
WELL. AT LEAST THAT.
YES. AT LEAST.
HIER ARBEITETE RECHTSANWALT DR. JULIUS BLUMENTHAL JG. 1900 ALS GEISEL INHAFTIERT SACHSENHAUSEN ERMORDET 3.12.1942
HIER WOHNTE ELI SCHNELLER JB. 1885 DEPORTIERT 1943 ERMORDET IN AUSCHWITZ
HIER WOHNTE ROSA SCHNELLER GEB. KLEIN JB. 1888 DEPORTIERT 1943 ERMORDET IN AUSCHWITZ

THE "STOLPERSTEINE" (STUMBLING BLOCK) WAS INITIATED AND CREATED BY ARTIST GUNTER DEMNIG.
HIERE WOHNTE: HERE LIVED. ARBEITETE: WORKED. DEPORTIERT: DEPORTED. ERMORDET: MURDERED.

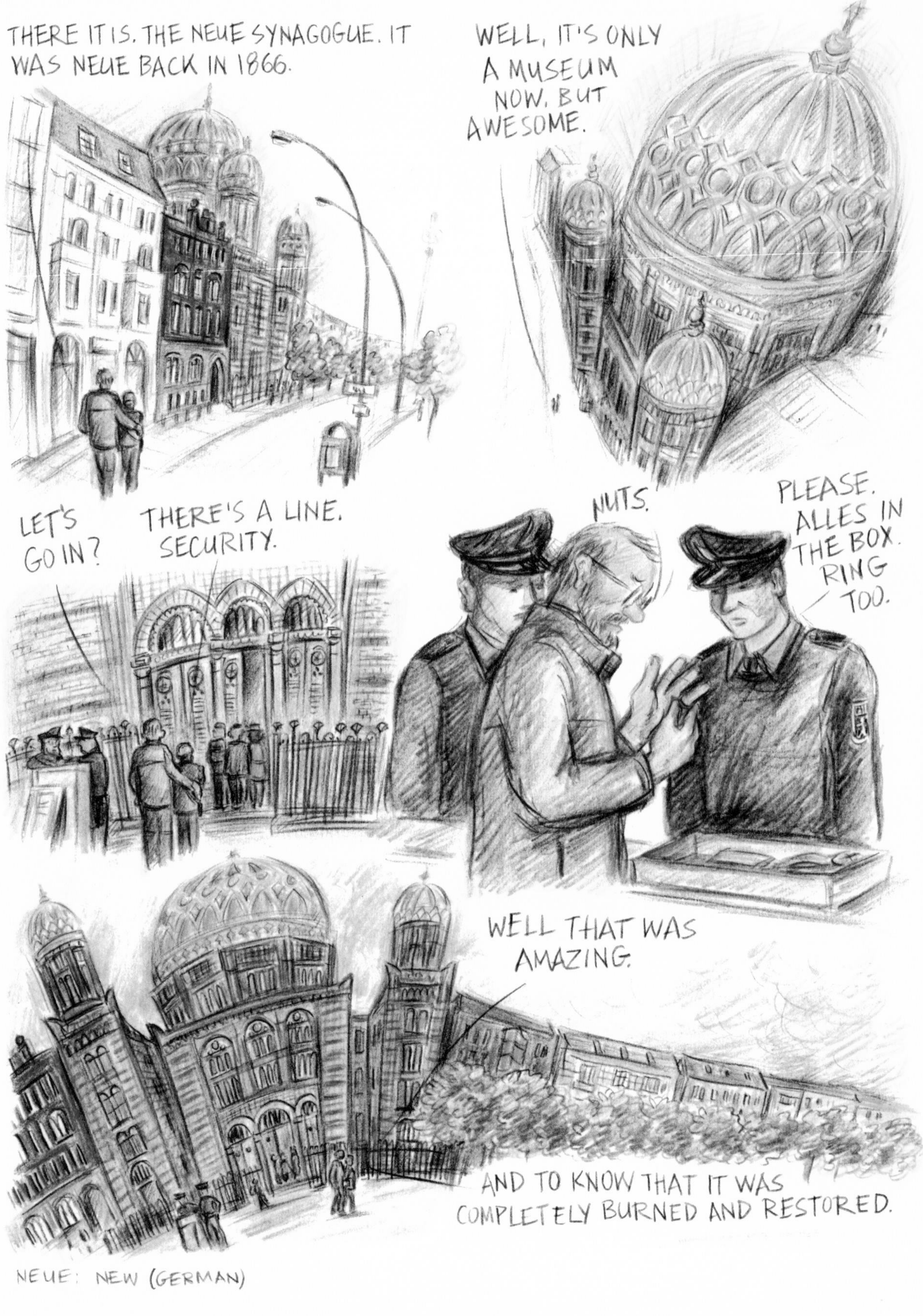
THERE IT IS. THE NEUE SYNAGOGUE. IT WAS NEUE BACK IN 1866.
WELL, IT'S ONLY A MUSEUM NOW, BUT AWESOME.
LET'S GO IN?
THERE'S A LINE. SECURITY.
NUTS.
PLEASE. ALLES IN THE BOX. RING TOO.
WELL THAT WAS AMAZING.
AND TO KNOW THAT IT WAS COMPLETELY BURNED AND RESTORED.

NEUE: NEW (GERMAN)

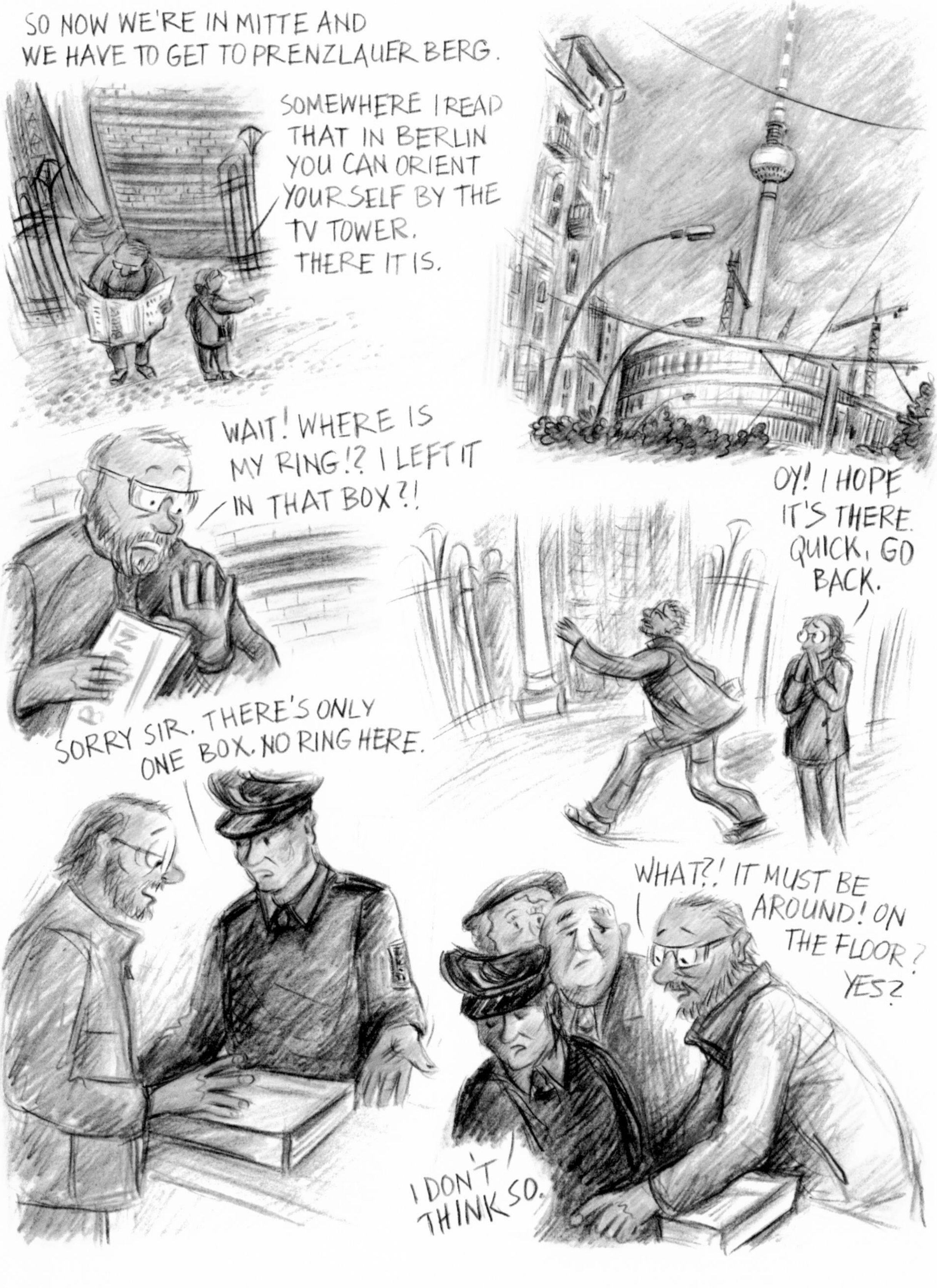
SO NOW WE'RE IN MITTE AND WE HAVE TO GET TO PRENZLAUER BERG.
SOMEWHERE I READ THAT IN BERLIN YOU CAN ORIENT YOURSELF BY THE TV TOWER. THERE IT IS.
WAIT! WHERE IS MY RING!? I LEFT IT IN THAT BOX?!
OY! I HOPE IT'S THERE. QUICK, GO BACK.
SORRY SIR. THERE'S ONLY ONE BOX. NO RING HERE.
WHAT?! IT MUST BE AROUND! ON THE FLOOR? YES?
I DON'T THINK SO.

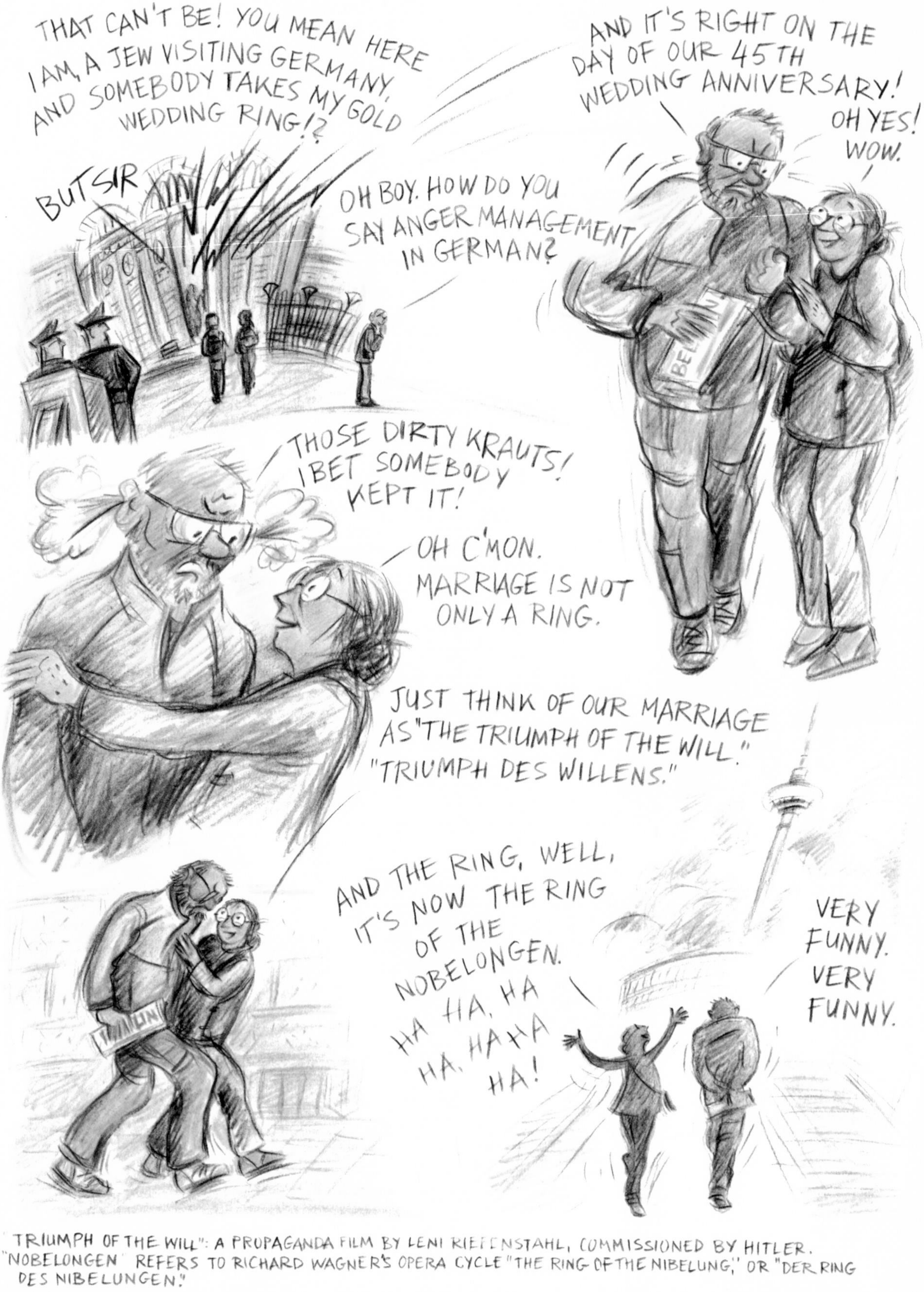
THAT CAN'T BE! YOU MEAN HERE I AM, A JEW VISITING GERMANY, AND SOMEBODY TAKES MY GOLD WEDDING RING!?
BUT SIR
OH BOY. HOW DO YOU SAY ANGER MANAGEMENT IN GERMAN?
AND IT'S RIGHT ON THE DAY OF OUR 45TH WEDDING ANNIVERSARY!
OH YES! WOW.
THOSE DIRTY KRAUTS! I BET SOMEBODY KEPT IT!
OH C'MON. MARRIAGE IS NOT ONLY A RING.
JUST THINK OF OUR MARRIAGE AS "THE TRIUMPH OF THE WILL." "TRIUMPH DES WILLENS."
AND THE RING, WELL, IT'S NOW THE RING OF THE NOBELONGEN.
HA HA, HA HA, HA, HA HA HA!
VERY FUNNY. VERY FUNNY.

"TRIUMPH OF THE WILL": A PROPAGANDA FILM BY LENI RIEFENSTAHL, COMMISSIONED BY HITLER.
"NOBELONGEN" REFERS TO RICHARD WAGNER'S OPERA CYCLE "THE RING OF THE NIBELUNG," OR "DER RING DES NIBELUNGEN."

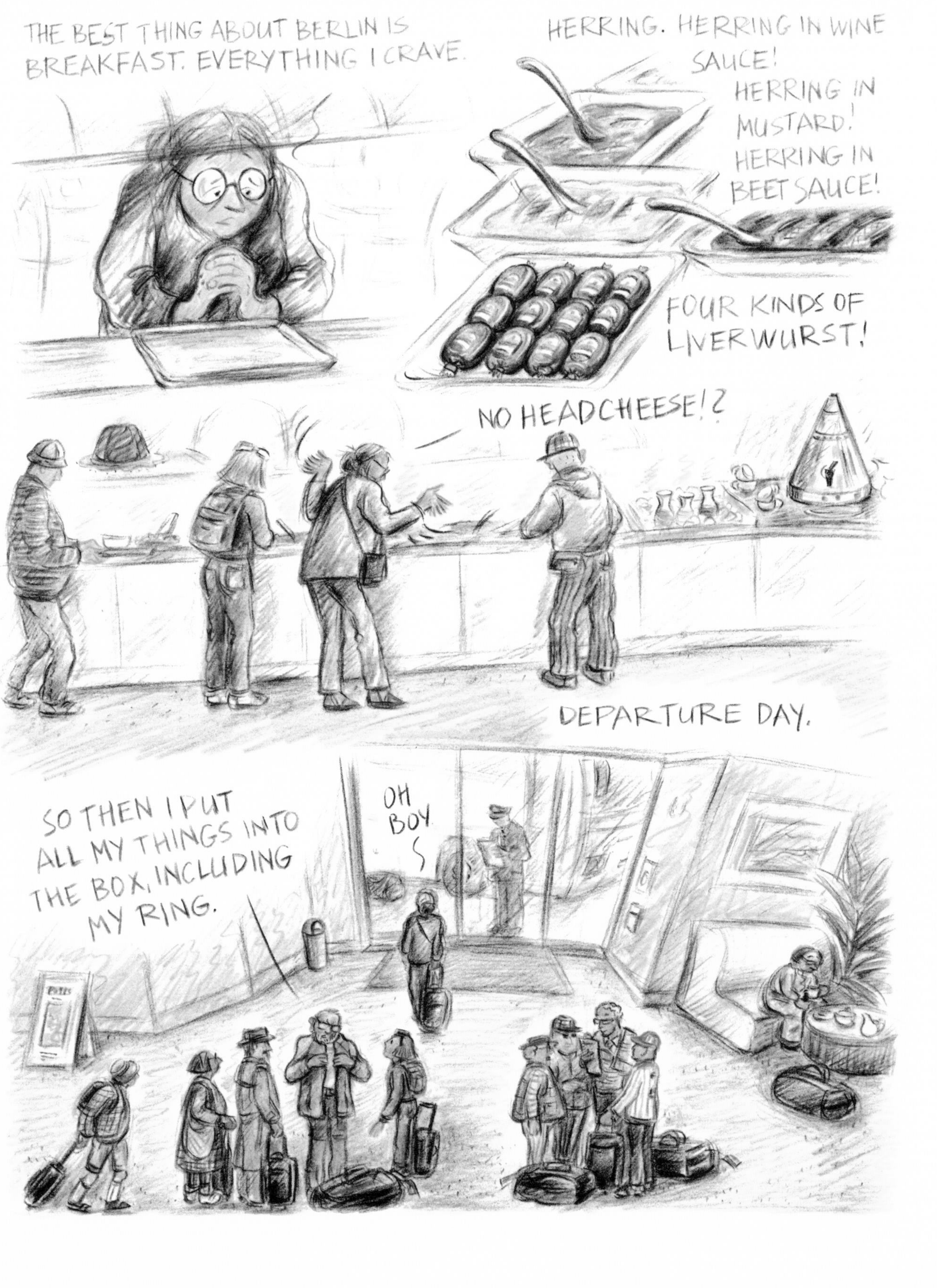
THE BEST THING ABOUT BERLIN IS BREAKFAST. EVERYTHING I CRAVE.
HERRING. HERRING IN WINE SAUCE!
HERRING IN MUSTARD!
HERRING IN BEET SAUCE!
FOUR KINDS OF LIVERWURST!
NO HEADCHEESE!?
DEPARTURE DAY.
SO THEN I PUT ALL MY THINGS INTO THE BOX, INCLUDING MY RING.
OH BOY

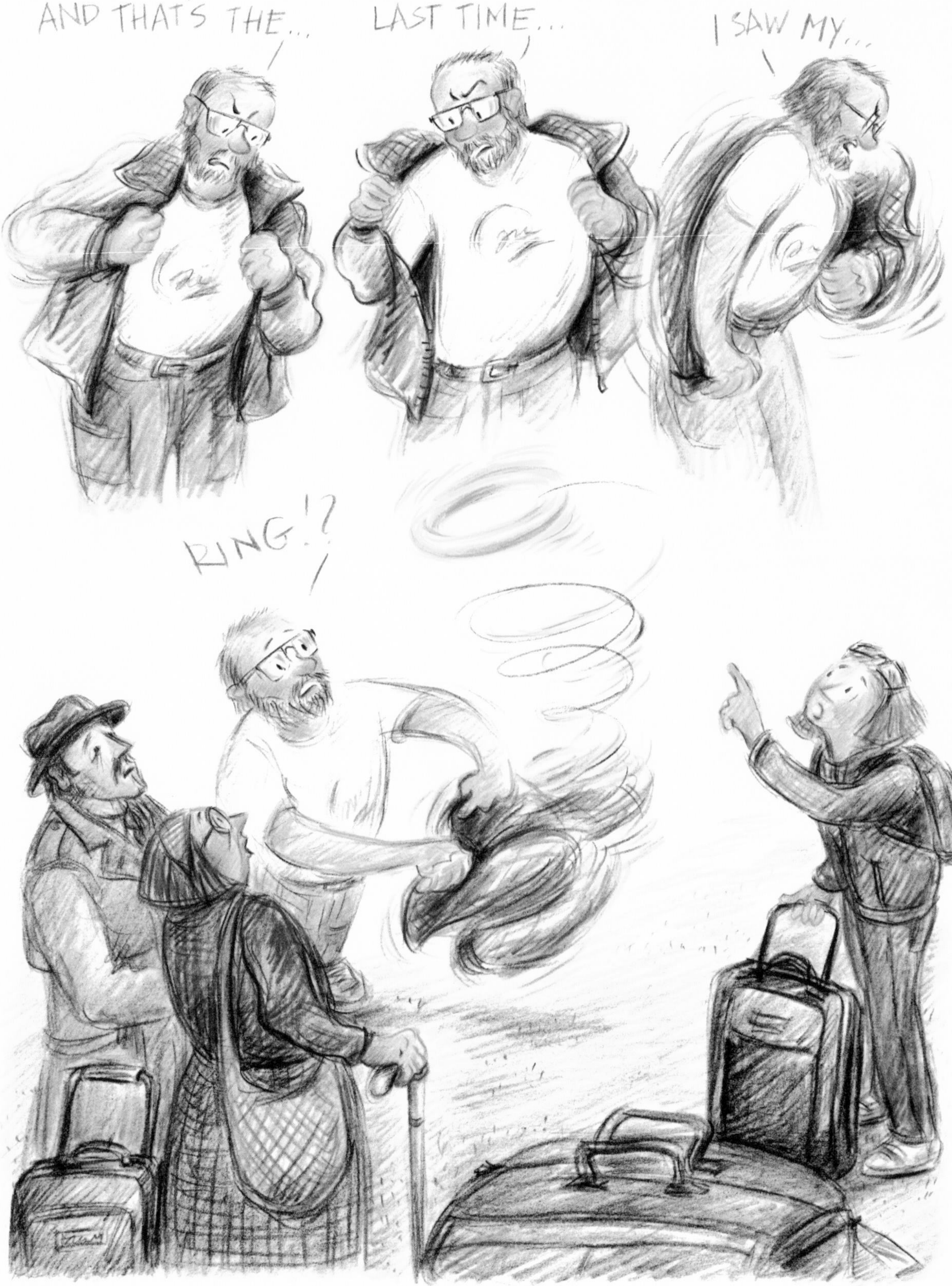
AND THAT'S THE...
LAST TIME...
I SAW MY...
RING!?

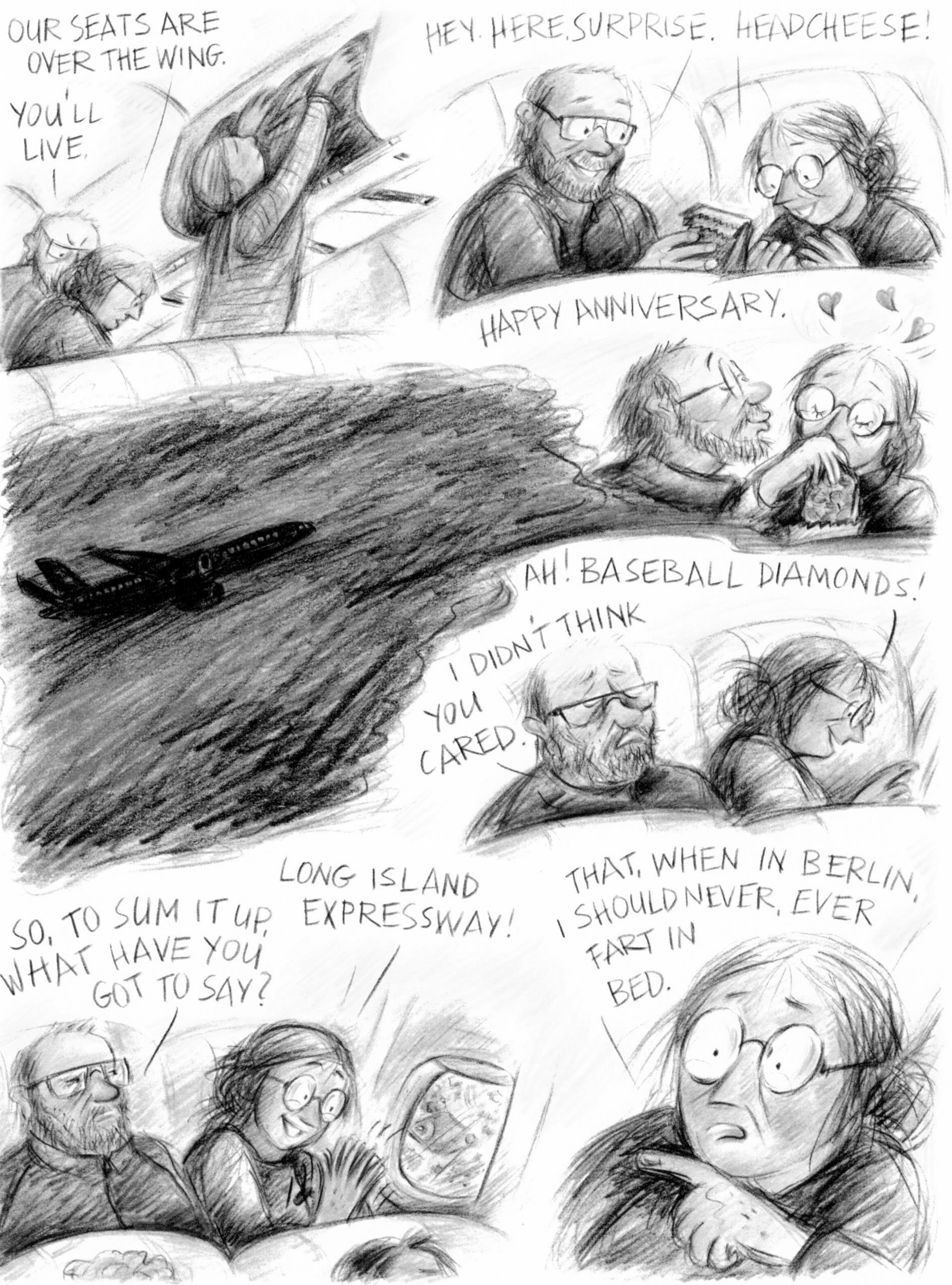
OUR SEATS ARE OVER THE WING.
YOU'LL LIVE.
HEY. HERE. SURPRISE.
HEADCHEESE!
HAPPY ANNIVERSARY.
AH! BASEBALL DIAMONDS!
I DIDN'T THINK YOU CARED.
SO, TO SUM IT UP, WHAT HAVE YOU GOT TO SAY?
LONG ISLAND EXPRESSWAY!
THAT, WHEN IN BERLIN, I SHOULD NEVER, EVER FART IN BED.

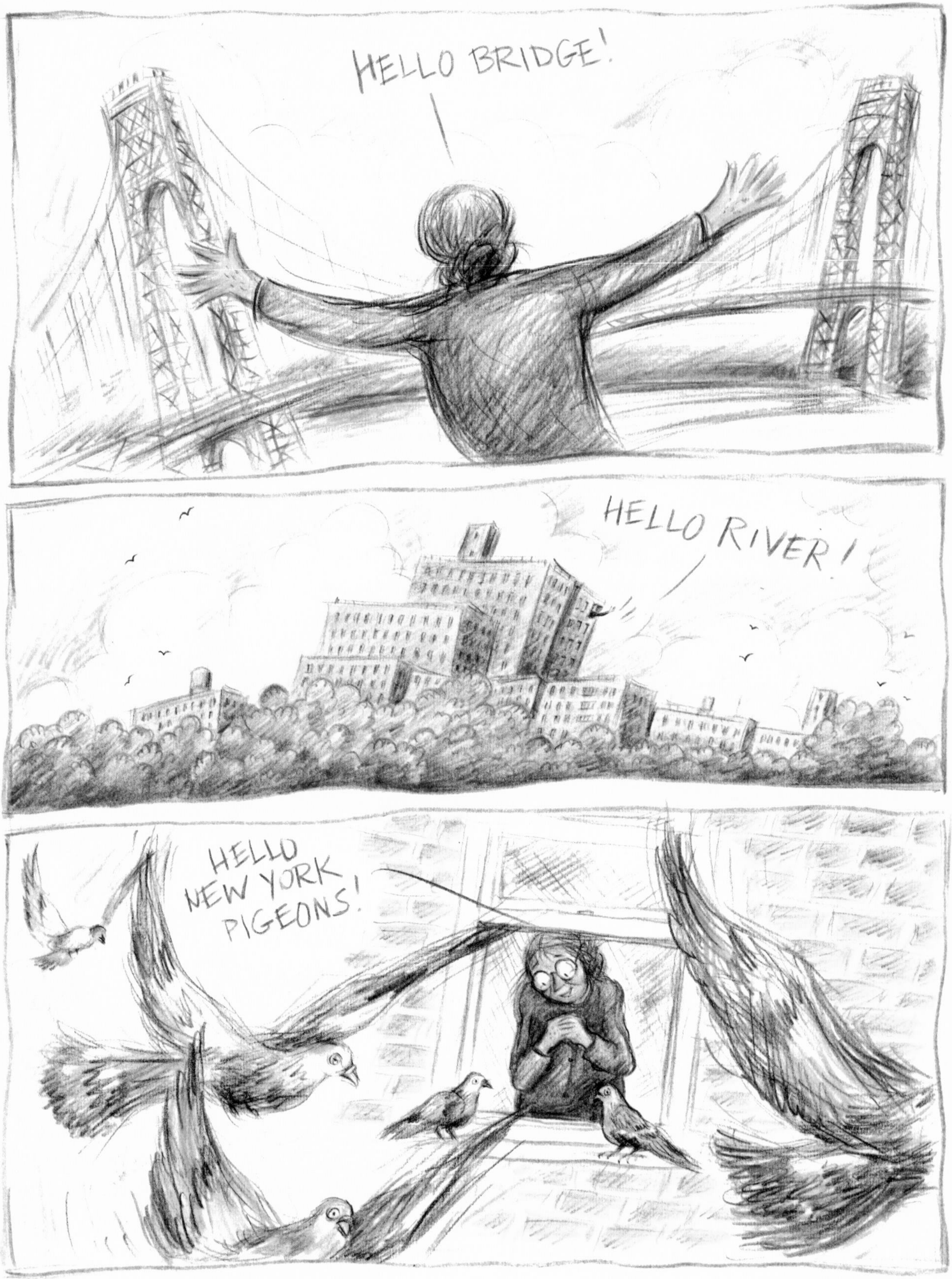
HELLO BRIDGE!
HELLO RIVER!
HELLO NEW YORK PIGEONS!

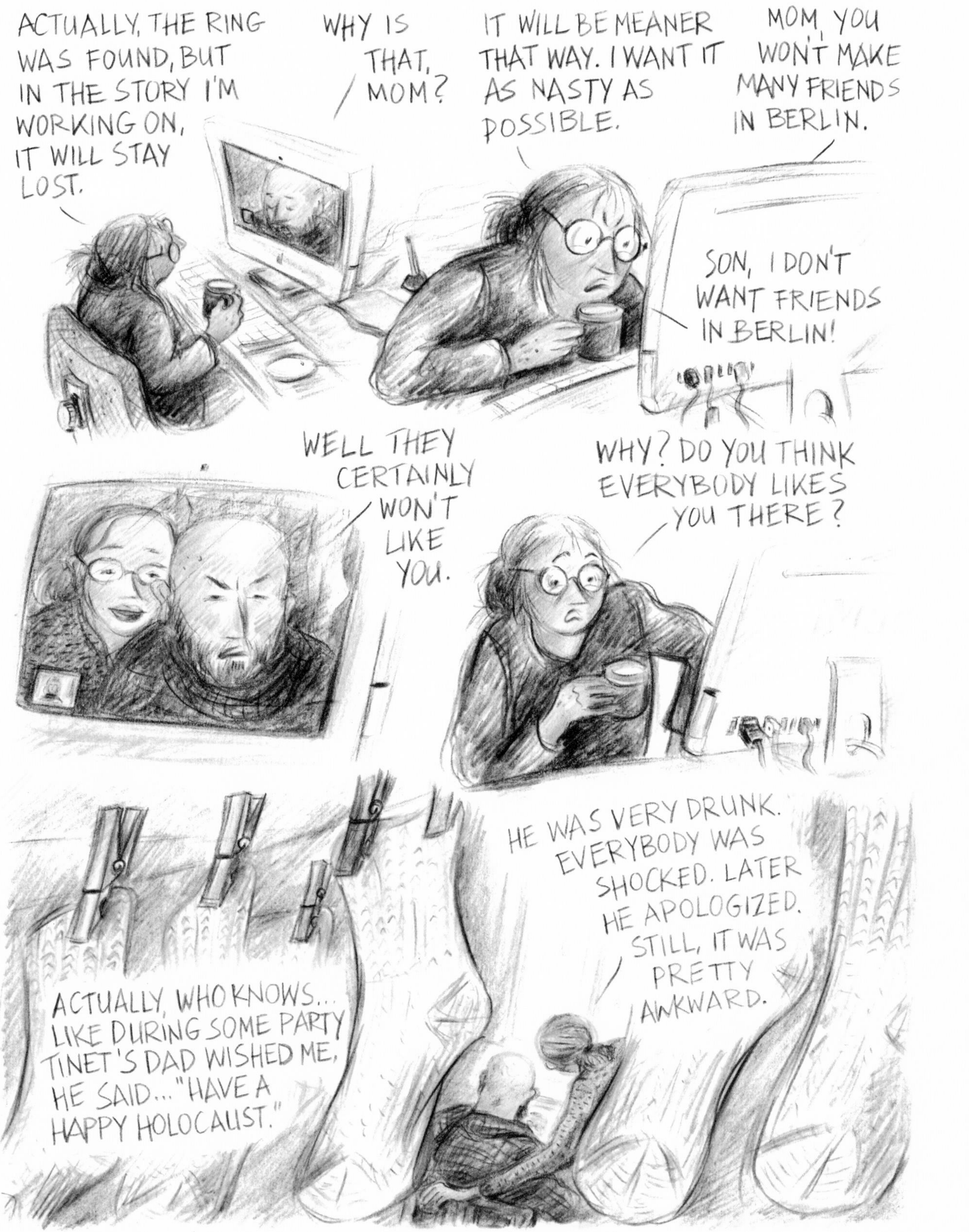
ACTUALLY, THE RING WAS FOUND, BUT IN THE STORY I'M WORKING ON, IT WILL STAY LOST.
WHY IS THAT, MOM?
IT WILL BE MEANER THAT WAY. I WANT IT AS NASTY AS POSSIBLE.
MOM, YOU WON'T MAKE MANY FRIENDS IN BERLIN.
SON, I DON'T WANT FRIENDS IN BERLIN!
WELL THEY CERTAINLY WON'T LIKE YOU.
WHY? DO YOU THINK EVERYBODY LIKES YOU THERE?
ACTUALLY, WHO KNOWS... LIKE DURING SOME PARTY TINET'S DAD WISHED ME, HE SAID... "HAVE A HAPPY HOLOCAUST."
HE WAS VERY DRUNK. EVERYBODY WAS SHOCKED. LATER HE APOLOGIZED. STILL, IT WAS PRETTY AWKWARD.

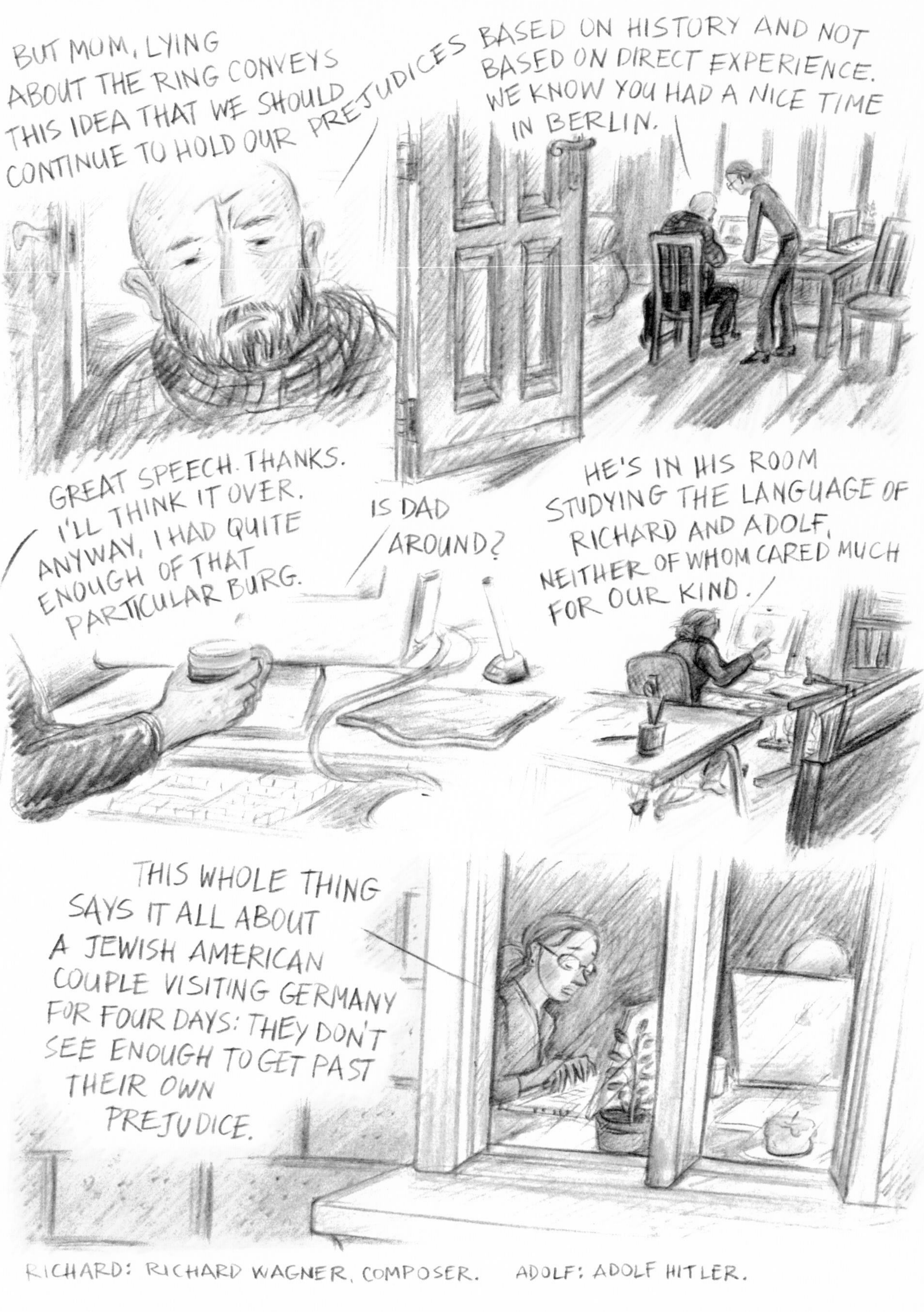
BUT MUM, LYING ABOUT THE RING CONVEYS THIS IDEA THAT WE SHOULD CONTINUE TO HOLD OUR PREJUDICES BASED ON HISTORY AND NOT BASED ON DIRECT EXPERIENCE.
WE KNOW YOU HAD A NICE TIME IN BERLIN.
GREAT SPEECH. THANKS. I'LL THINK IT OVER. ANYWAY, I HAD QUITE ENOUGH OF THAT PARTICULAR BURG.
IS DAD AROUND?
HE'S IN HIS ROOM STUDYING THE LANGUAGE OF RICHARD AND ADOLF, NEITHER OF WHOM CARED MUCH FOR OUR KIND.
THIS WHOLE THING SAYS IT ALL ABOUT A JEWISH AMERICAN COUPLE VISITING GERMANY FOR FOUR DAYS: THEY DON'T SEE ENOUGH TO GET PAST THEIR OWN PREJUDICE.

RICHARD: RICHARD WAGNER, COMPOSER. ADOLF: ADOLF HITLER.

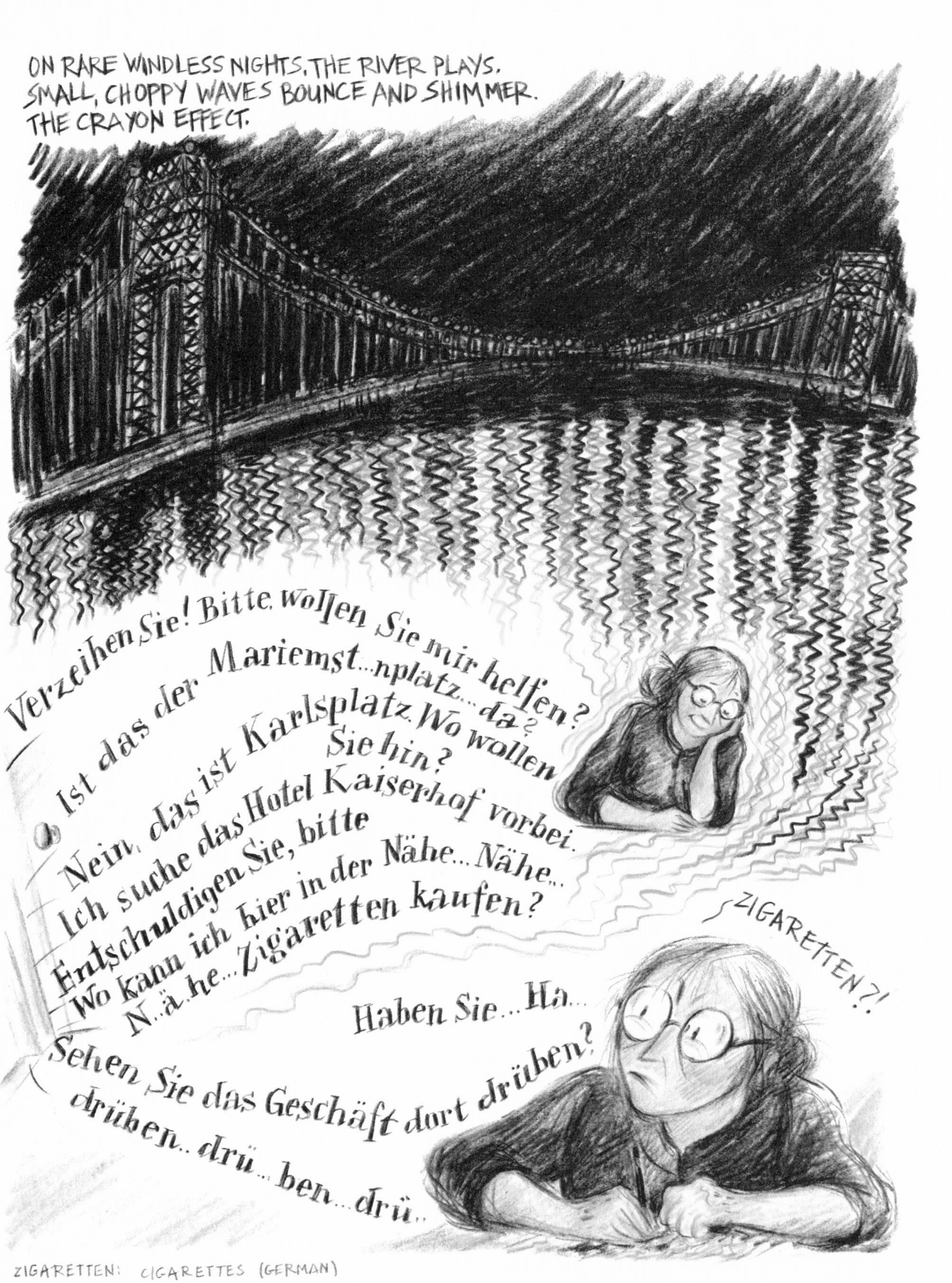
ON RARE WINDLESS NIGHTS, THE RIVER PLAYS.
SMALL, CHOPPY WAVES BOUNCE AND SHIMMER.
THE CRAYON EFFECT.
Verzeihen Sie! Bitte, wollen Sie mir helfen?
Ist das der Mariemst...nplatz...da?
Nein, das ist Karlsplatz. Wo wollen Sie hin?
Ich suche das Hotel Kaiserhof vorbei.
Entschuldigen Sie, bitte
Wo kann ich hier in der Nähe... Nähe...
N..ä..he... Zigaretten kaufen?
Haben Sie... Ha...
Sehen Sie das Geschäft dort drüben?
drüben.. drü... ben... drü..
ZIGARETTEN?!

ZIGARETTEN: CIGARETTES (GERMAN)

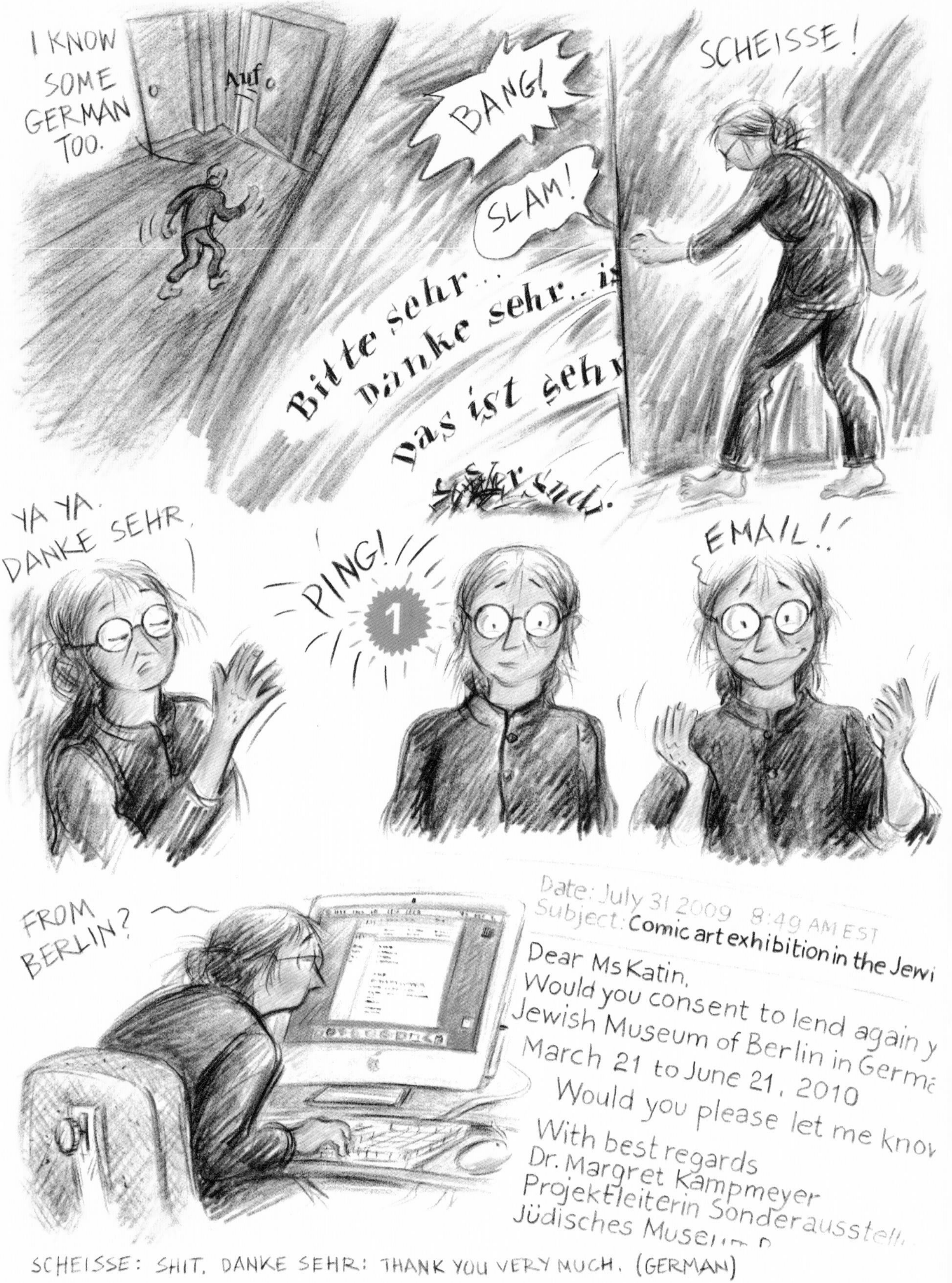
I KNOW SOME GERMAN TOO.
Auf
BANG!
SLAM!
Bitte sehr...
Danke sehr... is
Das ist sehr
SCHEISSE!
YA YA. DANKE SEHR.
PING!
1
EMAIL!!
FROM BERLIN?
Date: July 31 2009 8:49 AM EST
Subject: Comic art exhibition in the Jewi
Dear Ms Katin,
Would you consent to lend again y
Jewish Museum of Berlin in Germa
March 21 to June 21, 2010
Would you please let me know
With best regards
Dr. Margret Kampmeyer
Projektleiterin Sonderausstell
Jüdisches Museum

SCHEISSE: SHIT. DANKE SEHR: THANK YOU VERY MUCH. (GERMAN)

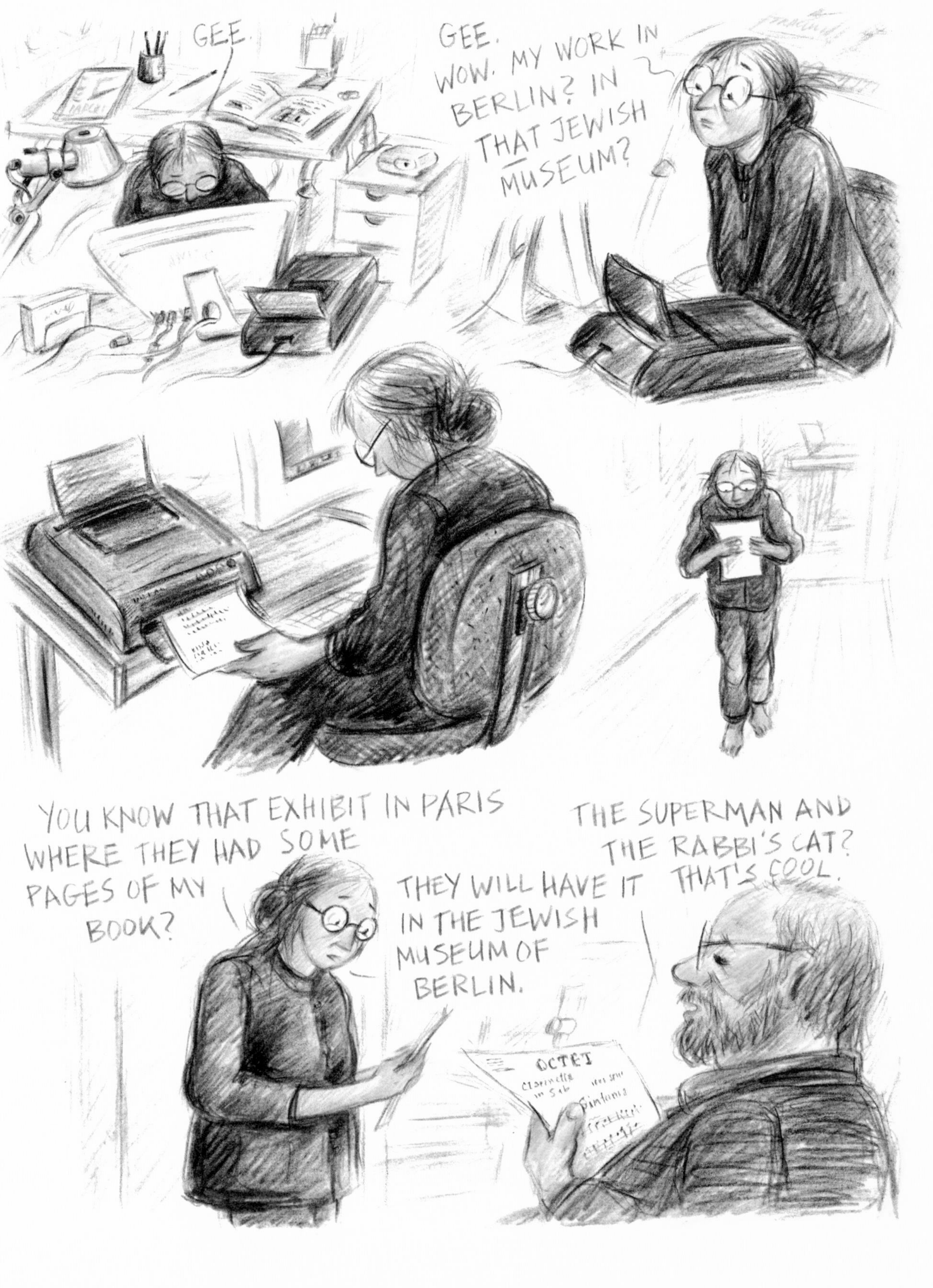
GEE.
GEE.
WOW. MY WORK IN BERLIN? IN THAT JEWISH MUSEUM?
YOU KNOW THAT EXHIBIT IN PARIS WHERE THEY HAD SOME PAGES OF MY BOOK?
THEY WILL HAVE IT IN THE JEWISH MUSEUM OF BERLIN.
THE SUPERMAN AND THE RABBI'S CAT? THAT'S COOL.
OCTET

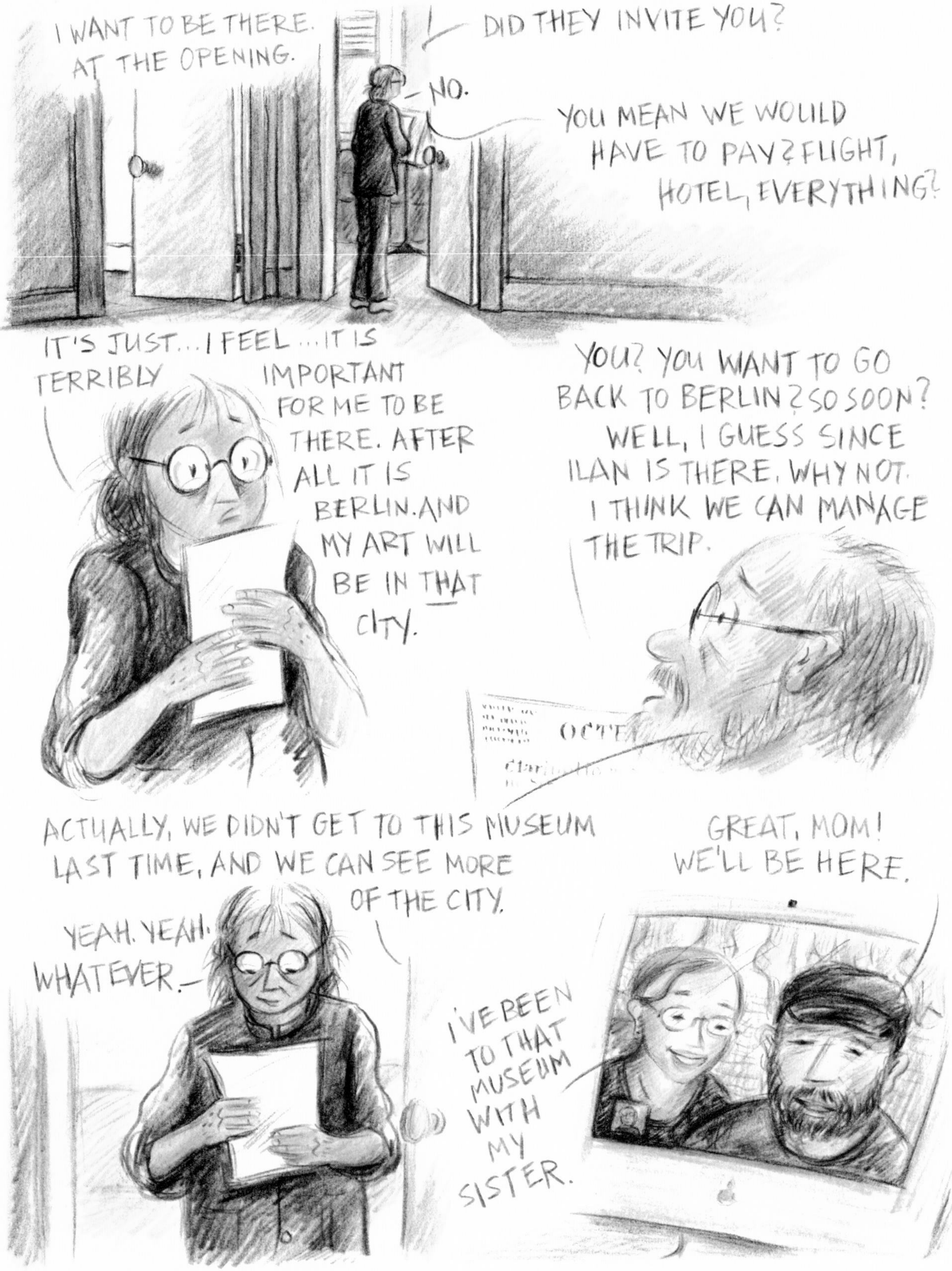
I WANT TO BE THERE. AT THE OPENING.
DID THEY INVITE YOU?
NO.
YOU MEAN WE WOULD HAVE TO PAY? FLIGHT, HOTEL, EVERYTHING?
IT'S JUST... I FEEL... IT IS TERRIBLY IMPORTANT FOR ME TO BE THERE. AFTER ALL IT IS BERLIN. AND MY ART WILL BE IN THAT CITY.
YOU? YOU WANT TO GO BACK TO BERLIN? SO SOON? WELL, I GUESS SINCE ILAN IS THERE, WHY NOT. I THINK WE CAN MANAGE THE TRIP.
ACTUALLY, WE DIDN'T GET TO THIS MUSEUM LAST TIME, AND WE CAN SEE MORE OF THE CITY.
YEAH. YEAH. WHATEVER.
GREAT, MOM! WE'LL BE HERE.
I'VE BEEN TO THAT MUSEUM WITH MY SISTER.

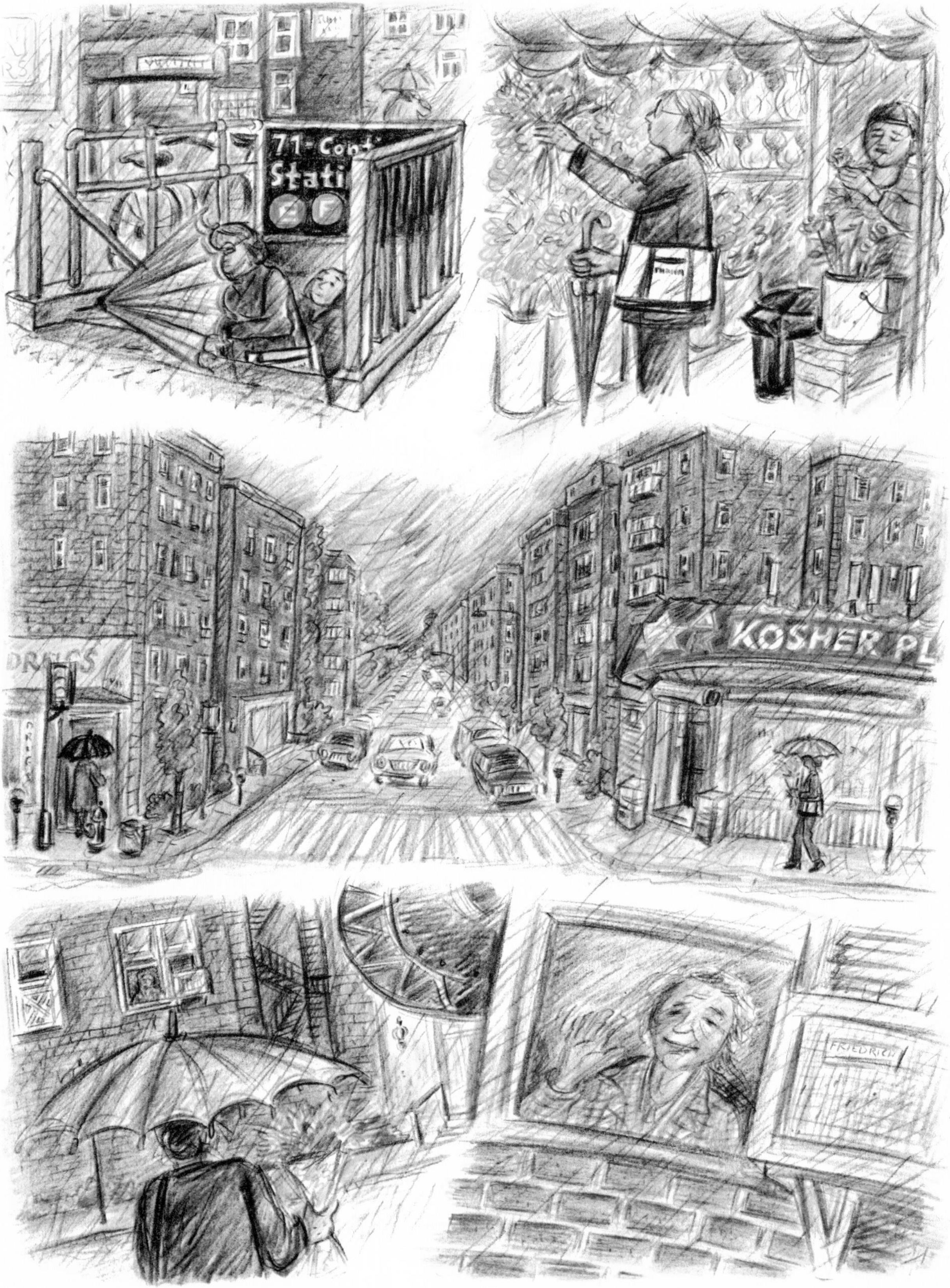
71-Cont
Stati
KOSHER PL
FRIEDRICH

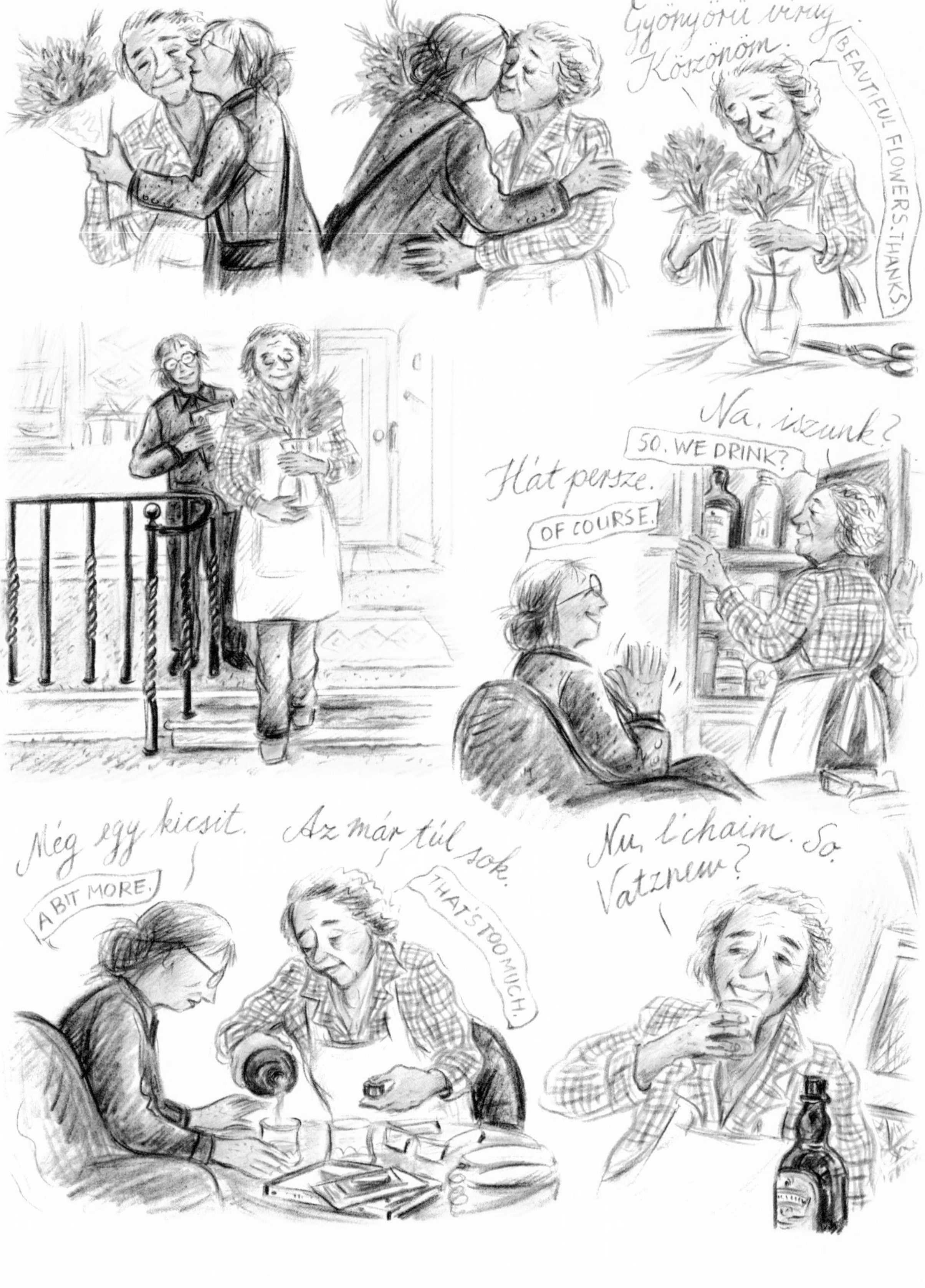

Gyönyörü virág Köszönöm.
BEAUTIFUL FLOWERS. THANKS.
Na, iszunk?
SO. WE DRINK?
Hát persze.
OF COURSE.
Még egy kicsit.
A BIT MORE.
Az már túl sok.
THAT'S TOO MUCH.
Nu, l'chaim. So. Vatznew?

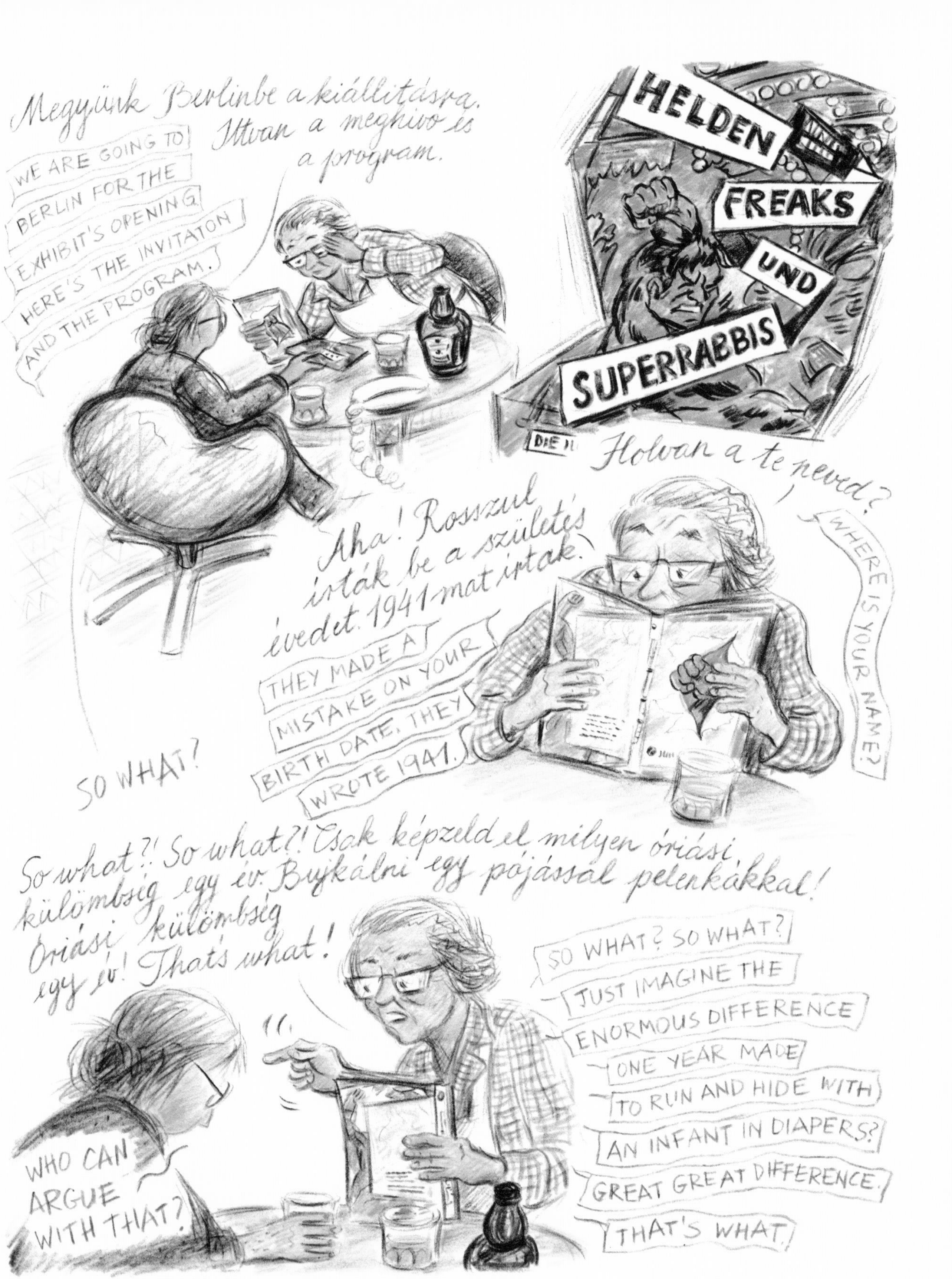

Megyünk Berlinbe a kiállitásra. Itvan a meghivo és a program.
WE ARE GOING TO BERLIN FOR THE EXHIBIT'S OPENING. HERE'S THE INVITATON AND THE PROGRAM.
HELDEN
FREAKS
UND
SUPERRABBIS
Holvan a te neved?
WHERE IS YOUR NAME?
Aha! Rosszul irták be a születés évedet. 1941-mat irták.
THEY MADE A MISTAKE ON YOUR BIRTH DATE, THEY WROTE 1941.
SO WHAT?
So what?! So what?! Csak képzeld el milyen óriási külömbsig egy év. Bujkálni egy pójással pelenkákkal! Óriási külömbsig egy év! That's what!
SO WHAT? SO WHAT? JUST IMAGINE THE ENORMOUS DIFFERENCE ONE YEAR MADE TO RUN AND HIDE WITH AN INFANT IN DIAPERS? GREAT GREAT DIFFERENCE. THAT'S WHAT.
WHO CAN ARGUE WITH THAT?

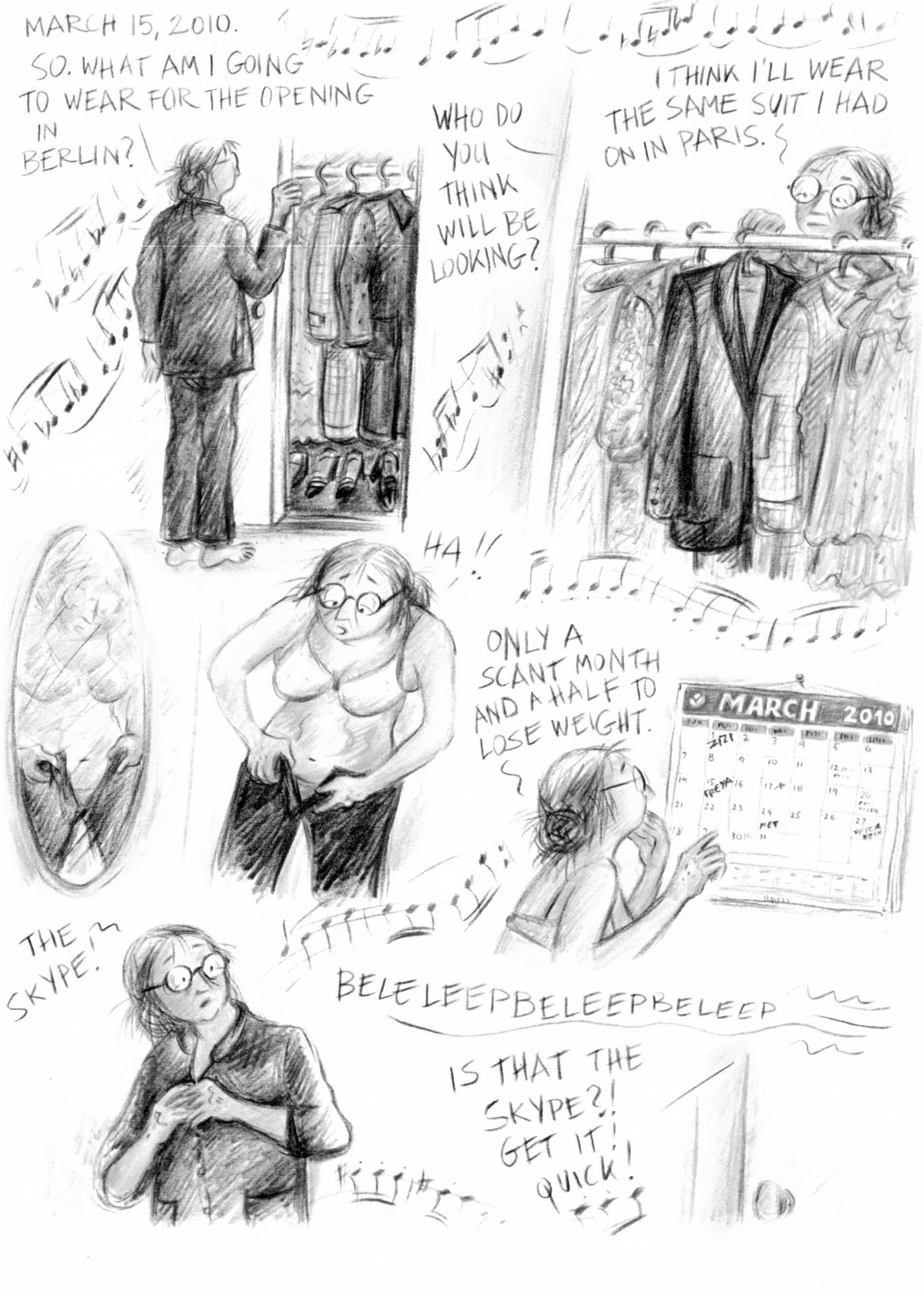
MARCH 15, 2010.
SO. WHAT AM I GOING TO WEAR FOR THE OPENING IN BERLIN?
WHO DO YOU THINK WILL BE LOOKING?
I THINK I'LL WEAR THE SAME SUIT I HAD ON IN PARIS.
HA!!
ONLY A SCANT MONTH AND A HALF TO LOSE WEIGHT.
MARCH 2010
THE SKYPE!
BELELEEPBELEEPBELEEP
IS THAT THE SKYPE?! GET IT! QUICK!

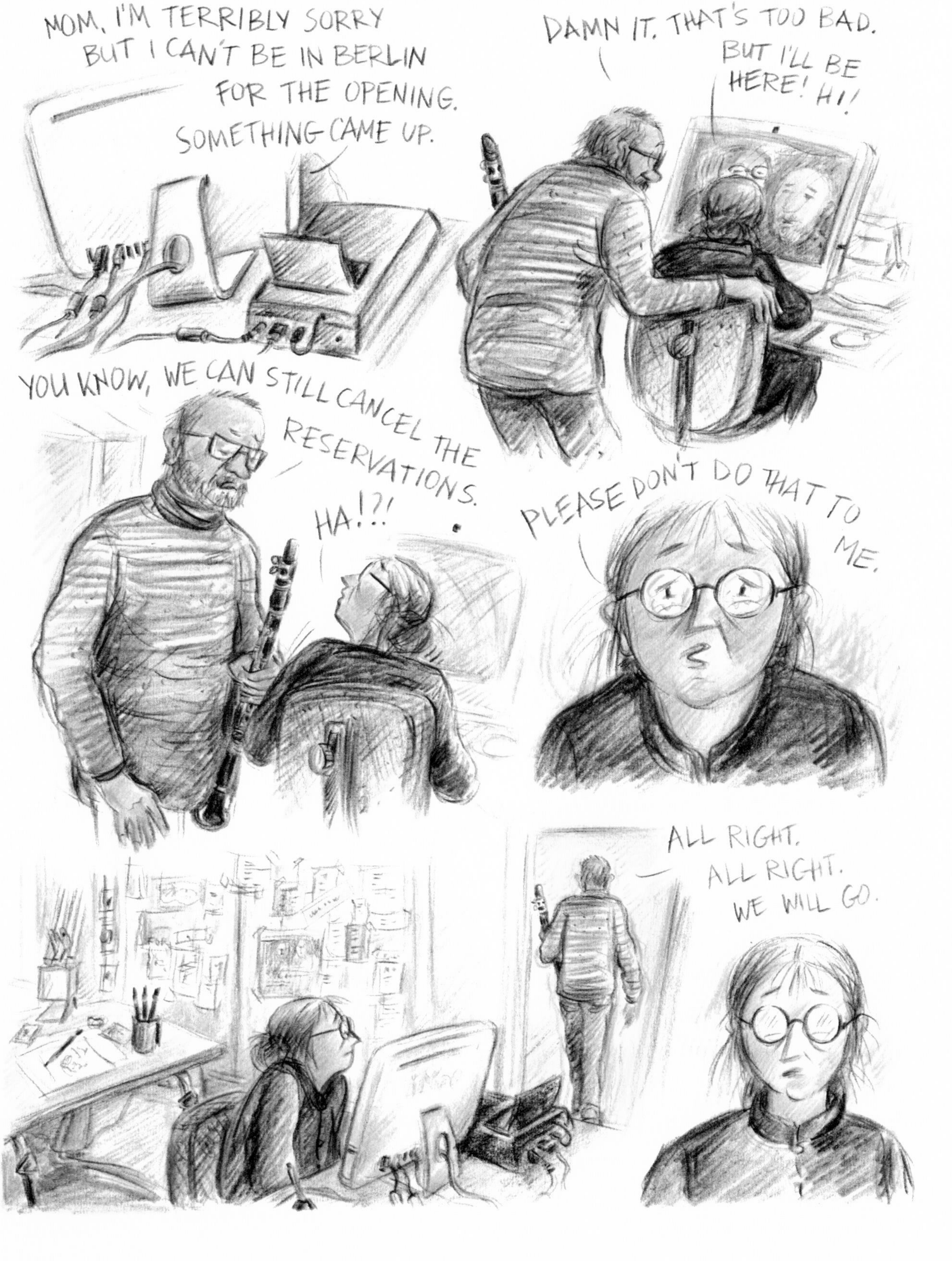
MOM, I'M TERRIBLY SORRY BUT I CAN'T BE IN BERLIN FOR THE OPENING. SOMETHING CAME UP.
DAMN IT. THAT'S TOO BAD.
BUT I'LL BE HERE! HI!
YOU KNOW, WE CAN STILL CANCEL THE RESERVATIONS.
HA!?!
PLEASE DON'T DO THAT TO ME.
ALL RIGHT. ALL RIGHT. WE WILL GO.

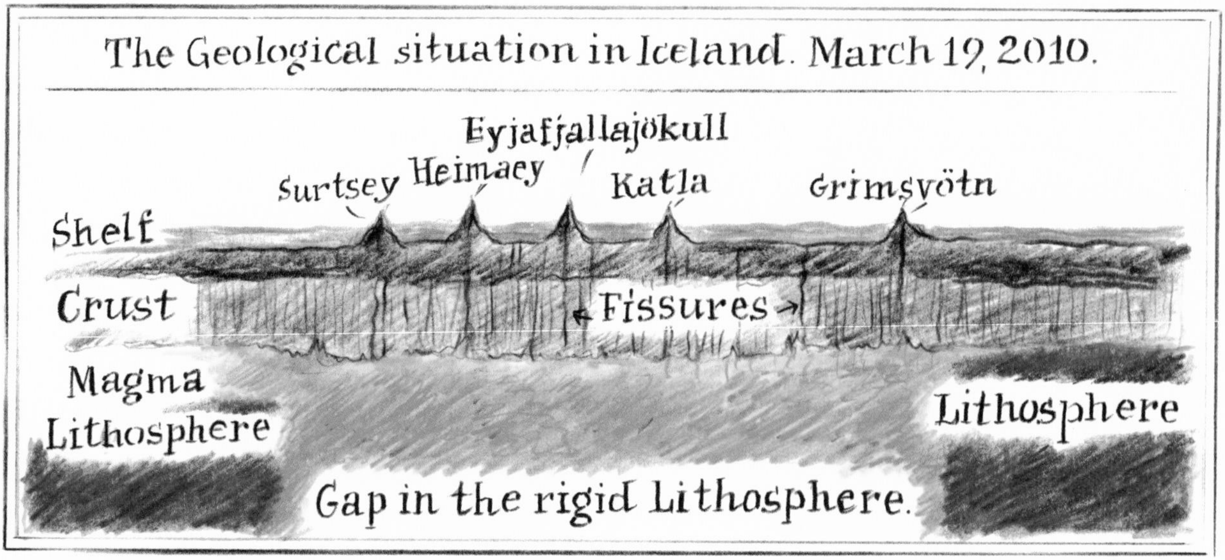
The Geological situation in Iceland. March 19, 2010.
Eyjafjallajökull
Surtsey
Heimaey
Katla
Grimsvötn
Shelf
Crust
Fissures
Magma
Lithosphere
Lithosphere
Gap in the rigid Lithosphere.

THE DENTAL SITUATION IN WASHINGTON HEIGHTS, MARCH 19, 2010, 5:40AM.

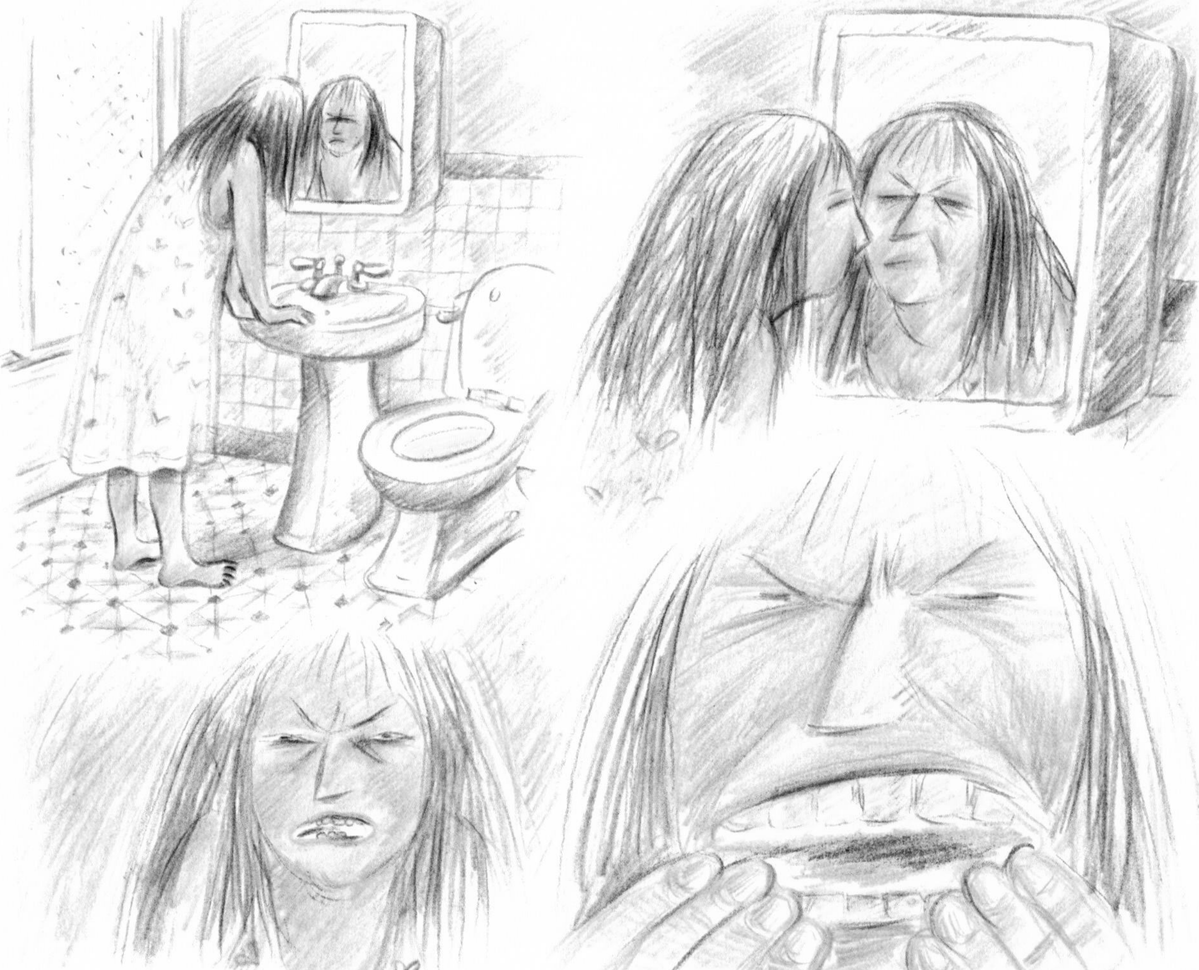

OY.

OK, SO THIS WHITENER WILL TAKE ABOUT FOUR WEEKS, JUST IN TIME FOR THE OPENING IN BERLIN.

ENAMEL SAF DENTAL WHITENING STRIPS

UPPER
LOWER

TEETH WHITENING KIT

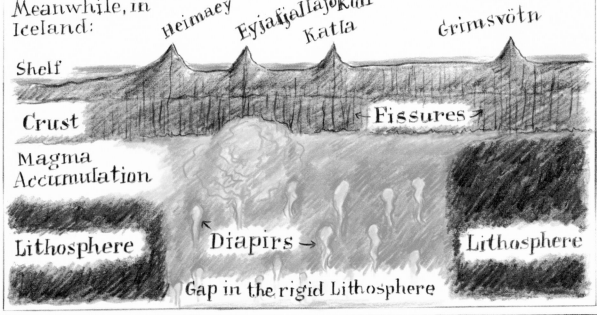

Meanwhile, in Iceland:

Heimaey   Eyjafjallajökull   Katla   Grimsvötn

Shelf

Crust

← Fissures →

Magma Accumulation

Lithosphere

Diapirs →

Lithosphere

Gap in the rigid Lithosphere

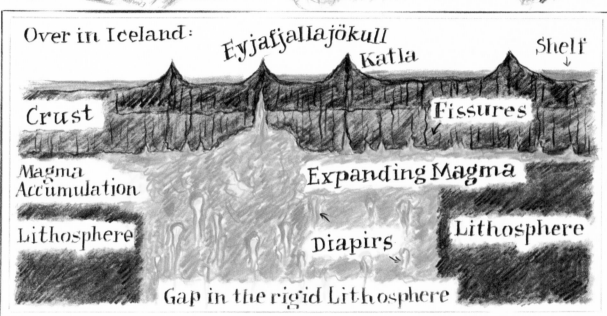

Over in Iceland:

Eyjafjallajökull

Katla

Shelf

Crust

Fissures

Magma Accumulation

Expanding Magma

Lithosphere

Diapirs

Lithosphere

Gap in the rigid Lithosphere

SO YOU CAN'T HAVE ANY RED WINE?

AH.. AH.

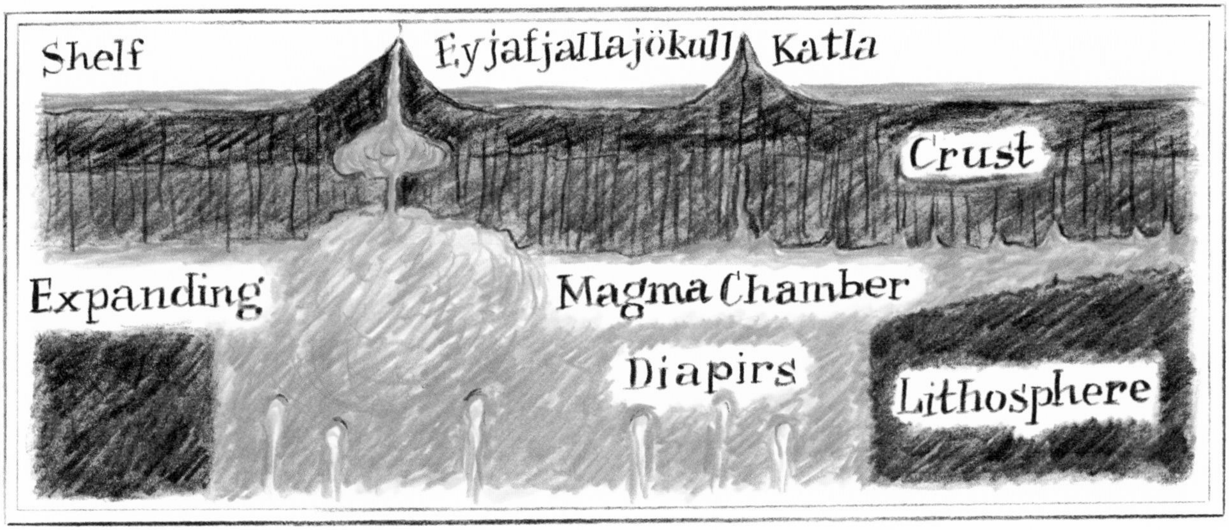
Shelf
Eyjafjallajökull
Katla
Crust
Expanding
Magma Chamber
Diapirs
Lithosphere

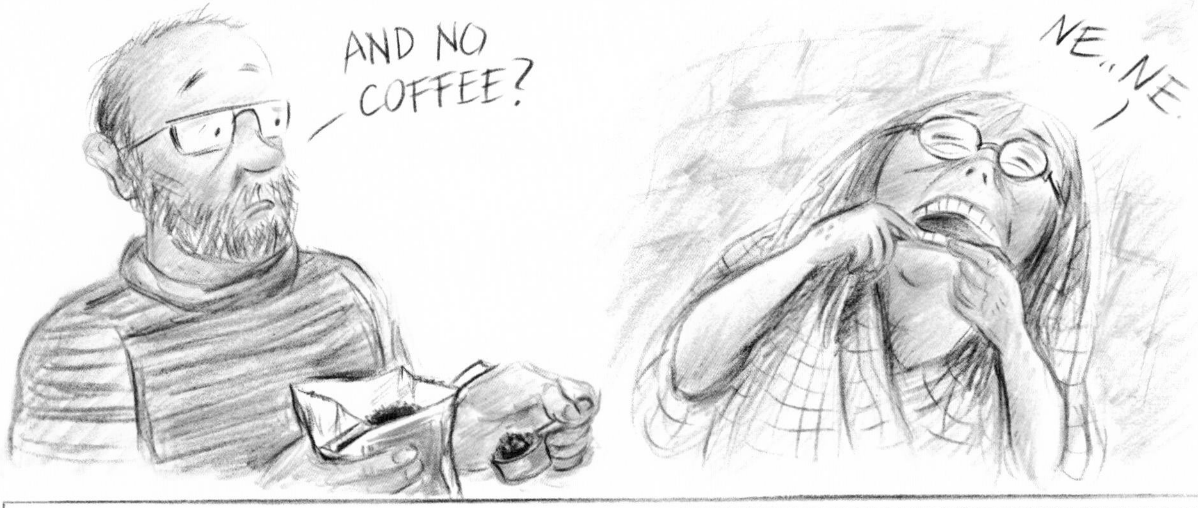
AND NO COFFEE?
NE..NE

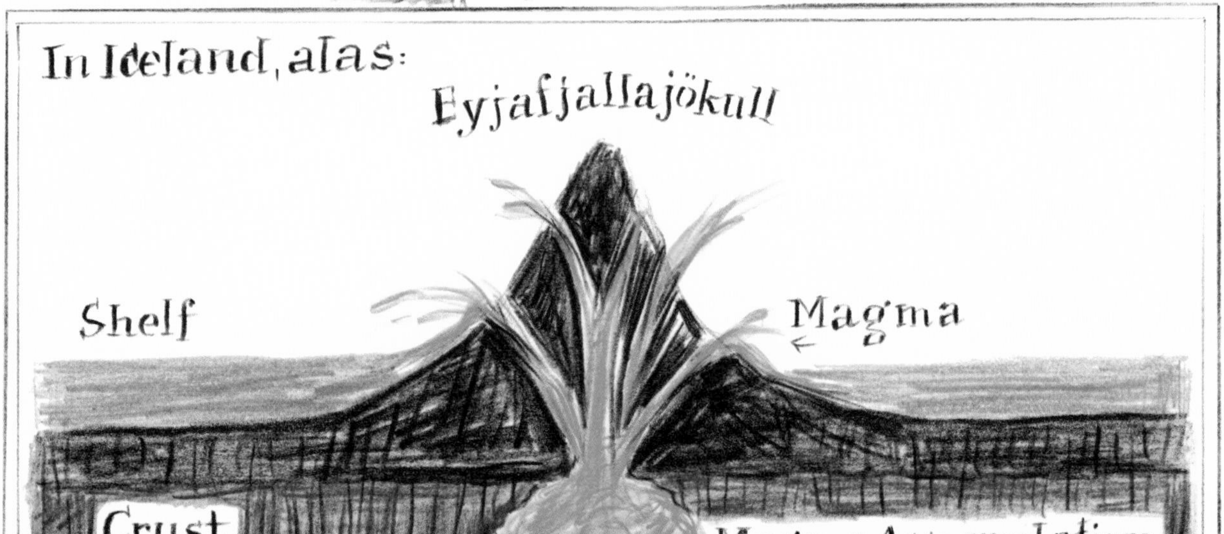
In Iceland, alas:
Eyjafjallajökull
Shelf
Magma
Crust
Magma Accumulation

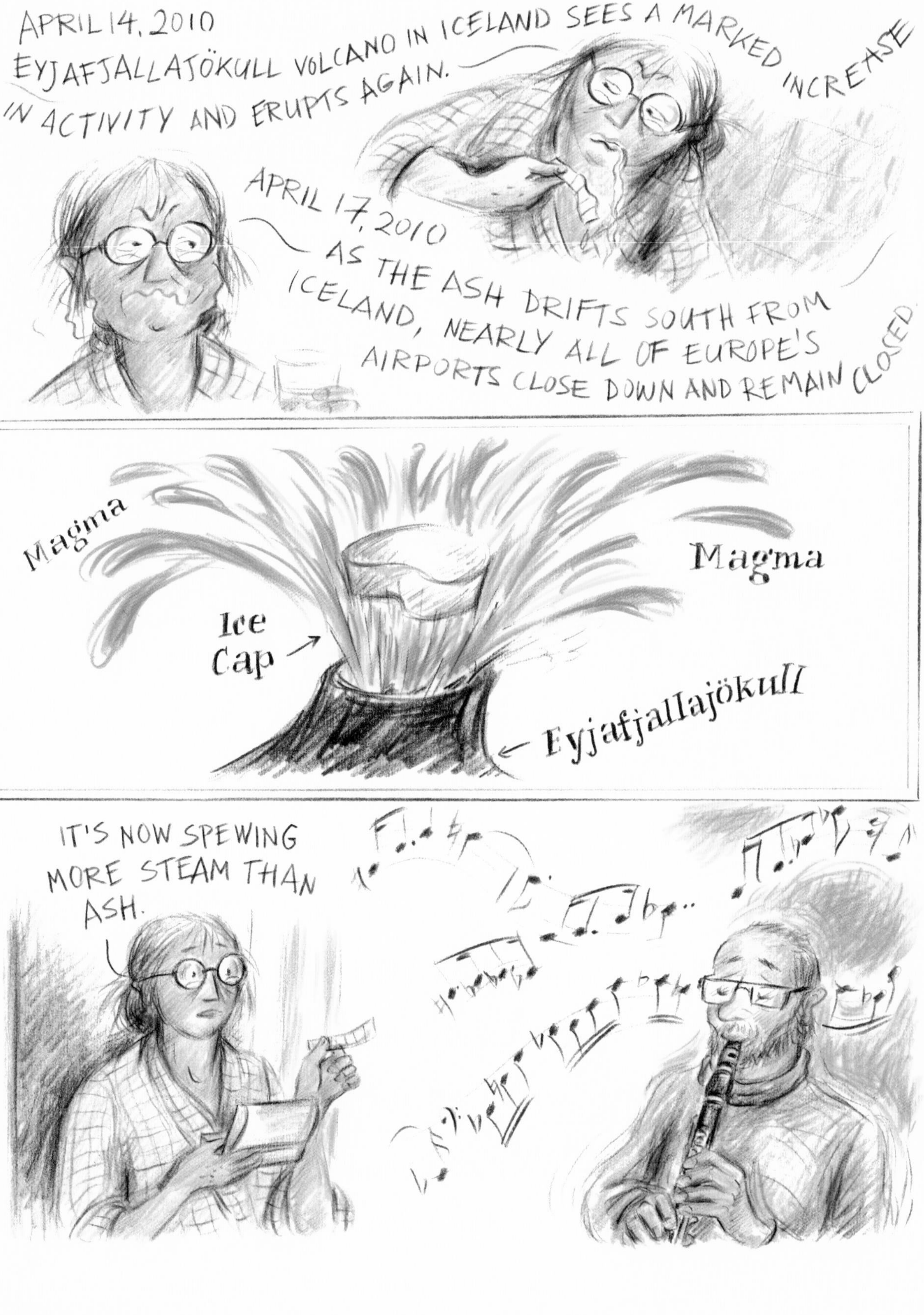
APRIL 14, 2010
EYJAFJALLAJÖKULL VOLCANO IN ICELAND SEES A MARKED INCREASE IN ACTIVITY AND ERUPTS AGAIN.
APRIL 17, 2010
AS THE ASH DRIFTS SOUTH FROM ICELAND, NEARLY ALL OF EUROPE'S AIRPORTS CLOSE DOWN AND REMAIN CLOSED
Magma
Magma
Ice Cap
Eyjafjallajökull
IT'S NOW SPEWING MORE STEAM THAN ASH.

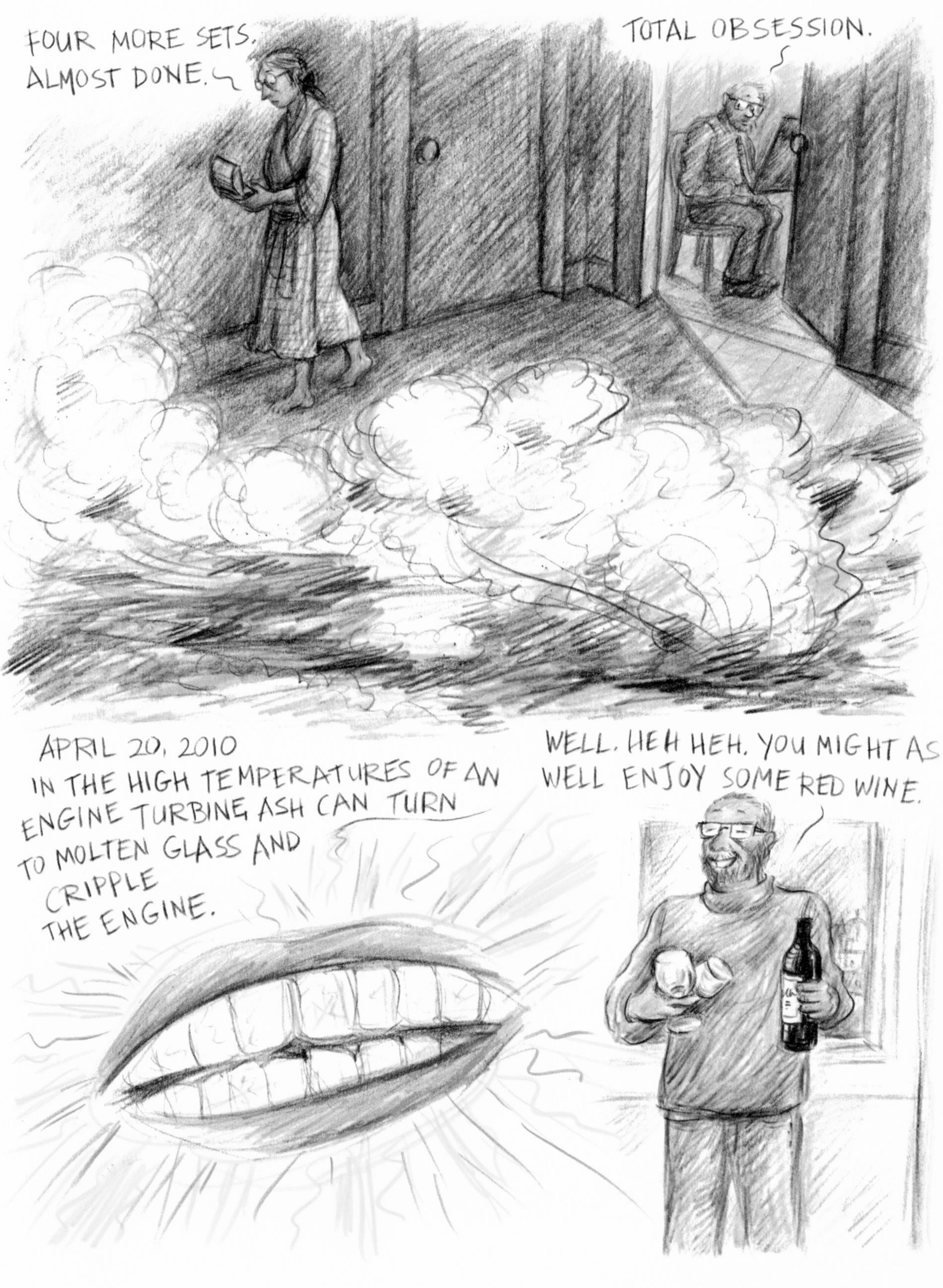
FOUR MORE SETS. ALMOST DONE.
TOTAL OBSESSION.
APRIL 20, 2010
IN THE HIGH TEMPERATURES OF AN ENGINE TURBINE ASH CAN TURN TO MOLTEN GLASS AND CRIPPLE THE ENGINE.
WELL. HEH HEH. YOU MIGHT AS WELL ENJOY SOME RED WINE.

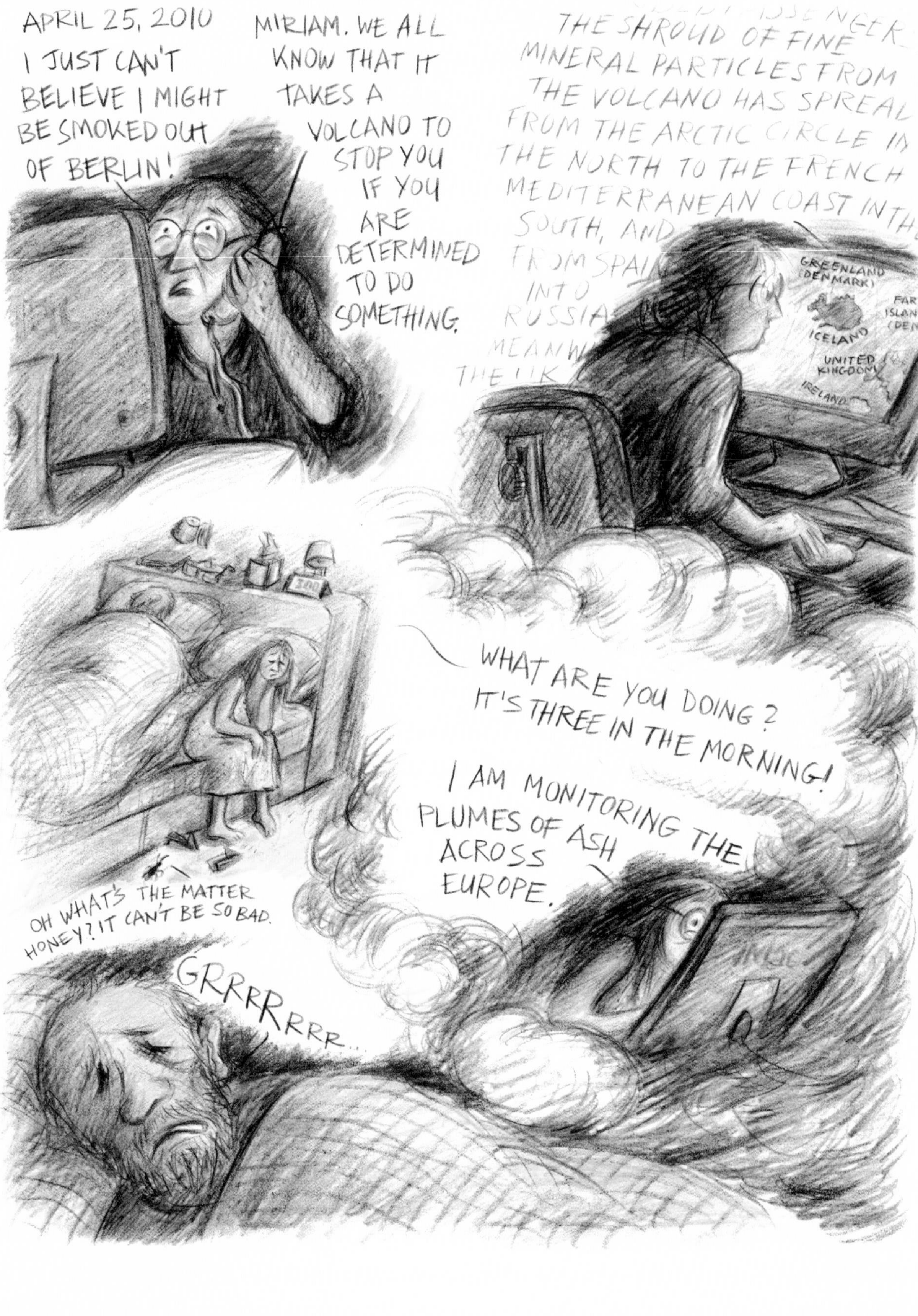

APRIL 25, 2010
I JUST CAN'T BELIEVE I MIGHT BE SMOKED OUT OF BERLIN!
MIRIAM. WE ALL KNOW THAT IT TAKES A VOLCANO TO STOP YOU IF YOU ARE DETERMINED TO DO SOMETHING.
THE SHROUD OF FINE MINERAL PARTICLES FROM THE VOLCANO HAS SPREAD FROM THE ARCTIC CIRCLE IN THE NORTH TO THE FRENCH MEDITERRANEAN COAST IN THE SOUTH, AND FROM SPAIN INTO RUSSIA
GREENLAND (DENMARK)
ICELAND
UNITED KINGDOM
IRELAND
WHAT ARE YOU DOING? IT'S THREE IN THE MORNING!
I AM MONITORING THE PLUMES OF ASH ACROSS EUROPE.
OH WHAT'S THE MATTER HONEY? IT CAN'T BE SO BAD.
GRRRRRrrr...

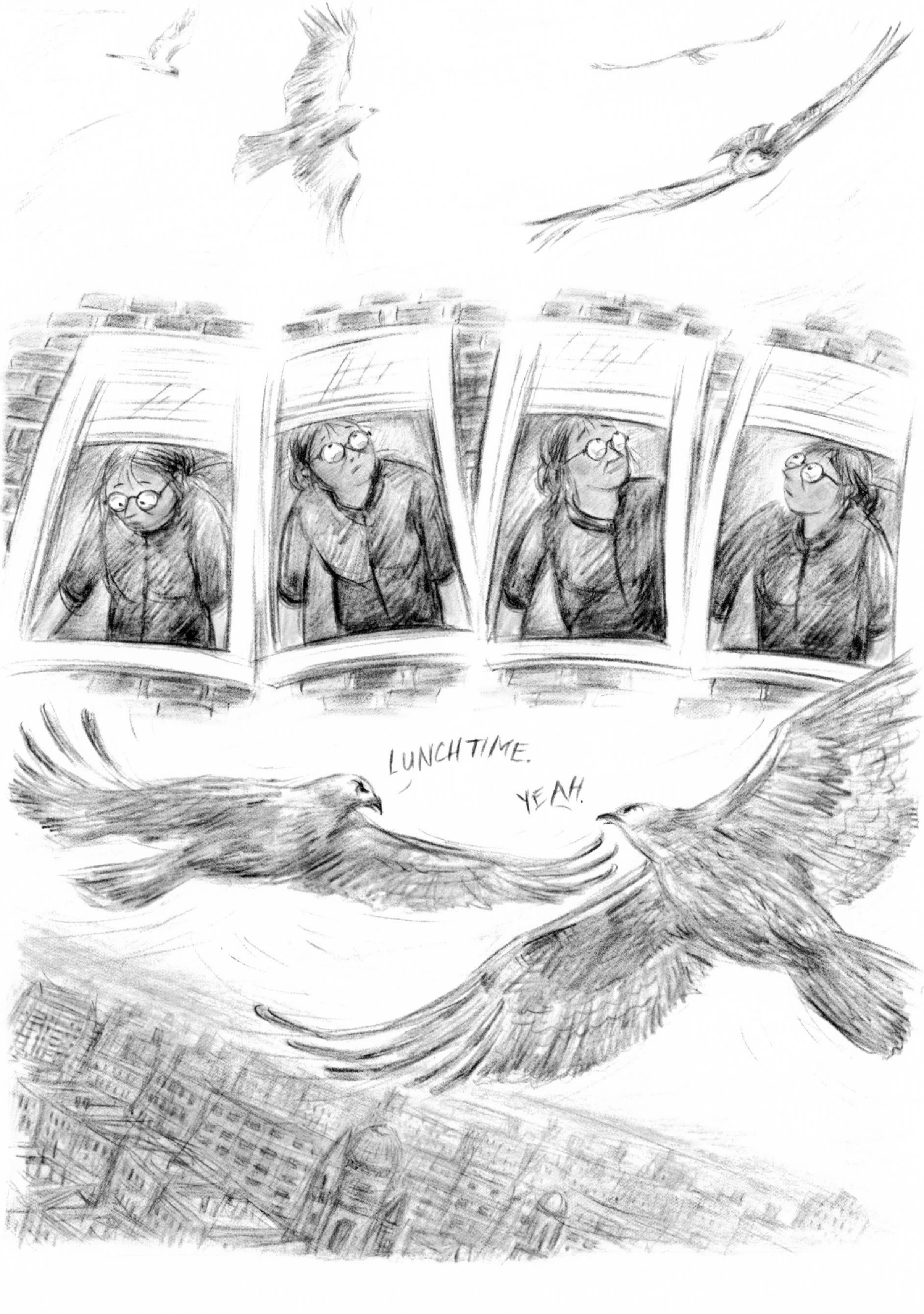
LUNCHTIME.
YEAH.

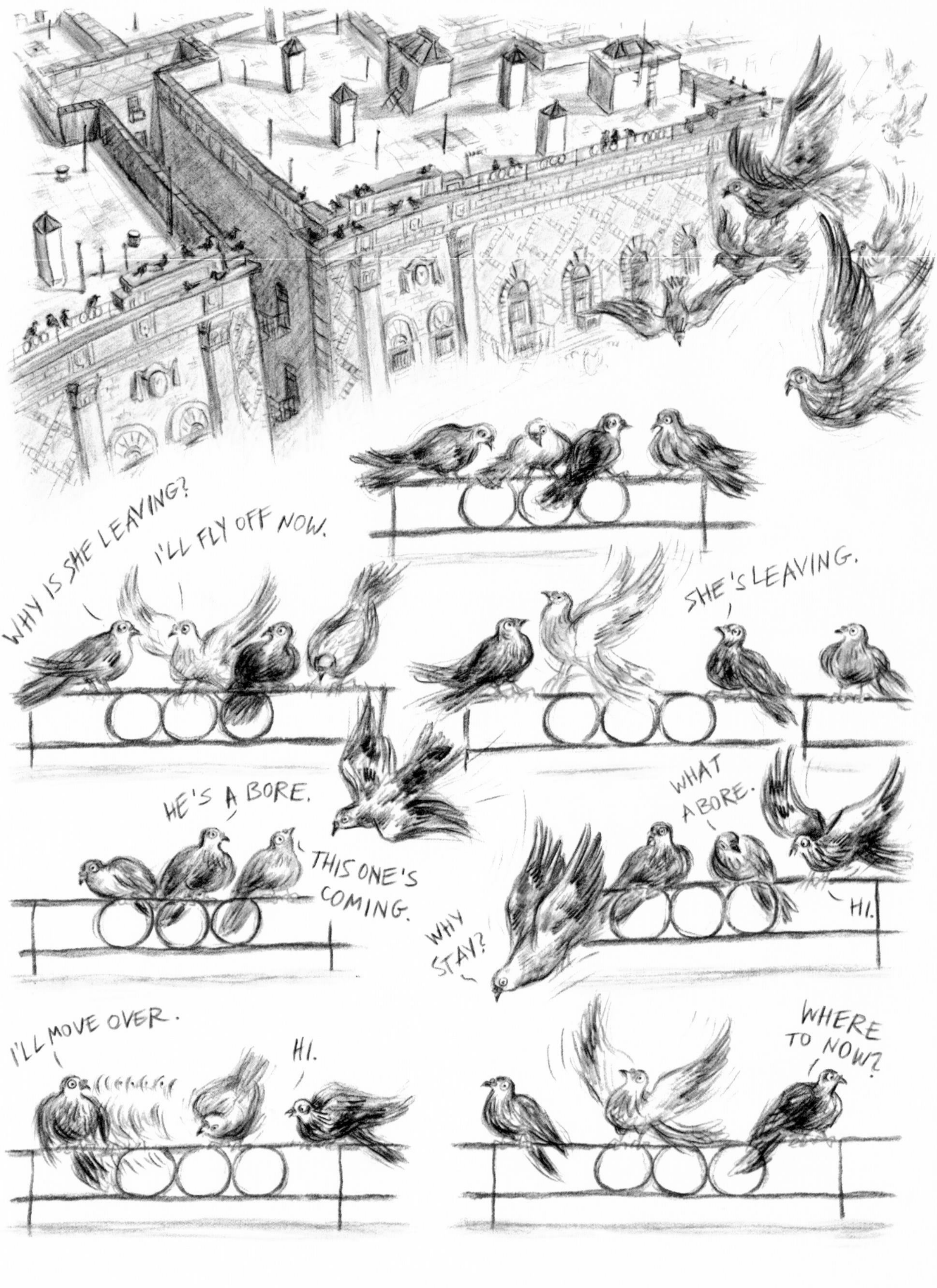
WHY IS SHE LEAVING?
I'LL FLY OFF NOW.
SHE'S LEAVING.
HE'S A BORE.
THIS ONE'S COMING.
WHAT A BORE.
WHY STAY?
HI.
I'LL MOVE OVER.
HI.
WHERE TO NOW?

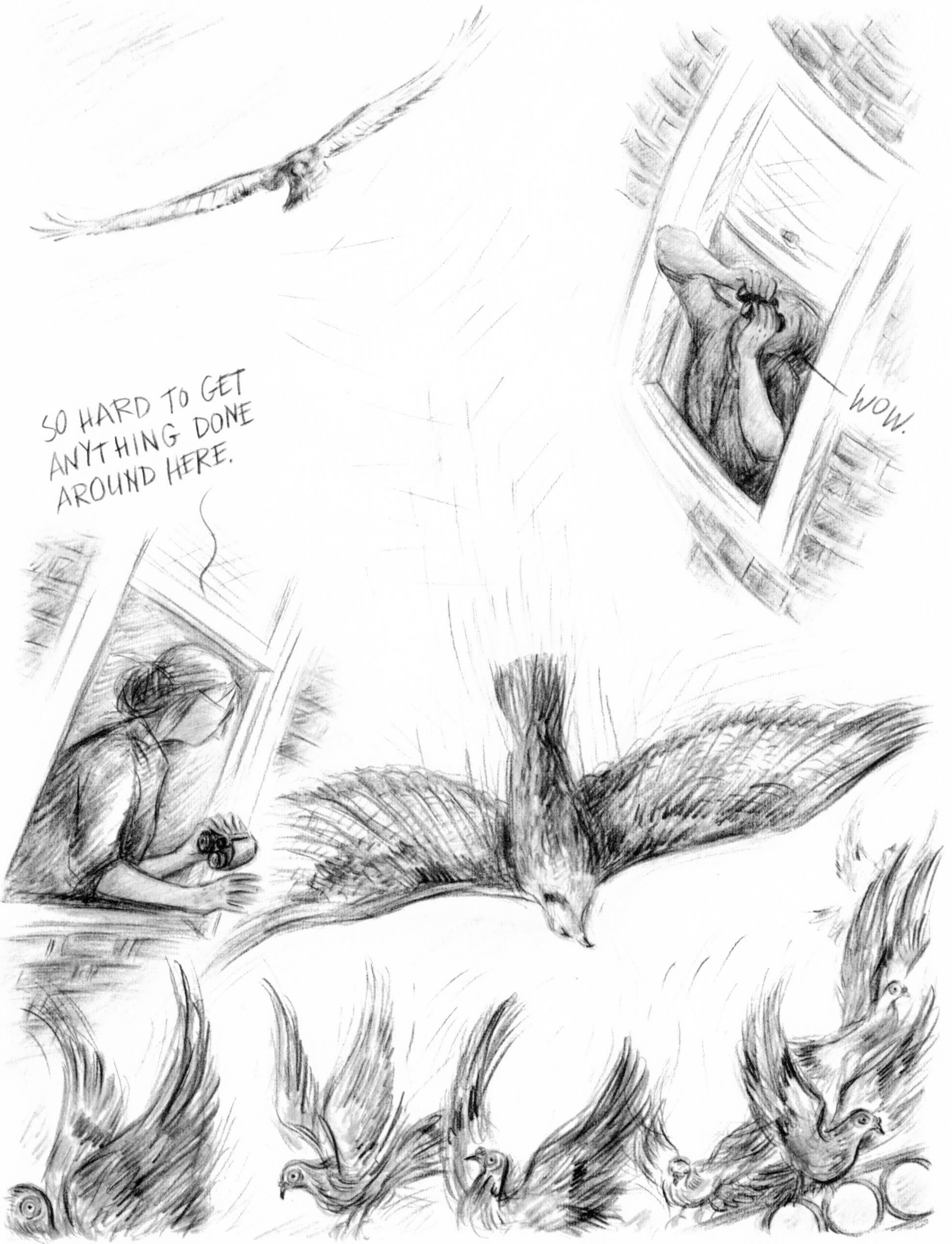
WOW.
SO HARD TO GET ANYTHING DONE AROUND HERE.

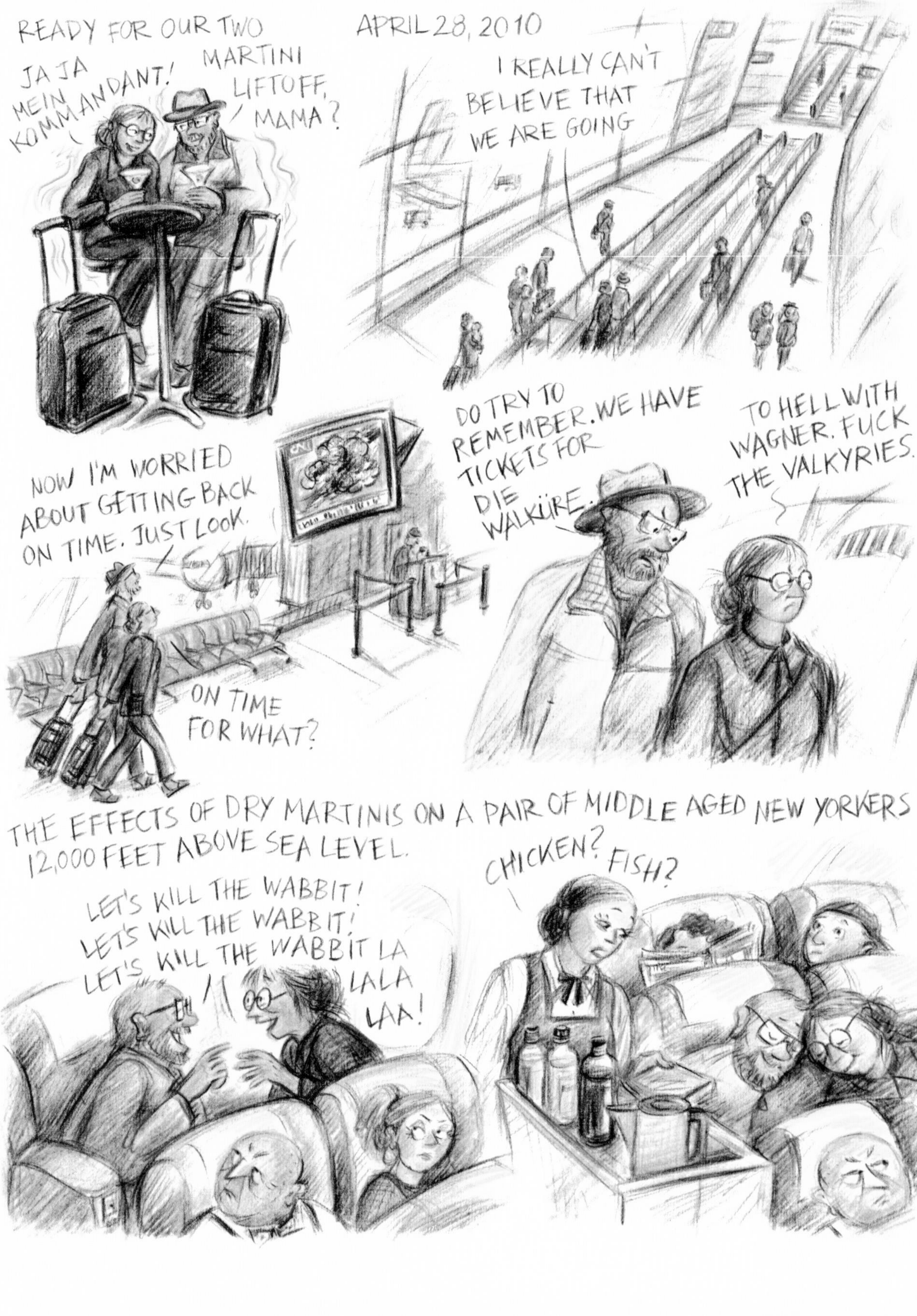
READY FOR OUR TWO
APRIL 28, 2010
JA JA MEIN KOMMANDANT!
MARTINI LIFTOFF, MAMA?
I REALLY CAN'T BELIEVE THAT WE ARE GOING
NOW I'M WORRIED ABOUT GETTING BACK ON TIME. JUST LOOK.
ON TIME FOR WHAT?
DO TRY TO REMEMBER. WE HAVE TICKETS FOR DIE WALKÜRE.
TO HELL WITH WAGNER. FUCK THE VALKYRIES.
THE EFFECTS OF DRY MARTINIS ON A PAIR OF MIDDLE AGED NEW YORKERS 12,000 FEET ABOVE SEA LEVEL.
LET'S KILL THE WABBIT! LET'S KILL THE WABBIT! LET'S KILL THE WABBIT LA LALA LAA!
CHICKEN? FISH?

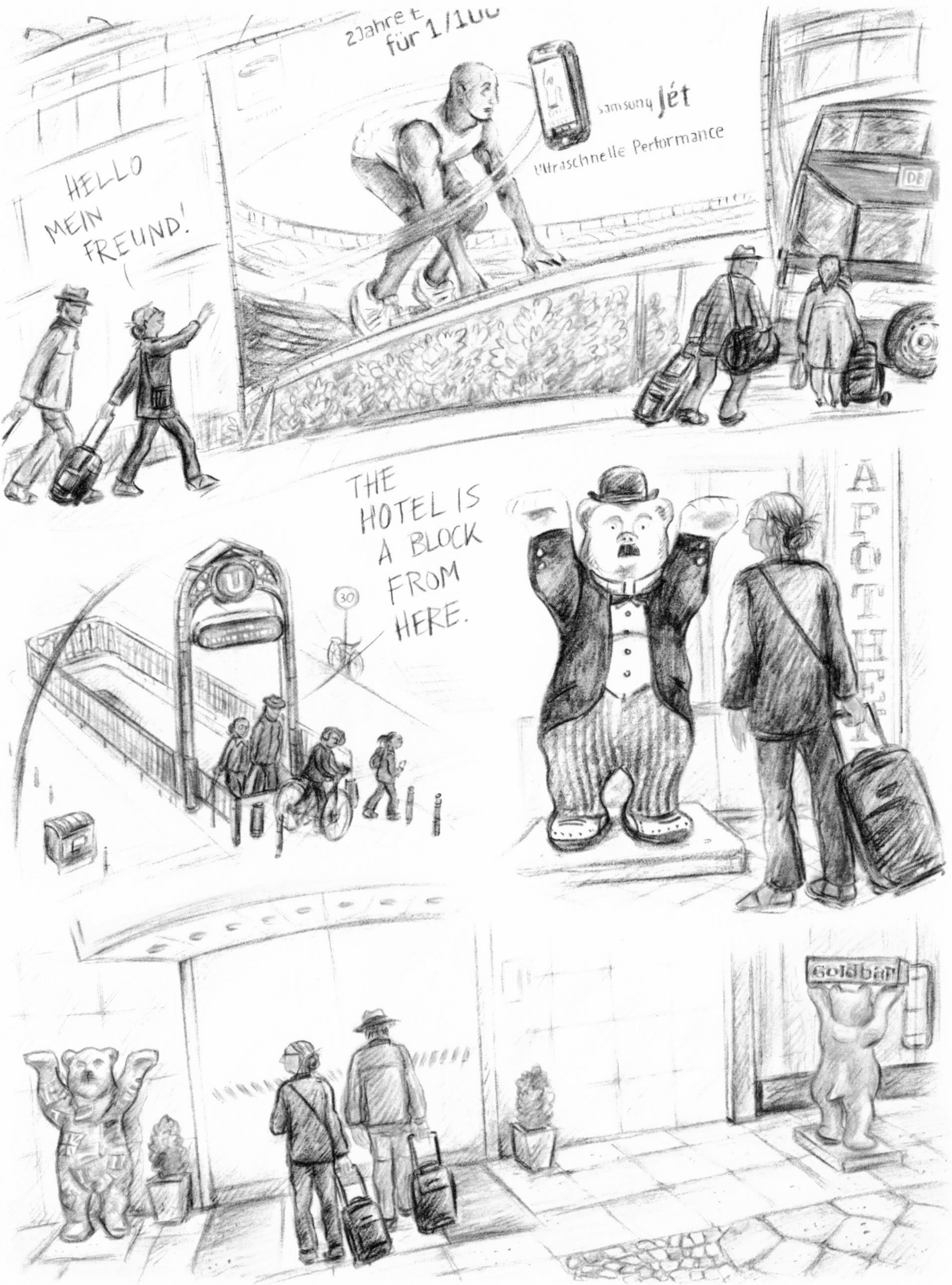
Samsung Jét
Ultraschnelle Performance
HELLO MEIN FREUND!
DB
THE HOTEL IS A BLOCK FROM HERE.
30
Goldbär

MEIN FREUND: MY FRIEND (GERMAN)

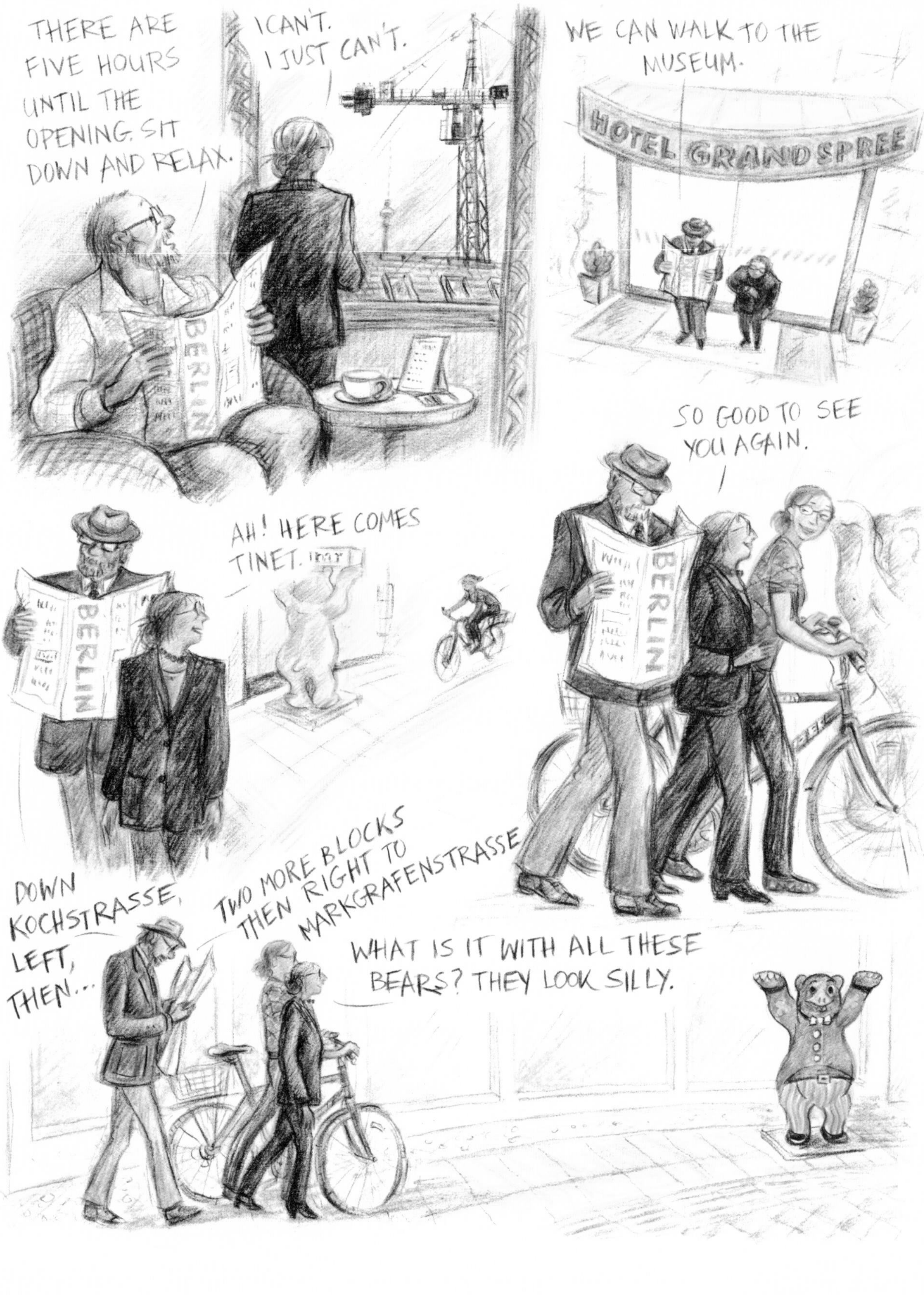
THERE ARE FIVE HOURS UNTIL THE OPENING. SIT DOWN AND RELAX.
BERLIN
I CAN'T. I JUST CAN'T.
WE CAN WALK TO THE MUSEUM.
HOTEL GRANDSPREE
BERLIN
AH! HERE COMES TINET.
SO GOOD TO SEE YOU AGAIN.
BERLIN
DOWN KOCHSTRASSE, LEFT, THEN...
TWO MORE BLOCKS THEN RIGHT TO MARKGRAFENSTRASSE
WHAT IS IT WITH ALL THESE BEARS? THEY LOOK SILLY.

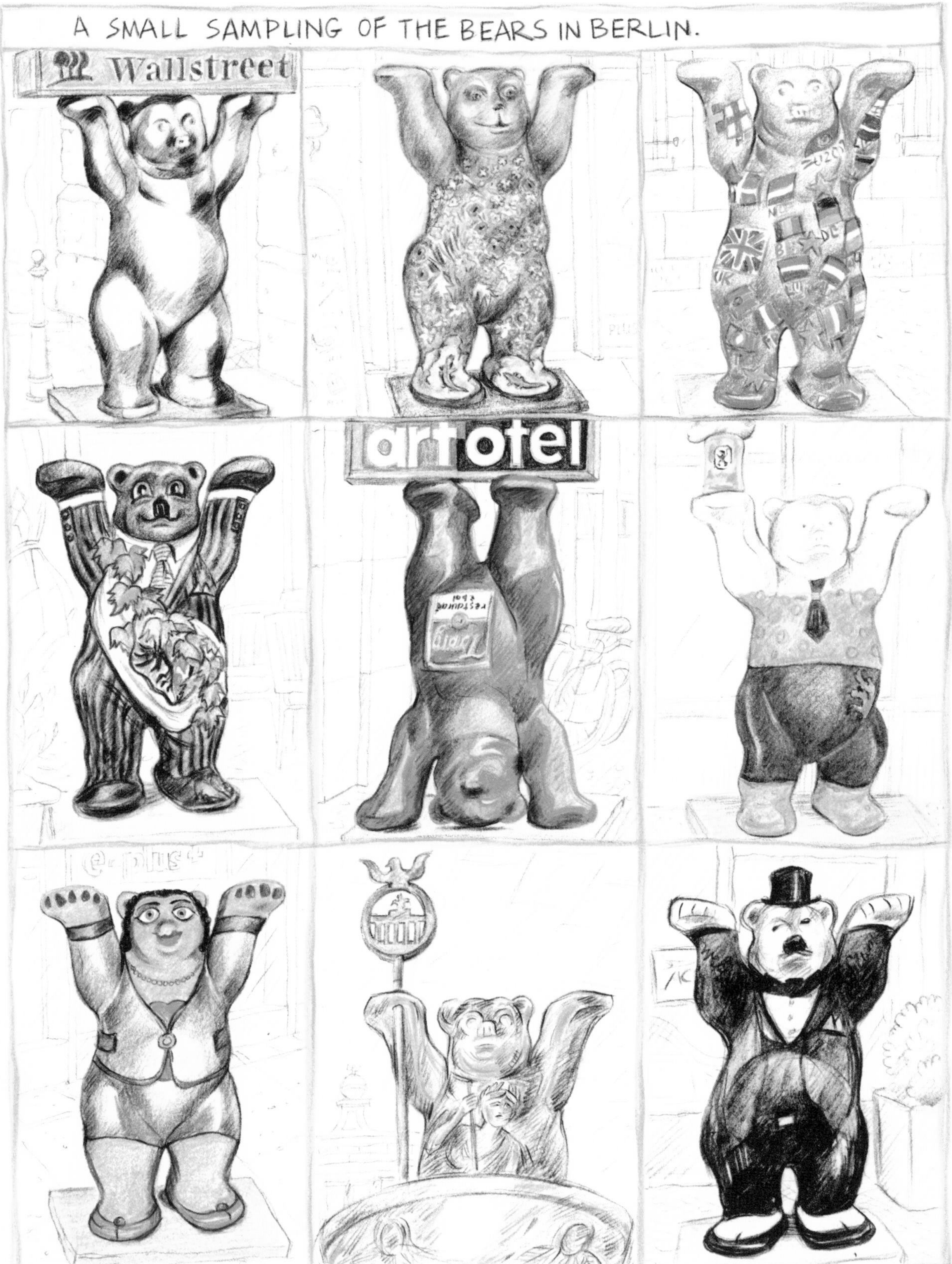
A SMALL SAMPLING OF THE BEARS IN BERLIN.
Wallstreet
artotel

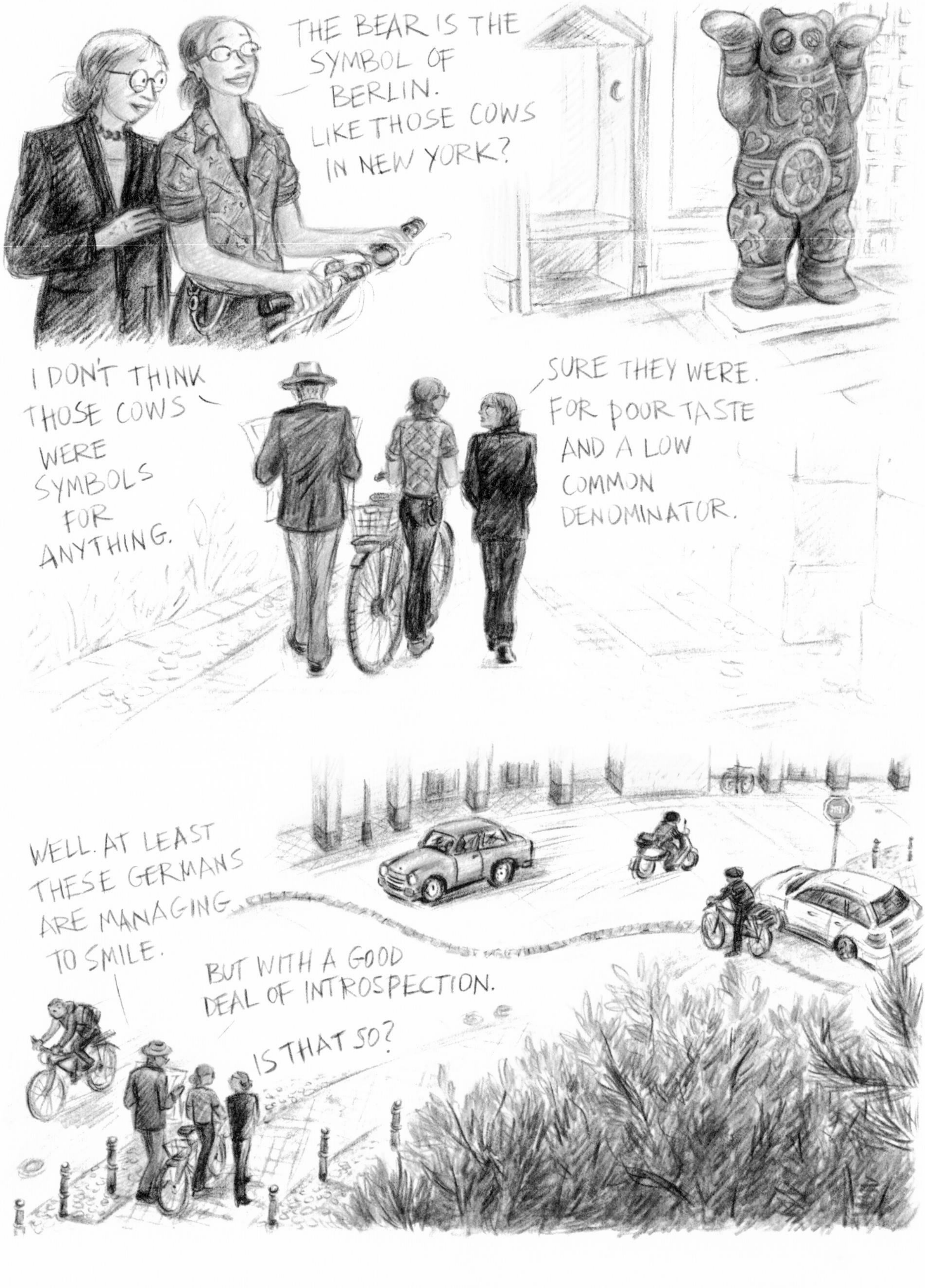
THE BEAR IS THE SYMBOL OF BERLIN. LIKE THOSE COWS IN NEW YORK?
I DON'T THINK THOSE COWS WERE SYMBOLS FOR ANYTHING.
SURE THEY WERE. FOR POOR TASTE AND A LOW COMMON DENOMINATOR.
WELL. AT LEAST THESE GERMANS ARE MANAGING TO SMILE.
BUT WITH A GOOD DEAL OF INTROSPECTION.
IS THAT SO?

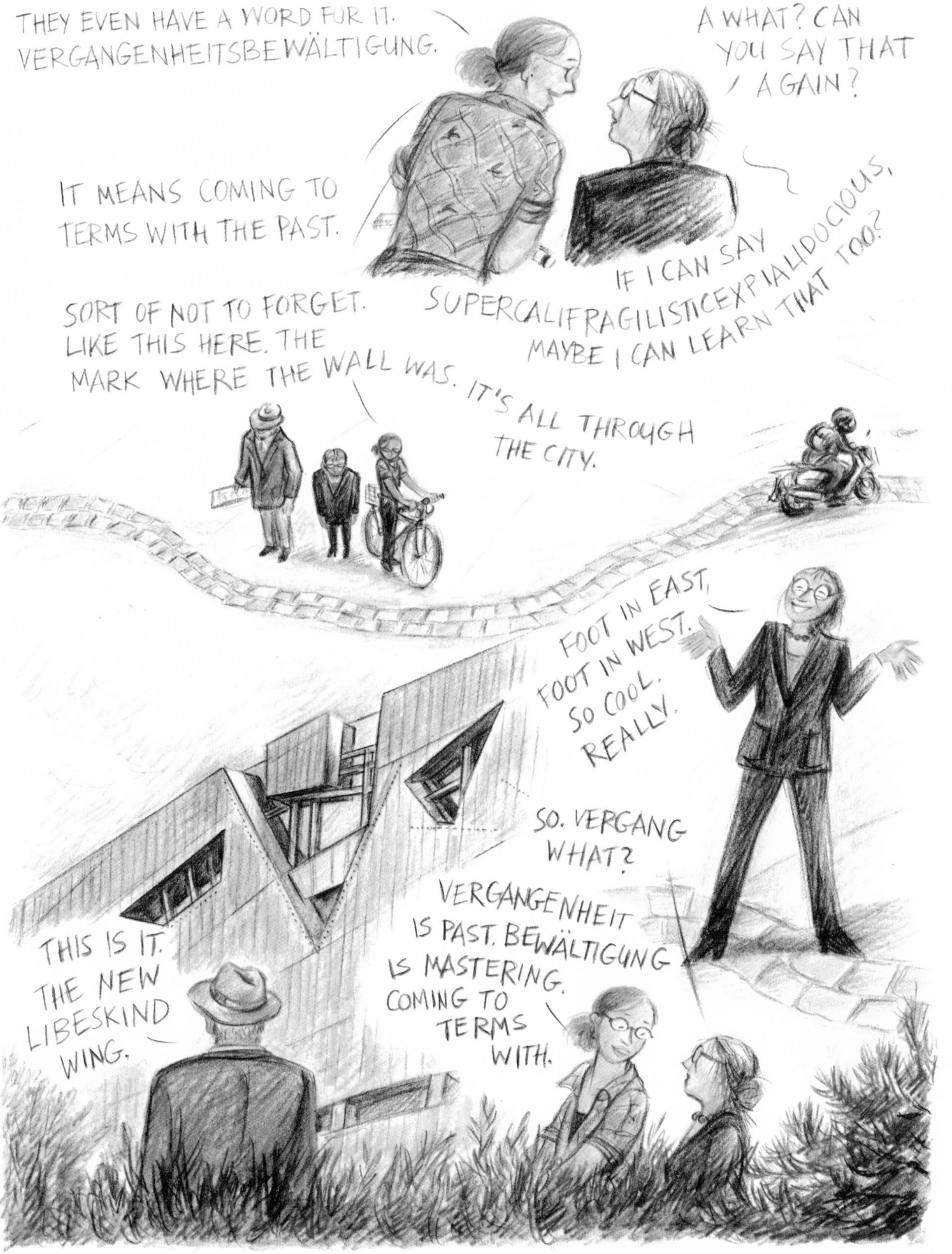
THEY EVEN HAVE A WORD FOR IT. VERGANGENHEITSBEWÄLTIGUNG.
A WHAT? CAN YOU SAY THAT AGAIN?
IT MEANS COMING TO TERMS WITH THE PAST.
IF I CAN SAY SUPERCALIFRAGILISTICEXPIALIDOCIOUS, MAYBE I CAN LEARN THAT TOO?
SORT OF NOT TO FORGET. LIKE THIS HERE. THE MARK WHERE THE WALL WAS. IT'S ALL THROUGH THE CITY.
FOOT IN EAST, FOOT IN WEST. SO COOL. REALLY.
SO. VERGANG WHAT?
THIS IS IT. THE NEW LIBESKIND WING.
VERGANGENHEIT IS PAST. BEWÄLTIGUNG IS MASTERING. COMING TO TERMS WITH.

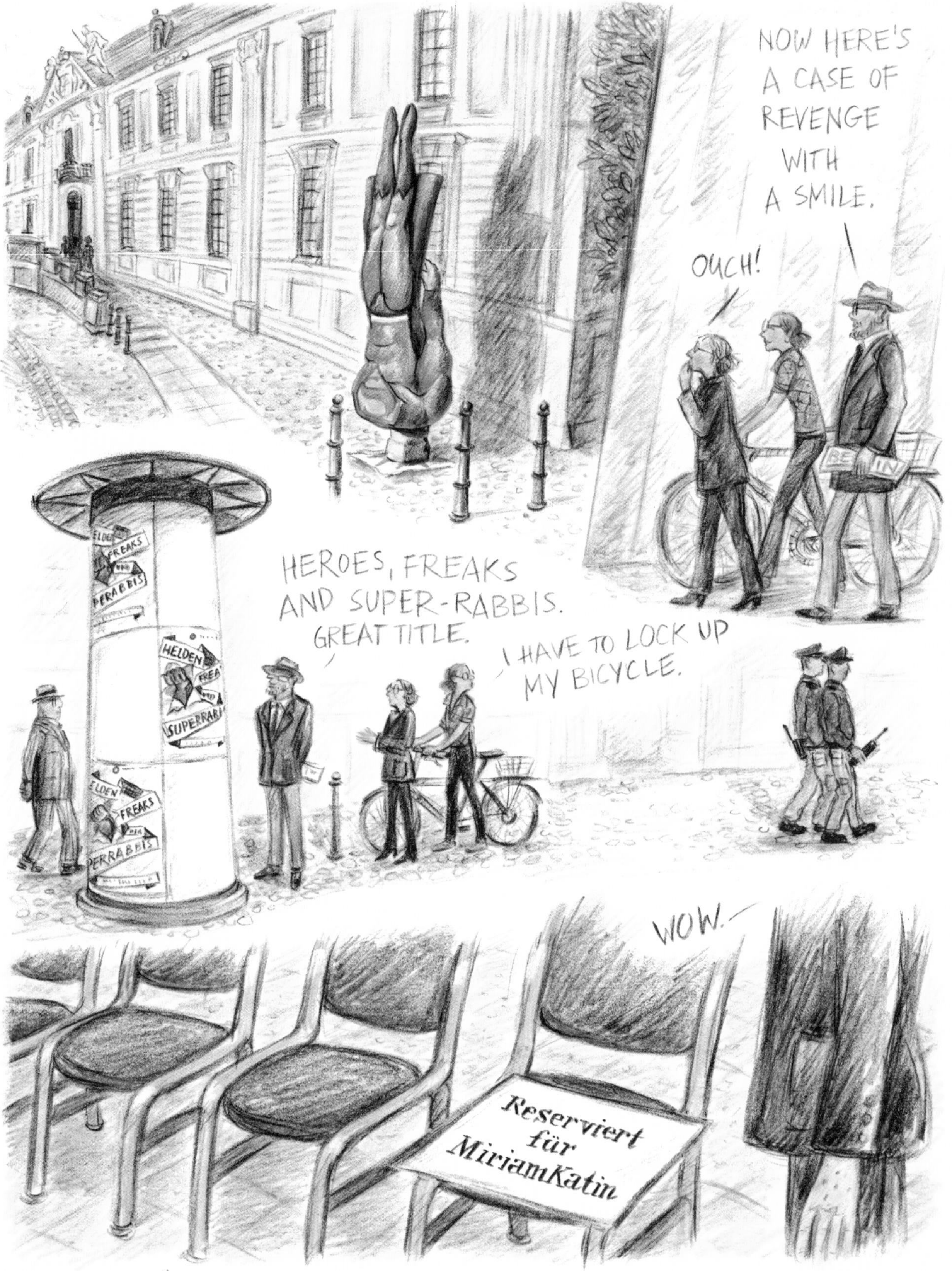
OUCH!
NOW HERE'S A CASE OF REVENGE WITH A SMILE.
HEROES, FREAKS AND SUPER-RABBIS. GREAT TITLE.
I HAVE TO LOCK UP MY BICYCLE.
WOW.
Reserviert für MiriamKatin

RESERVIERT FÜR: RESERVED FOR (GERMAN)

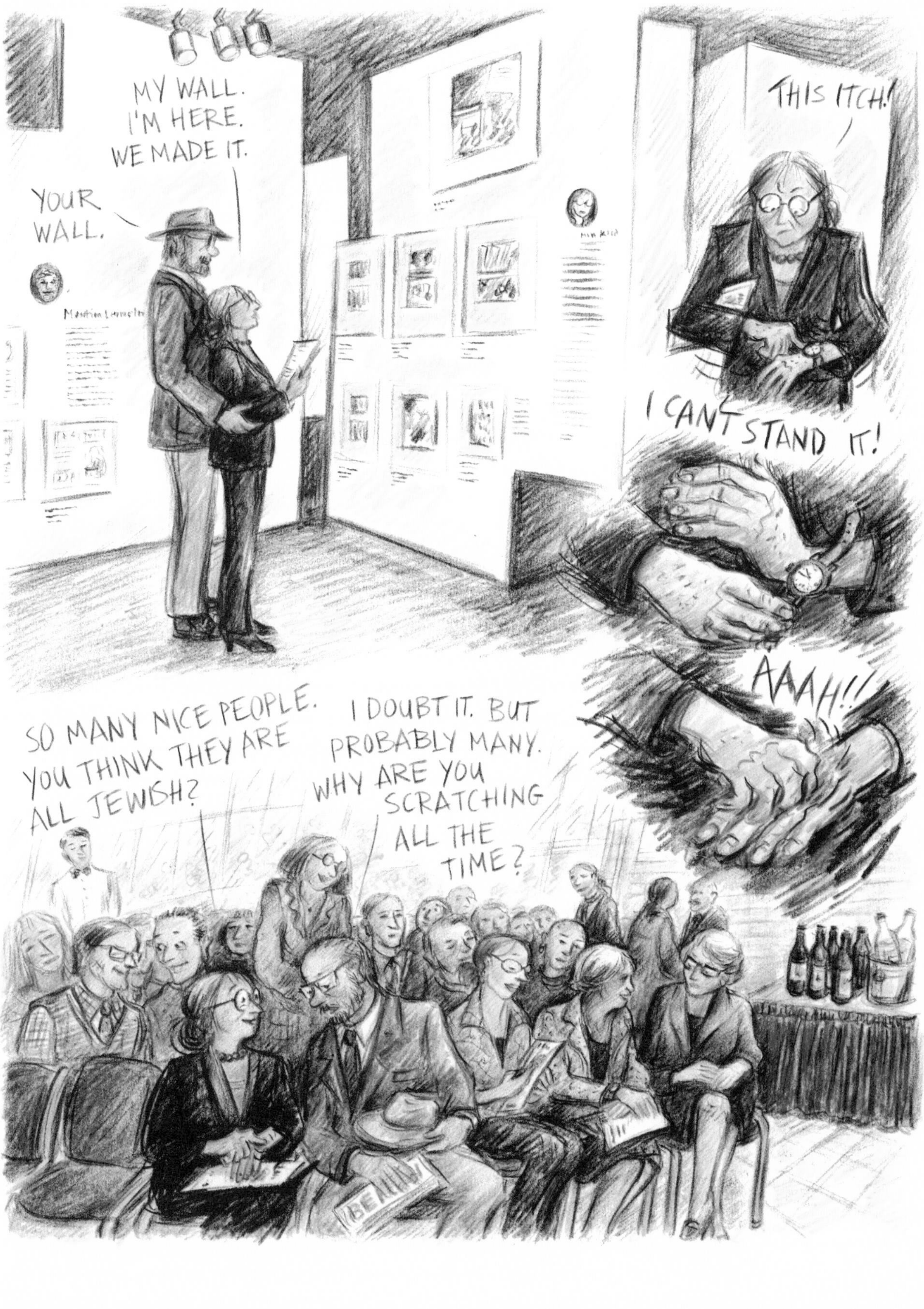
MY WALL. I'M HERE. WE MADE IT.
YOUR WALL.
THIS ITCH!
I CAN'T STAND IT!
AAAH!!
SO MANY NICE PEOPLE. YOU THINK THEY ARE ALL JEWISH?
I DOUBT IT. BUT PROBABLY MANY. WHY ARE YOU SCRATCHING ALL THE TIME?

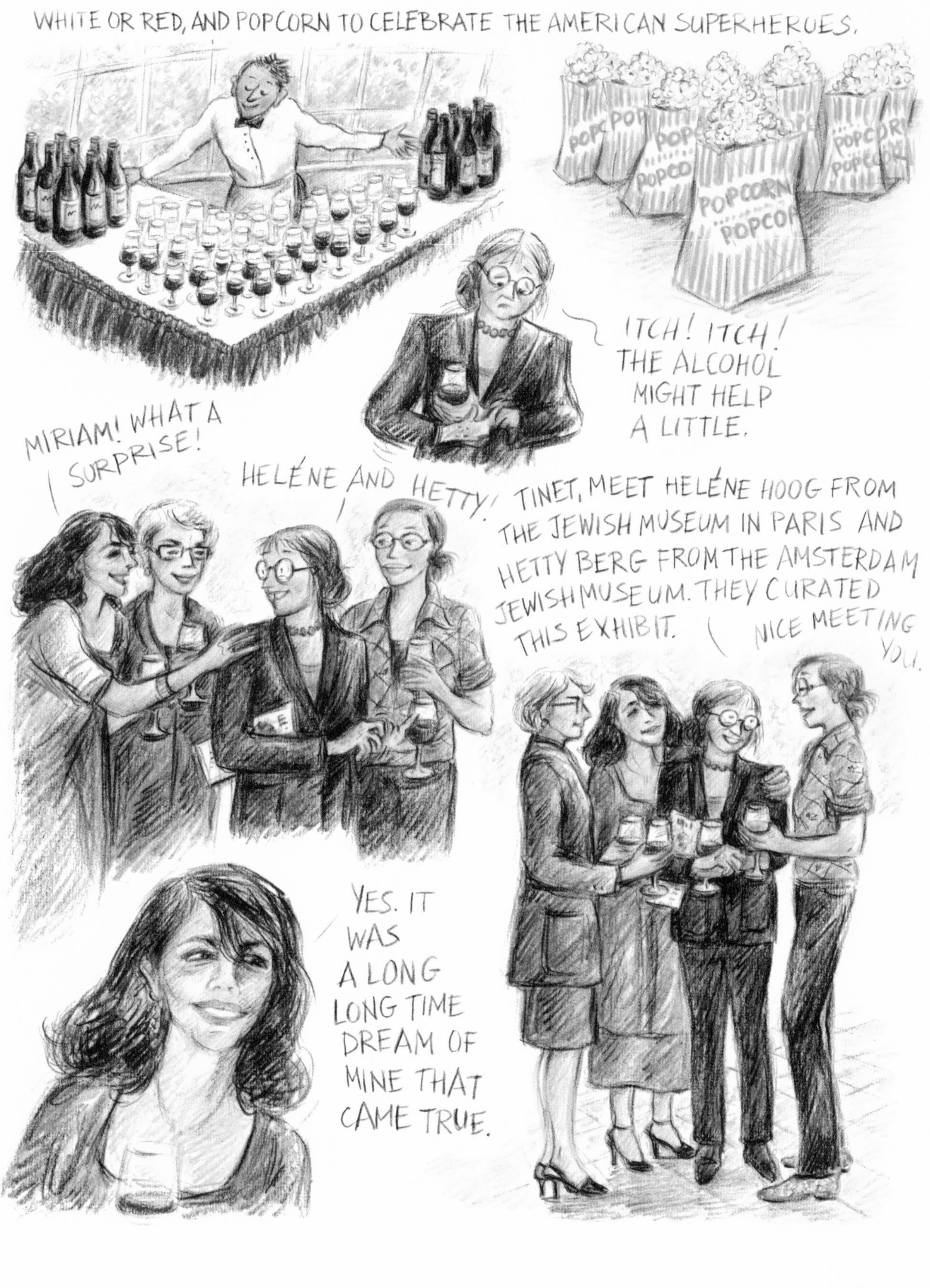
WHITE OR RED, AND POPCORN TO CELEBRATE THE AMERICAN SUPERHEROES.
POPCORN
ITCH! ITCH! THE ALCOHOL MIGHT HELP A LITTLE.
MIRIAM! WHAT A SURPRISE!
HELÉNE AND HETTY!
TINET, MEET HELÉNE HOOG FROM THE JEWISH MUSEUM IN PARIS AND HETTY BERG FROM THE AMSTERDAM JEWISH MUSEUM. THEY CURATED THIS EXHIBIT.
NICE MEETING YOU.
YES. IT WAS A LONG LONG TIME DREAM OF MINE THAT CAME TRUE.

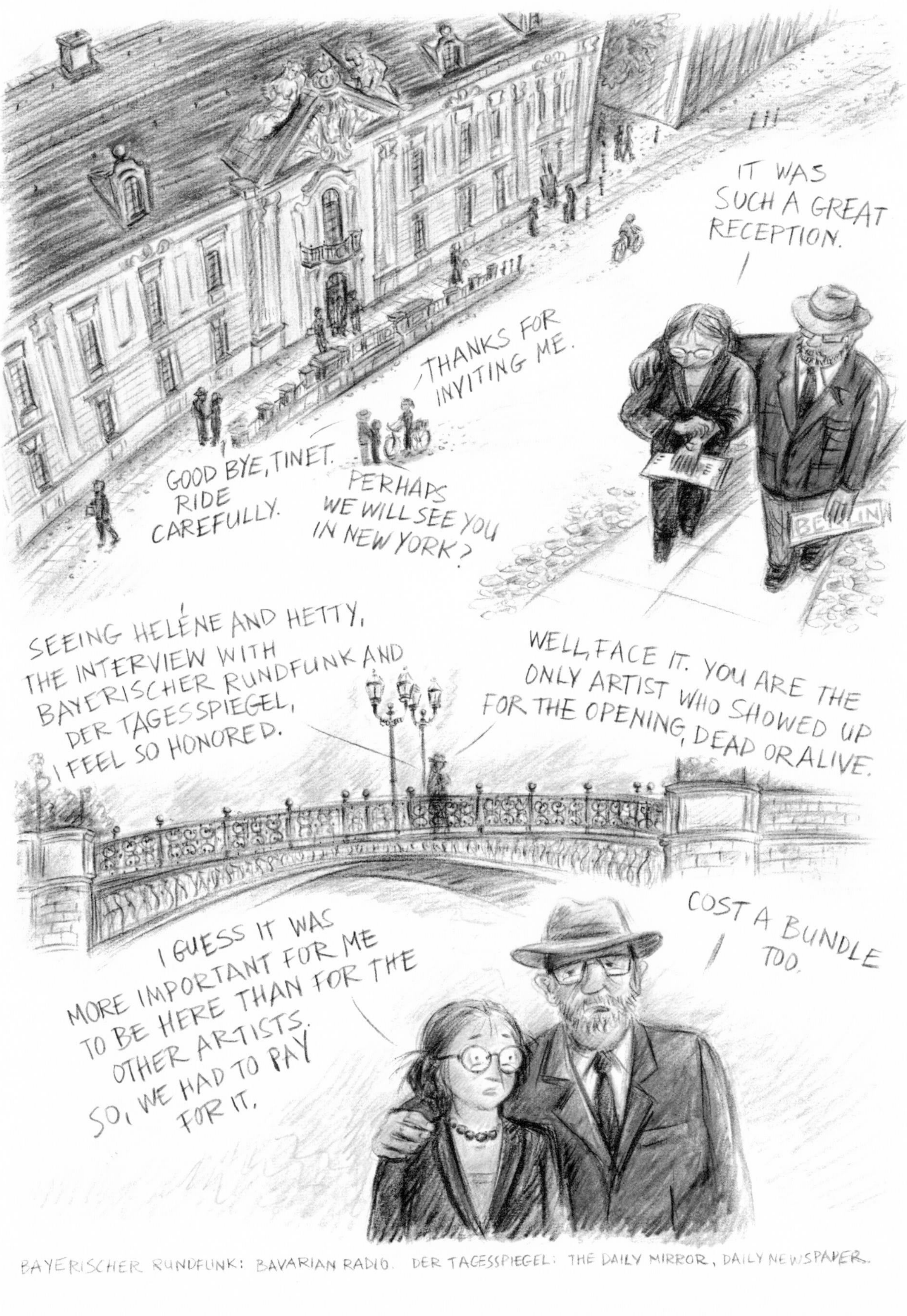
IT WAS SUCH A GREAT RECEPTION.
THANKS FOR INVITING ME.
GOOD BYE, TINET. RIDE CAREFULLY.
PERHAPS WE WILL SEE YOU IN NEW YORK?
BERLIN
SEEING HELÉNE AND HETTY, THE INTERVIEW WITH BAYERISCHER RUNDFUNK AND DER TAGESSPIEGEL, I FEEL SO HONORED.
WELL, FACE IT. YOU ARE THE ONLY ARTIST WHO SHOWED UP FOR THE OPENING, DEAD OR ALIVE.
I GUESS IT WAS MORE IMPORTANT FOR ME TO BE HERE THAN FOR THE OTHER ARTISTS. SO, WE HAD TO PAY FOR IT.
COST A BUNDLE TOO.

BAYERISCHER RUNDFUNK: BAVARIAN RADIO. DER TAGESSPIEGEL: THE DAILY MIRROR, DAILY NEWSPAPER.

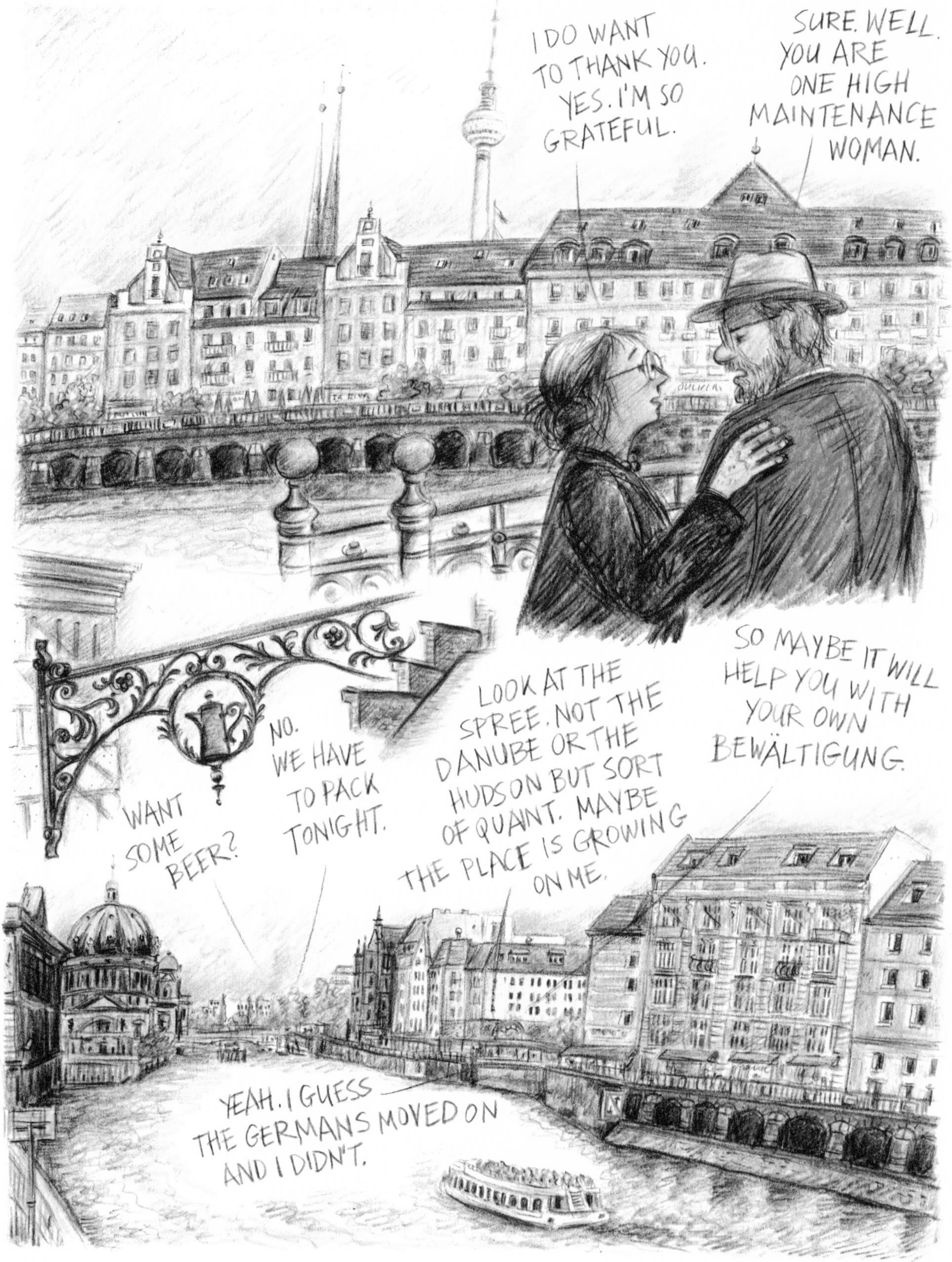
I DO WANT TO THANK YOU. YES. I'M SO GRATEFUL.
SURE. WELL. YOU ARE ONE HIGH MAINTENANCE WOMAN.
SO MAYBE IT WILL HELP YOU WITH YOUR OWN BEWÄLTIGUNG.
LOOK AT THE SPREE. NOT THE DANUBE OR THE HUDSON BUT SORT OF QUAINT. MAYBE THE PLACE IS GROWING ON ME.
WANT SOME BEER?
NO. WE HAVE TO PACK TONIGHT.
YEAH. I GUESS THE GERMANS MOVED ON AND I DIDN'T.

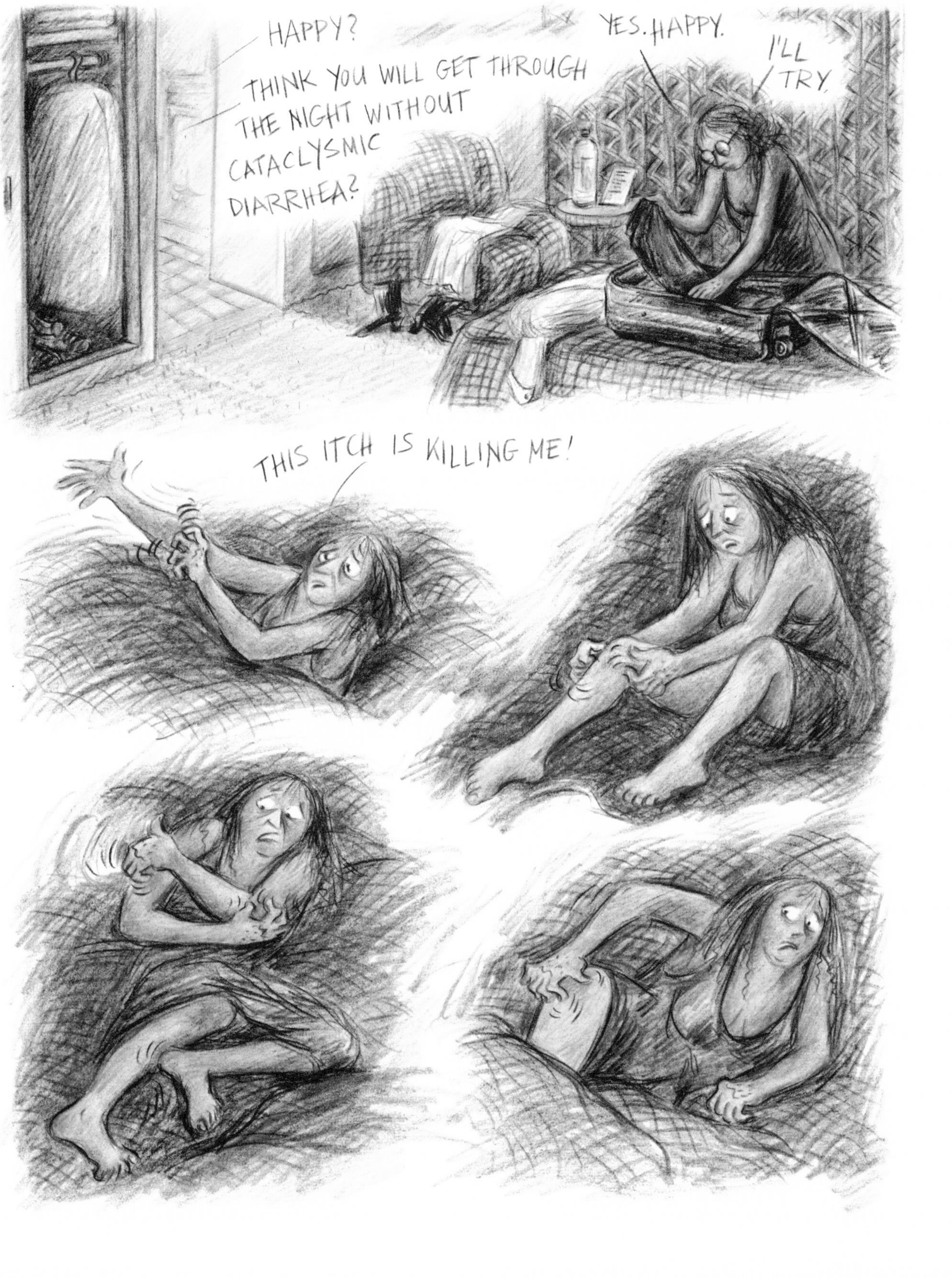
HAPPY?
THINK YOU WILL GET THROUGH THE NIGHT WITHOUT CATACLYSMIC DIARRHEA?
YES. HAPPY.
I'LL TRY.
THIS ITCH IS KILLING ME!

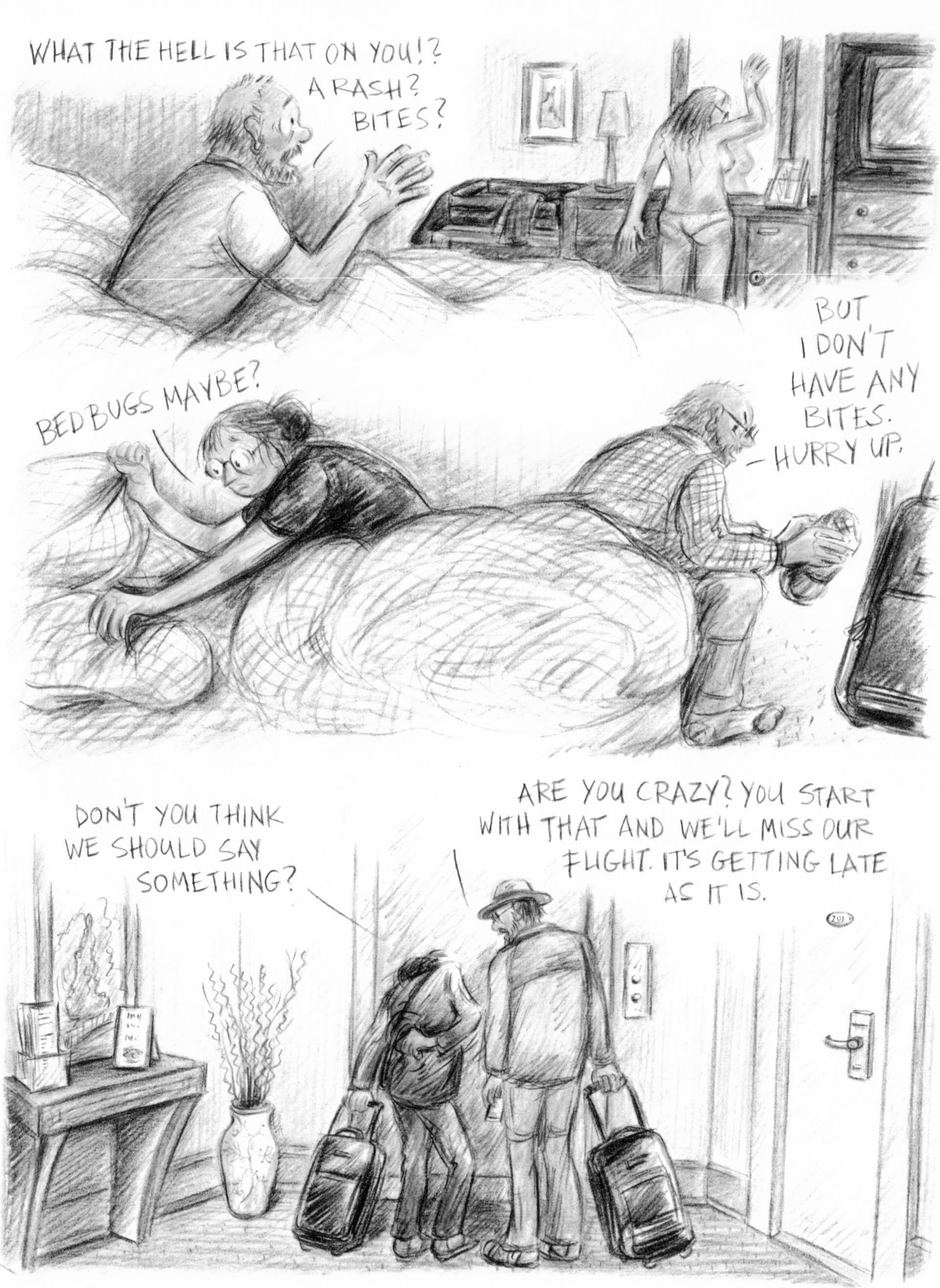
WHAT THE HELL IS THAT ON YOU!?
A RASH?
BITES?
BEDBUGS MAYBE?
BUT I DON'T HAVE ANY BITES. — HURRY UP.
DON'T YOU THINK WE SHOULD SAY SOMETHING?
ARE YOU CRAZY? YOU START WITH THAT AND WE'LL MISS OUR FLIGHT. IT'S GETTING LATE AS IT IS.

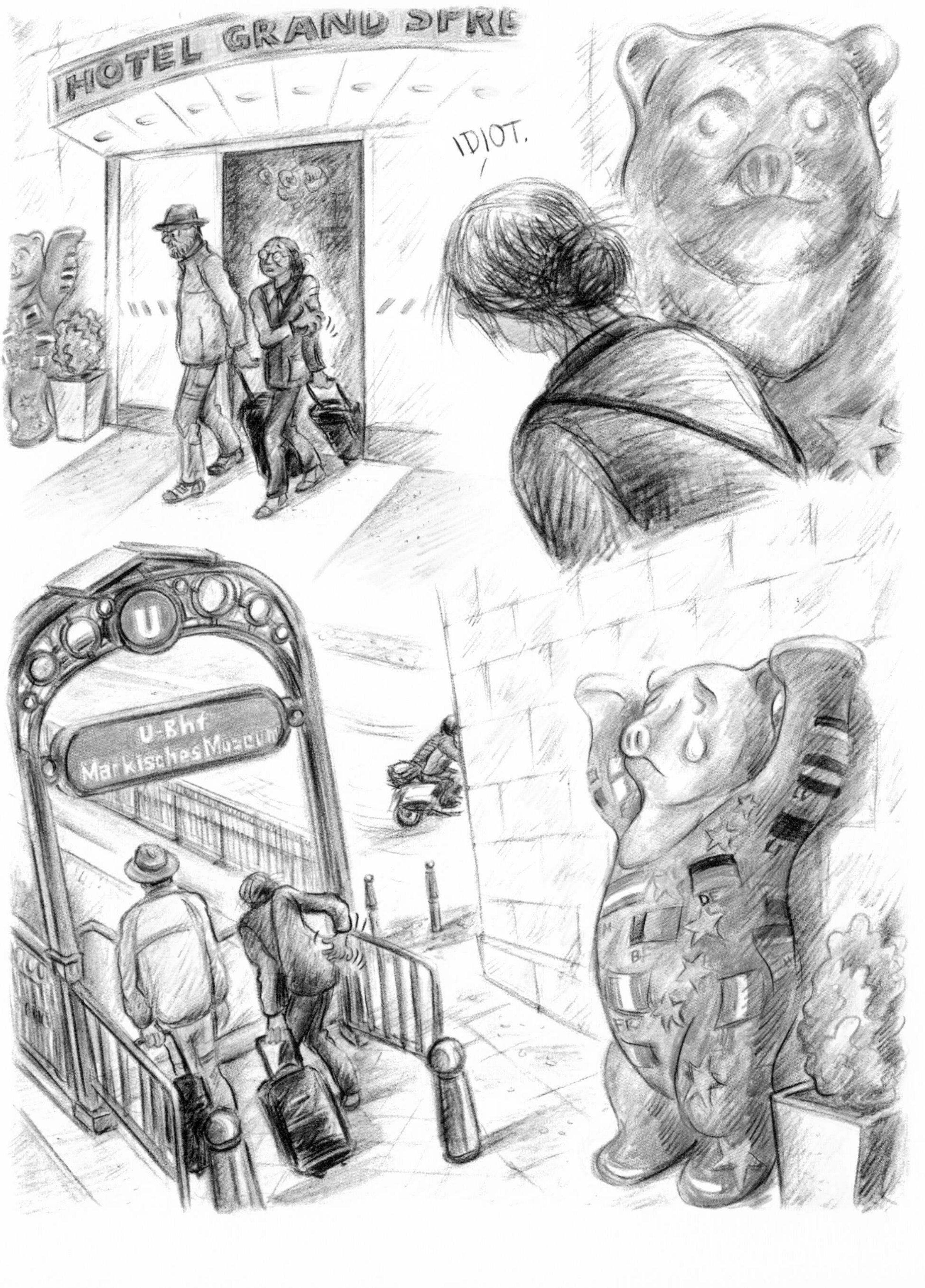
HOTEL GRAND SPRE
IDIOT.
U
U-Bhf
Markisches Museum

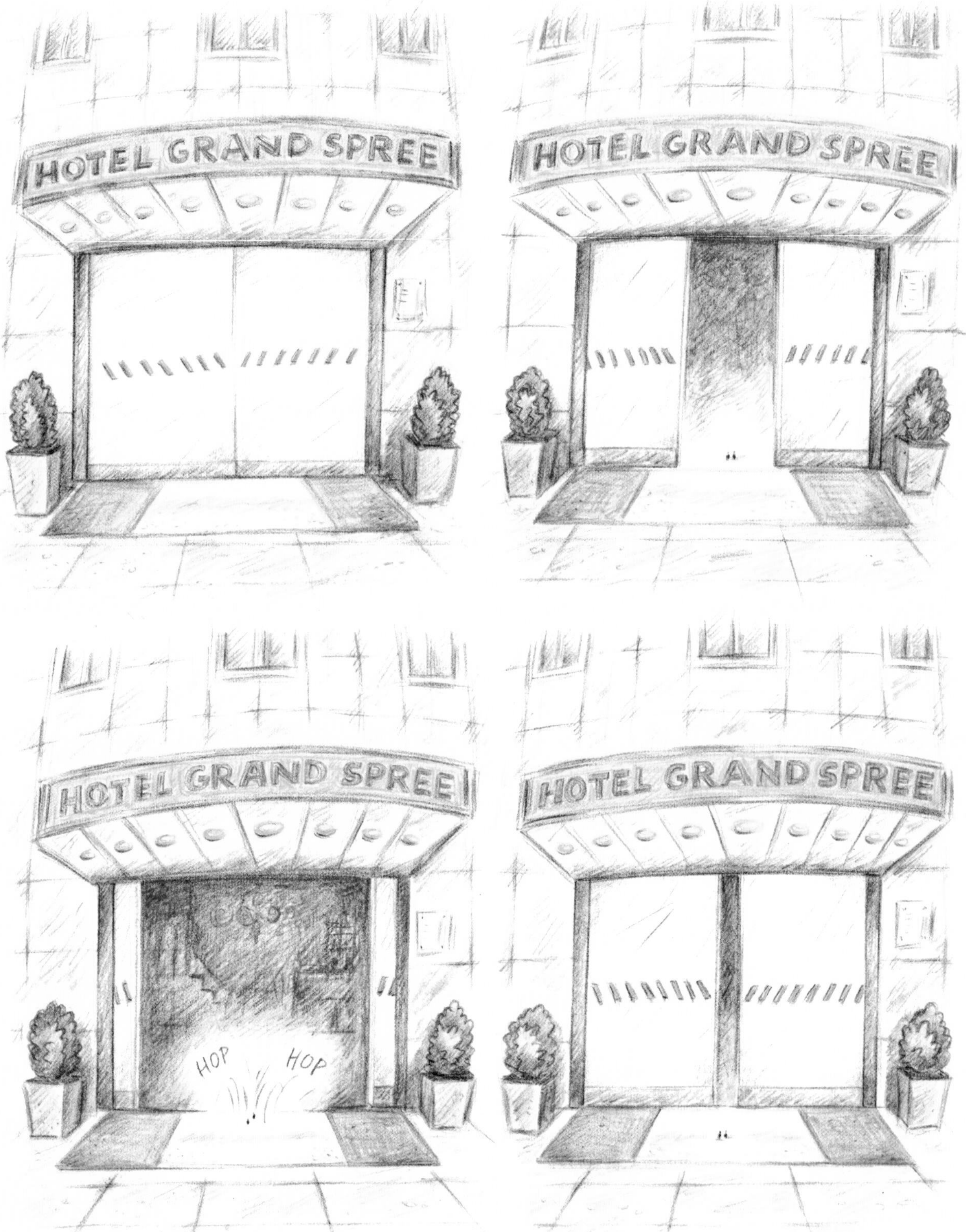
HOTEL GRAND SPREE
HOTEL GRAND SPREE
HOTEL GRAND SPREE
HOP
HOP
HOTEL GRAND SPREE

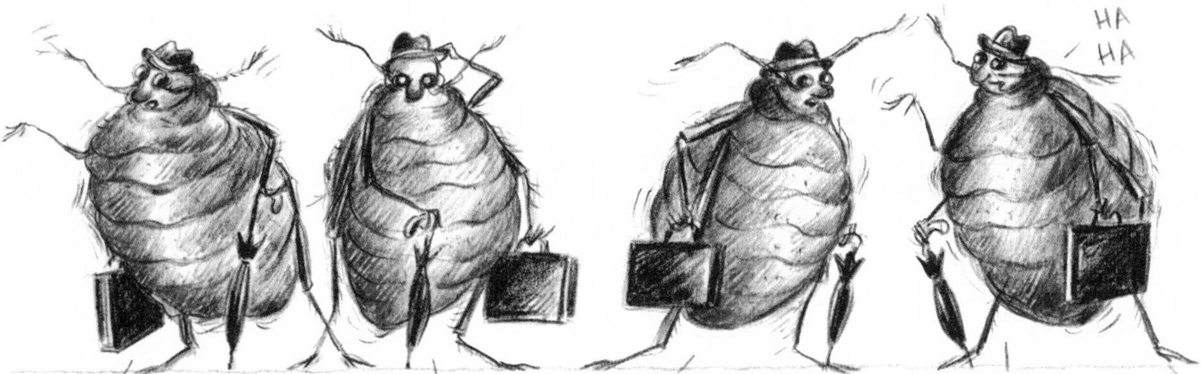
STOPPED RAINING.
MAN, I'M STUFFED.
SHE SAID SHE WILL NEVER COME BACK TO BERLIN.
HA HA
HER BLOOD WILL BE ALL OVER THE CITY. THAT WILL CALL HER BACK.

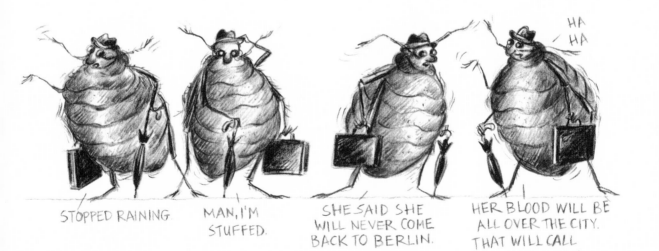

WHO WAS SENT
WITH HER?

KLAUS UND
MONIKA.

LUCKY BASTARD.
WELL, GOOD BITES.

JA, JA.
AUF WIEDERSEHEN.

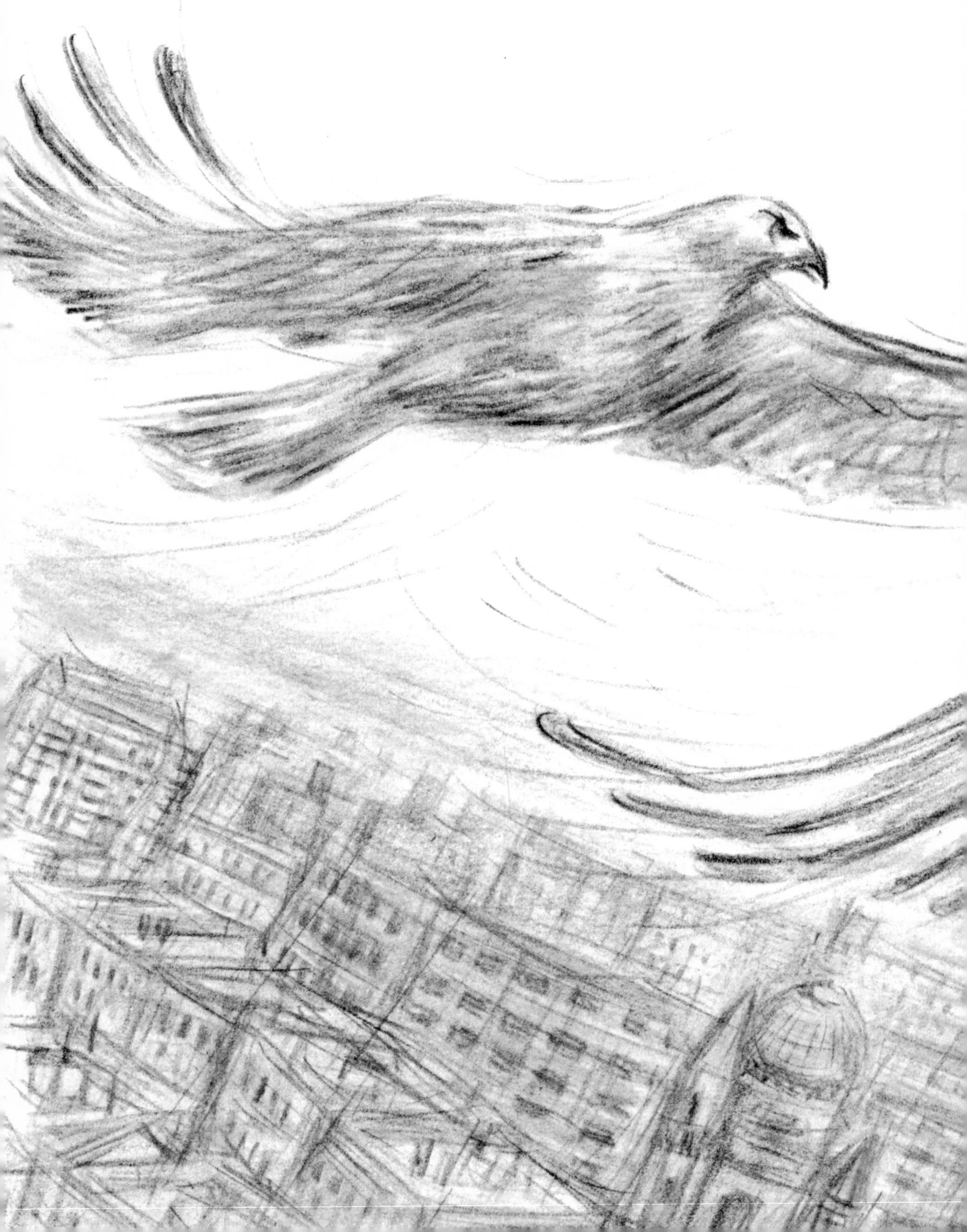